Jewish Life in

Twentieth-Century America

Jewish Life in Twentieth-Century America

Challenge and Accommodation

MILTON PLESUR

Nelson-Hall nh Chicago

973.04924
Plesur

LIBRARY OF CONGRESS CATALOGING IN PUBLICATION DATA

Plesur, Milton.
  Jewish life in twentieth-century America.

  Bibliography: p.
  Includes index.
  1. Jews—United States—Social conditions.
  2. United States—Social conditions—20th century.
  I. Title.
  E184.J5P58   973 '.04924   81-11196
  ISBN 0-88229-639-6 (cloth)   AACR2
  ISBN 0-88229-800-3 (paper)

Manufactured in the United States of America

10 9 8 7 6 5 4 3 2 1

The paper in this book is pH neutral (acid-free).

Contents

To the memory of my mother,
Sophie K. Plesur, much
of whose story is reflected in these pages

Acknowledgments ─────

I AM PLEASED TO RECORD my appreciation to former students who were of great assistance in seeking out materials and in performing other helpful tasks: Christine Berkowski, Ernest G. Brown, Kathleen Ann Buckley, John F. Dawson, James D. Hinga, John Jakubowski, Diane P. Janusz, William Johnson, James Mariano, Robert McDermott, Carol Pereicich, Ronald L. Sellers, Paul L. Stevens, and Stacey Walder.

My gratitude is also expressed to Judith Summer for her editorial aid, to Susan Grelick for her assistance in checking materials and in preparing the index, to Steve Lipman of the *Buffalo Jewish Review*, to Abraham Yanover, Executive Director of the Bureau of Jewish Education of Greater Buffalo, and especially, to my colleague, Selig Adler, Samuel Paul Capen Distinguished Service Professor Emeritus of American History at the State University of New York at Buffalo for his advisement, encouragement, and friendship in connection with this volume as well as with all my professional work in the more than thirty years of our association.

Introduction _____

IMMIGRANTS IN INCREASING numbers swelled the American ranks in the early twentieth century until the prejudicial quotas restricted this flow in the 1920s. It was ethnic Americans who built the great cities, worked on the docks, and railroads, and in mill, mine, and factory. Their neighborhoods and their ghettos were warm centers of communal energy and spirit. Proud and ambitious, many second-generation ethnics "made it" into prestigious businesses and professions. And American Jews, numbering 5,920,900 in 1981, were the most successful of minority groups. The American-Jewish community is the largest Jewish population in the world, consisting of slightly more than 40 percent of the world's Jews.

American-Jewish history has been the story of a search for acceptance, a quest for understanding from the Christian majority, and has paralleled the successful story of adjustment and accommodation to a changing industrial, urbanized milieu. From the tortuous challenge of Americanization confronting the non-English speaking immigrant in the secure ghettos of teeming cities to the contemporary pressures of affluent suburbia, American-Jewish life is the often contradictory story of assimilation and adjustments on the one hand, and the pursuit of traditional values on the other. American Jews have tended, however, to avoid the excesses of both ghettoization and complete integration.

The aftermath of the Second World War left the United States the center of world Judaism, and since the establishment of the State of Israel in 1948, Jewish life has polarized around these two countries. While concerned with the fate of Jews all over the world, the American-Jewish community has never abandoned its primary purpose of adjusting its Jewishness in order to achieve a uniquely American-Jewish way of life. And American Jews have, as a result, adopted the secular norm in such practices as their use of leisure time, their social life, their raising of smaller families, and in general the adoption of a stereotyped thinking. Not only has the American scene helped to shape the Jew, but he also, along with all other ethnic groups, has helped to mold what can be called "American culture." This obvious contribution to the American experience is all the more remarkable since Jews comprise slightly less than 3 percent of the population. It is the aim of the present volume to survey this two-fold relationship—that of the impact of Jews upon America and of contemporary America upon Jews.

The decade of the 1890s is a watershed in American history, for it was then that the United States passed from an agricultural economy preoccupied with domestic problems to an industrial, urbanized nation projecting its interests beyond the water's edge. The great East European-Jewish influx to America came at this time—when the Industrial Revolution was making its greatest strides, when the problems of metropolitan living offered never-ending challenges. Initially, we will attempt to measure this early adjustment of the Jewish masses to a new environment.

With the coming of the First World War in 1914, the American Jew was presented with his first major obligation to his overseas co-religionists, and agencies of all kinds proliferated. American-Jewish world leadership became a reality. The decade of the 1920s was an era of prosperity and business consolidation, or so it seemed. And the American Jew made giant strides in his drive for acceptance, but not without the vexation from anti-Semitic forces which was part of the conservative counter-attack of the period. In the 1930s came the Great Depression, and the adjustments American Jews were required to make proved to be of tremendous import. The New Deal of President Franklin D. Roosevelt appealed to Jews for a variety of reasons and they profited politically. FDR was, for Jews and for most ethnic minorities, a charismatic figure, and these groups formed an integral part of his winning political coalition.

Late in the 1930s and during the Second World War era, the ideal of a Jewish state loomed large, and American Jewry assumed substantial responsibility for the miracle of its creation. The defeat of Hitler and the successful prosecution of the war had been given the highest priority on the Jewish agenda. The Holocaust (the liquidation of six million Jews by the Germans) is, and will forever be, etched in the Jewish memory. Given the European catastrophe, Israel became increasingly the answer to Jewish homelessness, despite the fact that her creation demanded a number of adjustments. Since the war, American Jews have continued to face the ever-present challenges of a minority people, both within America and as the most powerful Jewish community in the world. These challenges came, however, when American Jews occupied an unprecedented position of respect and general affluence.

The story of Jewish-Americans and a review of their contributions and problems of adjustment will be surveyed in a series of chapters dealing with the early years of the century, the First World War era, the "Golden Twenties," "The Hungry Thirties," the period of the Second World War, and the time since the great victory over the Axis. Among the specific topics to be discussed are the Jewish agencies of culture and assimilation; immigrant adjustment; organizations which deal with communal concerns and those protective of overseas Jewry; the Orthodox, Conservative, Reform, and Reconstructionist enclaves within Judaism; the Jewish role in wars; American-Jewish contributions to both intellectual values and such mass cultural pursuits as entertainment; instances of anti-Semitism and Jewish counterattacks; the role of the American-Jew in establishing the State of Israel; the effect of Jewish-Americans on politics and education; and the Jewish component in the counter-culture of the 1970s. Great personalities who have traversed the Jewish-American stage in the twentieth century will also receive due mention.

The Jewish saga in America has been one of tremendous interest and value. Like all minority groups, Jews contributed to the uniqueness of the United States in ways that were themselves distinctive. The American soil nurtured a new type of Judaism, a Judaism of comfort and plenty. How this American-Jewish profile emerged is the theme of this volume.

1

The Ghetto and the Melting Pot: To 1914

IN 1880, WHEN THREE-FOURTHS of world Jewry lived in East Europe, only 3 percent (about 250,000) made their homes in the United States. By 1900, the character of American Jewry had been dramatically transformed by the arrival of some half a million immigrants from East Europe who represented a different culture and even a different variant of Judaism. They were the first contingents of the greatest population shift in Jewish history since the Exodus from Egypt. Over one-third of East European Jewry left their homes during the little more than three decades from 1880 to the outbreak of World War I, and 90 percent of them journeyed to America. By the turn of the century New York City had become the largest Jewish urban center in the world and the hub of a new American Judaism. And another 1.25 million Jewish immigrants were yet to land.

These Jews were one component of the so-called "new immigration" from eastern and southern Europe that crowded onto American shores in ever greater numbers from the end of the Civil War until the enactment of restrictive legislation in the 1920s. While Jewish immigrants had to face the problems that beset all newcomers, they had to undergo a double adjustment: from Europe to America and from village to city environment. Their own lives uprooted, Jewish immigrants were greeted by a strange, hostile America dominated by an impersonal industrial economy, a growing nativist anti-Semitism, and a Reform Judaism that did not seem to them Jewish at all. Above all, Jewish immigrants had to find means to preserve their identity as a religious-national community and escape being absorbed into the native Christian population.

Several factors led to a steady flowing of Jewish emigration from East Europe on a massive scale. Socio-economic dislocation, eventual displacement by a gentile middle class, and the conscious, calculated policies of governments intent upon making life impossible for Jews created a constant pressure to migrate. Outbreaks of anti-Jewish feeling, aggression, and violence sanctioned by church and state and known as pogroms intensified the desire for America and led to increases in flight over and above the normal trends of Jewish migration.

While available statistical data support the position that the accurate date for the commencement of the great migration was about 1870, popular interpretation, however, correlates its beginning with the outbreak of large-scale pogroms in Russia in the 1880s and the debarkation of the first group of eighteen refugees in New York City on September 9, 1881. During the ensuing years Jewish immigration grew in a geometrical progression. Nearly 200,000 (12 percent of the total number to come from East Europe, 1880–1914) arrived in the 1880s, over 300,000 (25 percent) in the next decade, and the remaining 1.4 million (64 percent) in the twentieth century. Jews from the domains of the Czar dominated the entire movement. From 1881 to 1900 those of Russian nationality formed a fairly constant 70 percent of the Jewish immigrants, while 24 percent came from Austria-Hungary and 4 percent from Rumania. Though these numbers seem impressive, East European Jews actually comprised less than 7 percent of the nearly 9 million immigrants who poured into the United States in the two decades before the turn of the century.

Although an integral part of the "new immigration," East European Jews were in many ways distinct from their fellow newcomers. Jews, far more than any other group, were "settlers," whose determination to stay was formed even before they left Europe. In general, fewer Jews returned to their homeland than any other national group, since many of the others often came to America only to earn a stake to take back to Europe. Moreover, Jewish immigration was a family movement, as evidenced by the large percentage of women and children among the immigrants.

Among all ethnic groups in the United States, Jews seem to have been the most proficient in providing their immigrants with some institutional source of minimal aid. The earliest refugees were cared for by the Russian Relief Committee of the United Hebrew Charities. Mass migration proved this inadequate, and the Hebrew Emigrant Aid Society (HEAS) came into existence by December, 1881. It was a makeshift organization facing an almost impossible task, and it survived only a year before returning the task of immigrant care in New York to the United Hebrew Charities. In its short life, however, the HEAS established an immigrant refuge on Ward's Island, cared for some 14,000 Russian immigrants, and helped East European Jews to settle in farm colonies. In 1892, another organization, the Hebrew Immigrant Aid Society, helped mediate between immigrants and immigration officials, protested steerage conditions of travel, and helped in securing employment. The United Hebrew Charities granted relief in kind—groceries, clothing, and furniture, and sponsored classes to teach unskilled women the needle trade. A profusion of other societies and committees sprang up to provide for such needs as burials, hospitalization, loans, and housing.

The vast majority of East European Jews, like most Gilded Age immigrants, settled in the expanding metropolitan centers of the United States, especially in New York City. Over 70 percent of the Jews landing in New York went no further. Opportunity was present and many did not have the fare to push westward. By 1890 about 135,000 of the city's Jewish population were concentrated in a small district on the Lower East Side of Manhattan. Many found their way to other large cities, where the New York phenomenon was repeated. By 1890, over 26,000 crowded into southeast Philadelphia, about 20,000 into west Chicago, and large numbers into Cleveland, Boston, Baltimore, and Milwaukee. The Jewish Agricultural and Industrial Aid Society helped relocate Jews as farmers, financing 161 agricultural settlements. By 1900, there were about 1,000 Jewish farm families; almost a decade later there were slightly more than 3,000. But most of the settlements, except those near cities like Carmel or Woodbine in southern New Jersey, were hardly successful. The Industrial Removal Office (1901) also helped settle almost 60,000 Jews in 1,474 smaller communities throughout the nation.

Before 1900 the great majority of Jewish immigrants had little experience with metropolitan existence because they had lived under a culture dominated by the smaller and circumscribed Jewish community. But, thereafter, they remained in American cities for practical reasons: they were their ports of arrival, cities often had agencies with funds at their disposal, and these cities were the places of residence of friends and relatives. Virtually penniless on arrival, Jews lacked the means to move on. Largely of semi-skilled commercial or artisan background, they found industrial and commercial centers to be a natural habitat where they became dependent on the apparel and tobacco trades and other light industries. The cheap tenement housing of urban slums, moreover, provided a psychological sanctuary for confused immigrants. It softened the break with the past by allowing immigrants to live in two worlds, retaining part of their customary habits and surroundings, yet touching the world outside. There everyone they might need to know was able to speak Yiddish, the Judaic-German "jargon" that remained the language of daily intercourse for many years. The newcomers consciously sought to locate where they could find synagogues, *mikvehs* (ritual baths), kosher butchershops, bakeries, and local or out-of-town Yiddish newspapers. Thus the mere presence of some East European Jews attracted others, and, once started, the trek to American cities snowballed. East European Jews were no different from other immigrant groups in responding to the economic and cultural magnetism of the metropolis.

Thus, like other ethnic groups, East European Jews fashioned their own neighborhoods in the cities, voluntary ghettoes where they tried to recreate the *shtetl* (community) environment of the Old Country. Jews, at first, were perhaps just a little more clannish than most newcomers. They not only avoided other ethnic groups but also clustered according to their separate national Jewries. On New York's Lower East Side, Hungarian, Galician, Lithuanian, Rumanian, and Russian Jews lived together—but side by side. Jewish ghettoes remained features of large cities as long as immigrants continued to pour in. They did not, however, remain static. As soon as they had been moderately acculturated and had accumulated sufficient funds, rising and successful Jewish immigrants would move to a better section of town. The ghetto itself survived because it constantly received new lifeblood from each boat arriving from the Old World. Only when the Great War disrupted the flow did the process of the ghetto's disintegration slowly proceed to its conclusion.

The Jewish quarter of the city was easily identifiable. Its signs were unmistakable. The streets resounded with Yiddish and were crowded with pushcarts. Fear of being labeled "greenhorns" prompted many Jews to rush off to buy American clothing soon after landing, but the skull-cap, beard, long-skirted *kaftan* (long coat), and women's wig still abounded. A Jewish man almost invariably sported a shiny black derby and often a Prince Albert frock coat in place of a worn-out kaftan. Even from a distance one knew that he was approaching "Jewtown"—he was informed by the sound of sewing machines, worked at high pressure from earliest dawn until mind and muscle gave out together.

The Jewish ghetto shared the squalor, filth, noise, and impoverishment of all ethnic slums. Living quarters were gloomy, dingy tenement houses built on narrow lots, one hundred feet deep by twenty-five feet wide. Many of the worst tenements were in the hands of East European Jews who acquired ownership by obtaining a loan at 4½ percent interest, then placing a large mortgage on the property with the loan. To pay back the loan, maintain the mortgage, and still show a profit, they had to charge exorbitant rents. Newer tenements, or "double deckers" dating from Theodore Roosevelt's incumbency as governor of New York (1899–1901), were six or seven stories high. Each floor generally had four sets of apartments. The front apartments had four rooms each, the rear, three, so that there were fourteen rooms to each floor. Only four rooms received direct light and air from the street and small back yard of the building. Of these four rooms, only two were large enough to be called rooms. The kitchen, directly behind the parlor, received air from an "air-shaft." Because of the narrowness of the air-shaft and its use as a garbage receptacle, the air emanating from it was ordinarily foul. Ventilation, therefore, was at a minimum. There was no light or air in the bedrooms. The water closets in the hallway served two apartments. The vast majority of tenement apartments had no bathrooms, and sometimes one bathtub served an entire building. Outside of New York, in smaller cities, there were seldom the high rise tenements. Instead, Jews often made private dwellings into storefronts and built cottages in the rear.

Jewish immigrants created no new or special problems and merely accentuated the numerous existing problems of urbanization. During the day, the streets resembled an old-time market, clogged with goods and enveloped in a terrific din. The newcomers crowded into dark, damp tenement rooms where privacy was rare. Few families could afford the $10 to $20 monthly rental of a three- or four-room flat. Therefore, the male boarder soon became an integral part of the Jewish-immigrant family. Summer heat made rooms unbearable, and whenever possible immigrant Jewry fled to porch or roof.

While the Jewish family held up surprisingly well under immigrant conditions, crowded ghetto life did affect the young. Youth could not receive their friends easily in such quarters. As a result, their social intercourse took place on the streets, in cafes, dance halls, and vaudeville theaters, or at prize fights and card games. These disintegrating influences combined with old world parental discipline and relaxation in the Jewish religious practices led to some juvenile delinquency, wife desertion, and general disorder.

Although the children were remarkably good students, many had to leave school to work in the streets as shoeshine boys, newsboys, or porters. Some of their number soon became members of gangs who took part in crimes, ranging from petty thievery to robbery by assault. Some of their minor crimes stemmed from misunderstanding or ignorance of the laws in the United States. Language proved a barrier when the accused tried to explain their actions to the police or in court, and the means of obtaining legal advice were at first unknown to them. As time went by, organizations, such as the Bureau of Personal Service in Chicago and the Educational Alliance in New York were opened for the purpose of giving legal aid as well as many other types of assistance.

In 1907, although their overall rate of crimes of violence was lower than that of other immigrants, the Jewish community, in a typical gesture of self-help, opened the New York Jewish Protectory for juvenile delinquents. Settlement houses were established and social workers, like Lillian Wald of New York and Jane Addams of Chicago, not only combatted juvenile delinquency, but also inspired many a young street urchin to rise above ghetto aspirations.

With their search for a new home, Jewish immigrants brought a dream of earning a comfortable living in the United States. This dream evaporated immediately upon arrival. The majority of East European Jews landed with practically no money in their pockets. As part of a family movement they often had dependents to support. Immediate entry into gainful employment was imperative. Like all immigrants, Jews had to adjust to the forces they found at work in the American economy. In America industry was an even more dominant economic force than some of them had experienced. Many of the newcomers stayed in commerce, but a new semi-industrial proletariat rose among them, armed with needle, sewing machine, and flat-iron.

Jewish immigrants grabbed whatever jobs they could in America in order to avoid starvation. Work was often temporary as they went from one job to another. Prior to 1900 the migration consisted primarily of "tailors" and *Luftmenschen* (those of no particular trade—teachers, idlers, petty tradesmen, and agents). They were physically and mentally unprepared to compete with peasant Slav immigrants for manual labor in factories or other heavy industries. Although poverty and lack of skill forced many Jews to put in a few weeks or months at day labor, as soon as they were able they turned to what they considered more promising fields. Those who were skilled artisans had a somewhat easier time in finding employment, but such persons constituted only a small fraction of Jewish immigration before 1900. Often even they had to abandon their crafts in face of competition from goods turned out by specialized and mechanized factories.

Other factors also handicapped immigrant Jews seeking work in industrial America. Inability to speak English hampered entry into many commercial fields. Orthodox religious observance proved an economic embarrassment. Many of the devout refused to work on Saturdays or the many Orthodox holy days, thus excluding themselves from most factories which operated six or even seven days a week. In most trades suspension of work for the two days a week—both Jewish and Christian Sabbaths—exposed the observant Jew to too much competition. The preference of East European Jews for economic independence also caused newcomers to eliminate many occupational possibilities. Very often, they would rather earn less wages and be in business for themselves than earn more money working for someone else. To be independent they needed pursuits that required relatively little capital outlay and yet would provide employment for the entire family.

Therefore, Jews funneled into those employments which offered them a chance to practice their religion, remain independent, and advance to a better station, and which were similar to those they had pursued in East Europe. Relatives and *landsleute* (fellow townsmen) played a major role in directing immigrants to an occupation, especially those who became factory workers. Many of the East European Jews had been needle workers in their homelands and became tailors after they arrived in America. The ready-to-wear clothing boom provided abundant opportunity for them, and the garment industry ultimately became the predominantly Jewish trade. Sixty percent of Jews employed in the Lower East Side of New York were shopworkers in the needle trades. In keeping with their background, many East European Jews also became tradesmen—peddlers, clerks, and small retailers. A small percentage remained artisans. Carpenters, painters, glazers, and locksmiths could be seen searching for work daily on the streets of the Jewish districts. The only industry other than the garment trade which Jews entered in sizable numbers was tobacco—many savored America's freedom while rolling cigars and cigarettes in tenement rooms. Thus, the overwhelming number of immigrant Jews were involved either in the production of consumer goods or in consumer services, as they had been in East Europe.

Simultaneously with debarkation, Jewish immigrants began to recreate their East European Jewish communal existence. The immigrants were composed, in great part, of the dissenters, the poor and underprivileged, the unlearned or less-learned, and most secularized of East European Jewry. Nevertheless, they did want to partake in a Jewish group life with the traditional paraphernalia. Life had been difficult in

Europe, but for some the security and status gave the individual a sense of personal worth and sustained morale, even under the czars. Jewish immigrants, isolated in the American melting pot, found that traditional social forms, religious brotherhoods, and charitable associations could help them keep their bearings and provide, as well, for their practical needs.

But establishing a new Jewish community did not prove to be an easy task. Immigrants brought with them the many divisions which had threatened Jewish solidarity in Europe: intense and bitter strife between Orthodox groups of *Hassidism* and *Mitnagdim*, between enlightened Orthodox *(Maskilim)* and traditionalists, between ardent Hebraists and Yiddishists, between radicals or labor unionists and believers in laissez-faire, and between Orthodoxy and such non-religious movements as Marxian socialism and Jewish secular nationalism. Moreover, East European Jews, experienced in the conduct of their own small communities, were a minority in American cities and inexperienced in relations with the broader, outside world. They found it difficult to identify with and participate in the new society of the United States. On the other hand, once armed with the resources of their new American rights and a revitalized Yiddish, immigrant Jews not only re-established much of East Europe in the metropolis but also evolved new-world institutions of their own making.

As soon as they were able, Jewish immigrants made every effort to assist their own, establishing *landsmanshaft* fraternal societies whose members came from the same town or neighborhood in East Europe. These organizations provided members with funeral and cemetery benefits, visitors to the sick, insurance, interest-free loans, and, perhaps most important, friendship. Although immigrant Jews lived in poverty, they were proud that they depended on neither city nor private charity—their own organizations could care for the needy.

The immigrants, most of whom practiced Orthodoxy, took

refuge in traditional religious institutions as a bulwark against an alien environment. Their most elementary require-ment was a place to pray daily or weekly, to say *kaddish* (memorial prayer), to observe *Yahrzeit* (anniversary of death), or to celebrate a *Bar Mitzvah* (confirmation of males). So a synagogue was one of the first creations shortly after the arrival of a handful of Jews in any city. Synagogues in the United States numbered 270 in 1880, 533 by 1890, and 1,769 by 1906. East European Jews were chiefly responsible for this increase. Orthodox East Europeans would not attend existing Reform synagogues, where services were strange and unfamiliar, so they had to build their own, in fact, so many that the immigrant community was actually overwhelmed with synagogues. Instead of a central community organizing religious life and exercising authority over the synagogues, as there had been in each Old World village, group after group in metropolitan America formed independent syna-gogues defiant of all ecclesiastical authority beyond their own walls. Differences in national origins, liturgy, and social and economic backgrounds contributed to this synagogue proliferation.

It soon became difficult to locate a sovereign religious authority within any immigrant congregation. This authority in East Europe belonged to the rabbi, who was not primarily a preacher but rather the ecclesiastical head of the community and judge on matters of ritual and law. The role of rabbi, however, for some decades lost most of its influence and honor in the New World and, in fact, financially hard-pressed congregations often preferred a cantor *(Hazzan)* if they could afford only a single functionary, since he was more necessary in a traditional service. When rabbis did appear, they found their authority and role undefined and their jobs at the mercy of congregational power to hire and fire at will.

Most immigrants retained their Orthodoxy, but often in a modified, less rigid form. Modification of traditional folkways was neither intentional nor approved, but American conditions soon stretched the range of permissiveness. In the harsh life of the slums, violations of custom and tradition came to be regarded more leniently. For example, while still wrong in religious eyes and considered unfortunate, it was no longer a disgrace to work on Saturdays. In some ways, Orthodoxy adapted to its new surroundings; for example, daily services were held well before first light in order to accommodate the laboring man. Caught up in the bustle of America, however, fewer Jewish immigrants were deeply concerned about the fate of Orthodoxy.

The large attendance of Jewish children in schools was often noted, and the free public schools proved to be the most important factor in developing a new Jewish community in America. Approximately 25 percent of those children over fourteen years who migrated to America could not read or write in any language, and Jews, probably more than any other immigrant group, associated free and equal education with their image of America, because they had been denied such opportunities in the Old World. Public schools made Americans of Jewish immigrants within a single generation and became the vehicle for upward mobility, status, and influence within the community. Immigrant parents were appalled at the rapid acculturation caused by public schools, but, nevertheless, proletarian parents gave their wholehearted blessings to sons and even daughters taking advantage of this new opportunity. So they sent their children through the elementary grades, though many went no further, because they had to enter the sweatshops at age twelve or thirteen.

However, a large percentage of those who did well in the secondary schools went on to the free City College of New York, called the "Jewish College of America," because by the turn of the century, it was mainly Jewish in population. By 1914, City College had a 75 percent Jewish enrollment and, within a generation, more than half of New York City's physicians, dentists, and teachers were Jewish. By 1900, youngsters of East European background had become the majority in the city's free educational institutions. Outside New York, Jews also crowded into the municipal equivalents of City College. Of note, too, was the founding, in Philadelphia in 1907, of Dropsie College for Hebrew and Cognate Languages, a small, nonprofit, nonsectarian graduate institution. Jewish college students were numerous enough by 1906 to found the Menorah Society, a group stressing Judaism as a positive element.

Because every child was expected to spend the greater part of his day in the American public school system, the early immigrants were faced with the problem of religious education for the children. This problem was solved in some cities by the Hebrew Sunday School which had been in existence many years before and which established schools in sections where the new immigration settled. Parents supplemented this religious instruction by hiring teachers to come to their houses to instruct the children every day after school in the rudiments of Hebrew, especially that which was used in public worship. These teachers eventually opened schools where Hebrew was the only subject of instruction, and there were several such schools in Philadelphia supported by voluntary contributions. Sessions were held every day of the week including Saturdays and Sundays.

Hedarim, religious elementary schools in single rooms where Hebrew, the prayer book, and the Bible were taught, were also set up in New York City by East European Jews, much to the consternation of the uptown Jewish community. More advanced or professional schools, like the *Talmud Torahs* with a number of graded classes were conducted after public school hours and were supported by tuition fees and contributions of both East European Jews and generous German Jews. Again this schooling was supplementary. It was difficult for parents to force Jewish children to attend instruction after a full day of school. As a result, the children rejected more and more the customs of the Old World and became Americanized just by after-school play in the streets and also in the Young Men's Hebrew Association and Educational Alliance, formed and encouraged by German Jews to help Americanize immigrant groups.

On a different level, the first full-time elementary religious school, the Etz-Chaim Talmudical Academy, was founded in New York in 1887. And in 1896 East European Jews of the same city set up the Rabbi Isaac Elchanan Theological Seminary (eventually to evolve into Yeshiva University), the first *yeshiva* in the United States. A private agency, the Educational Alliance, was formed in the 1890s with the aim of Americanizing the foreign Jew. Free technical schools, one for boys called the Hebrew Technical Institute and the Hebrew Technical School for girls, as well as the free Baron de Hirsch Trade School, were also founded in New York City. By 1910, Socialist-oriented Zionists organized the first Yiddish school system, and six years later the Workmen's Circle, an anti-Zionist socialist organization, organized its own network of schools.

Yet all these educational efforts reached only a small proportion of immigrant children. Poverty, indifference, and weakened parental control kept many away from formal Jewish education. A 1908 report revealed that about 75 percent of Jewish children between six and sixteen received no religious education, although the usual pattern whereby children attended for only a few years meant that a greater number among a generation would have been exposed to some religious instruction than might show in a count taken at any one time. More than the 75 percent were bar-mitzvahed, but few girls attended religious classes.

Jews also shared all immigrants' experiences with the settlement houses that grew from the guilty consciences that Gilded Age conditions imparted to some Americans. Settlement work became an avocation among American Jews, especially among "emancipated" Jewish women. Christian missionary organizations usually preceded Jewish relief houses, much to the dismay of immigrant mothers who saw their children attracted to these non-Jewish places. The first Jewish settlement house for immigrants opened in Chicago in 1888. Upper-class Jewish reformers took up full-time residence in the slums to deal with the problems of health and home care, schooling, recreation, culture, and civics. They also spurred the building of parks and public baths, the formation of labor centers and libraries, and they helped to arouse respect for Jewish customs, ceremonies and environment. Jewish settlement work, however, proved only a passing phase. Jews moved out of the hardship class earlier than other groups and also out of the depressed areas of the cities.

The education and Americanization of Jewish immigrants often had unhappy results, such as the growing hostility between Old World parents and their New World offspring. Synagogue elders were especially anxious, as they noted the wild behavior of young people, their frequent violation of religious taboos, their nonattendance at the synagogue, their violation of dietary laws, and, eventually most important of all, intermarriage. Americanized youngsters sometimes came to despise their parents because they were "foreigners." This generation gap, common to all immigrant groups, was more serious to Jews because it involved not only a loss of parental authority and abandonment of Old World habits, but also a threat to traditions which constituted the roots of Judaism. In spite of his American environment and pride in his limited English vocabulary, the Jewish ghetto father remained pretty much as he was when he landed: patriarchal, devoted to the law and prayer, trained in a narrow sectarian direction, and often insensitive to modern conditions. The Jewish mother, who spoke only Yiddish, was absorbed in observing the religious law and taking care of her numerous children. Drab and plain in appearance, she tried desperately to fulfill religious obligations, while at the same time laboring to make her children Americans as quickly as possible. Usually she became partially accustomed to change, but all through her life she continued to be dismayed by the precocity, irreligion, and Americanism of her children.

Enticed by the American economic lure, and acquiring a feeling of loyalty for this nation, the East European Jew quickly desired to assimilate in matters outside of religion. He wanted to become a part of America. He did not want to be considered a foreigner in this new land which he considered his home.

One of the main vehicles used to aid the Jew in the

assimilatory process was the Yiddish newspaper. In an era when newspapers and periodicals were growing rapidly in number and quality, the Jewish yearning for free expression that had been stifled in the Old World erupted in the New. Between 1885 and 1914 over one hundred fifty daily, weekly, monthly, quarterly, and festival journals and yearbooks in Yiddish appeared in New York City, the largest number of periodicals published by any immigrant group. They espoused all points of view: traditional and anti-traditional, humorous and philosophical, commercial, recreational, literary, anarchist, socialist, Zionist, and pro-labor. Most important were the newspapers—12 in New York alone in 1891. They played a leading role in the life of the immigrant Jew, giving him information he could get nowhere else because he could not read English. Indeed the Yiddish press, on its editorial pages, devoted 64 percent of its space to American topics.

The *Yiddish Tageblatt (Jewish Daily News)*, founded in New York in 1885, claimed to be the first Yiddish daily in America, although it appeared only three or four times a week. The dailies' most successful period began in the late 1890s. Three out of four founded in the mid-1890s survived for a respectable length of time, and by the turn of the century America had seven Yiddish dailies, six in New York and one in Chicago. The most important socialist paper was the *Arbeiter Zeitung* (1890–1902), the organ of the United Hebrew Trades.

After 1901, the dedicated socialist, Abraham Cahan transformed one of its successors, the *Jewish Daily Forward* (founded in 1897), into the pacemaker of Yiddish journalism. One of its features, letters of advice from the editor, the *Bintel Brief (Bundle of Letters)*, provided a warm and human insight into ghetto life. The Yiddish newspaper was perhaps the most important of the new cultural developments of immigrant Jewry. At a penny a day, it kept thousands of Jews of diverse backgrounds, confused in a crowded alien world, aware of their common heritage. Cahan's tenure as editor ended only with his death in 1951.

Also vital as a popular medium of Jewish immigrant culture and recreation was the Yiddish theater. It attracted all the people of the ghetto: sweatshop mothers and their babies, day laborers, small shopkeepers, socialists, scholars, poets, and journalists. The Yiddish theater reflected the world of the ghetto—the serious as well as trivial interests of the entire Jewish immigrant community. It portrayed in grotesque fashion American customs and satirized the old Orthodox ways. It offered a mass of vaudeville, light opera, and historical and melodramatic plays, as well as a more serious element demanded by the intellectuals. Especially popular among immigrant Jews was Shakespeare's *King Lear*, probably because it dealt with ungrateful children, a common complaint of ghetto life. Noteworthy, too, was the fact that Lear was portrayed as a businessman.

Yiddish theater of course began in Europe but eventually became an institution unique to America. The first performance of a Yiddish play in the United States was held in 1882 in New York, and the first permanent theater was a transformed music hall on the Bowery. By 1900 New York supported three Yiddish theaters whose seventy or eighty professional actors and dozen playwrights presented over one thousand performances annually before an estimated two million patrons. On weekday evenings the theaters were let to guilds or clubs for a continual round of benefits. On Friday, Saturday, and Sunday nights the house was always sold out at twenty five cents to one dollar a seat. Yiddish actors such as Maurice Schwartz (founder of the Yiddish Art Theater in 1918), Jacob Adler, who turned from musicals and melodramas to serious works, David Kessler, Boris Thomashefsky, Cantor Zelig Mogalesco, and the beautiful Mrs. Bertha Kalisch were all very popular. Jacob M. Gordin, the author of the Jewish Lear as merchant, and Joseph Latteiner were the best-known playwrights. As Jewish districts began to blend into the cities, they were invaded by ten-cent vaudeville and ten-cent movies, and along with the plays, had been a vital factor in the survival of Yiddish culture in America. They had amused the public, and had brought a little variety and pleasure into the monotonous lives of the immigrant Jews.

Yiddish theater was one of the signs of a revitalization of the Yiddish tongue in the United States. Immigrant intellectuals developed Yiddish, an imprecise, vernacular dialect in East Europe, into an agent of enlightenment and Americanization. Perhaps the most important means was an impressive literary culture. Harkavy's *Complete English-Jewish Dictionary* appeared in 1891. Escapist popular literature in Yiddish found an eager market in the tenement; women desired romantic fiction and the men, adventure stories. New York City became the largest Yiddish book mart in the world. Book publishing itself developed more slowly, but the merger of a number of bookseller printers of New York into the Hebrew Publishing Company in 1901 augured better times for Yiddish publishing.

That the Jews were finally becoming economically self-sufficient and comfortable in the United States was attested to by their contribution to literature and the arts. For example, Charles Frohman, David Belasco, and the Shubert Brothers became famous producers for the American stage. Belasco is remembered for bringing realism to the stage, Frohman for his numerous, successful productions, and the Shuberts as vaudeville entrepreneurs for the entire nation. Still another producer, Oscar Hammerstein's main goal was to popularize opera. And on-stage performers included many music and comedic notables. One very outstanding Jewish artist was Moses Jacob Ezekiel, a talented sculptor who became nationally known for a bust of President Woodrow Wilson. Literature abounded with Jewish talent such as Mary Antin, Abraham Cahan, and Edna Ferber. Mary Antin's *The Promised Land* (1912) was a syrupy account of an impoverished immigrant who became successful in the manner of the dream most immigrants were imagined to have. Abraham Cahan's classic, *The Rise of David Levinsky* (1917), provided a sober and realistic insight into the ghetto, the clothing industry, Jewish immigrant life, and the Americanization of immigrants. Edna Ferber's *Fanny*

Herself (1917), described a Jewish community in Wisconsin where the Americanized Jew lived among his Gentile neighbors with greater ease than ever before. Morris Rosenfeld's poetry was filled with references to the sweatshops, the immigrants, and their quest for the better life. There were many other artists but these examples are typical and symbolic of the contributions American Jews were beginning to make to the life of the mind.

The story of Jewish labor as well as the radical tendencies of some of the workers also served as an agency of acculturation. At the turn of the century, unions in the needle trades, whose Jewish membership was their largest ethnic component, were not as strong as the oldest American unions. Rudimentary collective bargaining existed, but the low wages, long hours, and child labor in the sweatshops attested to the fact that the problems were too extensive to be solved overnight. In 1911, a fire broke out in the Triangle Shirtwaist Company killing 146 people, mostly Jewish women. Numerous laws were passed in New York City, Boston, and Philadelphia to control sanitation, unsafe conditions, and slowly the contract system, where piecework was done in the home, gave way to work in small factories. One of the main reasons the East European Jews did not at first support trade unions and labor organizations to the same extent as other nationalities was their strong belief that they did not intend to be workingmen all their lives. Tammany Hall, New York's Democratic party organization, assisted Jews and other groups in order to perpetuate its power, and when a Jewish socialist was elected to the House of Representatives in 1914, Tammany was unhappy, realizing that a strong socialist party in the East Side was a threat to its control.

However, not surprisingly, many Jewish immigrant intellectuals turned to radical solutions for the problems of the urban slums. Although the total number of true Jewish revolutionaries was small, all sorts of Jewish radicals appeared—socialists, anarchists, positivists, and even visionary utopian reformers. The anarchists were dedicated to the task of unfrocking traditional orthodox beliefs, using such strategems as irreverent "Yom Kippur Balls," featuring music, dancing, and food.

More important were the socialists, for they were influential in the labor movement and had non-Jewish Marxist connections. Socialists of all varieties were anti-religious and divided into two groups during this period: those who wanted Marxist universalism and those who favored a Yiddishist secular culture divorced from religion. The latter founded their own schools and are still partly active through YIVO (*Yiddisher Vissenshaftlicher Institut*, Yiddish Scientific Institute), which moved to New York from Vilna in Poland in 1940 as a result of World War II. Abraham Cahan had delivered the first Yiddish socialist speech as early as 1882 and during the 1880s, radicals established several short-lived organizations such as the Jewish Workingmen's Association, the Russian Progressive Association, and the Pioneers of Liberty. Socialists played a major role in founding the UHT (United Hebrew Trades) in 1888, a union for Jews working in the garment industry. In the early 1890s the largely Jewish Russian and Hungarian sections of the Socialist Labor party in New York City had only 140 members, and the Party continued to be dominated by Germans. Not until the turn of the century, after Daniel DeLeon had managed to split the Socialist Labor Party, did socialist politics lose its appeal to German trade unionists and socialist leadership fall to Russians and East European Jews.

Socialism and radicalism never became strong enough to destroy Judaism in America. Immigrant Jews, though knowing poverty and endless toil, had no experience in class conflict. Moreover, East European Jews came in large enough numbers to be able to create a flourishing religious life as well as an intense Jewish secularism in radical political organization and unions. It was not uncommon for a Jewish worker to read an anti-religious Yiddish paper, vote socialist, join a socialist union and yet attend a synagogue regularly and observe most Jewish laws. In fact, even though socialist papers attacked the Spanish-American War (1898) as a capitalist enterprise, Jewish workmen saw it as a test of their newly acquired patriotism and nine hundred recent Jewish immigrants enrolled as army volunteers to swell the total number of Jews who served to at least 4,000.

At the beginning of the twentieth century, the Jewish labor movement had established its own secular Yiddish schools, press, (the *Forward* was in essence the UHT organ), welfare agencies, and even its own popular national fraternal order, the Workmen's Circle, which afforded medical and insurance benefits. The labor-radical secularists, the leaders of the Jewish unions, directed their followers towards the socialism they had carried from Russia.

By 1900, there were eighty nine unions supporting the United Hebrew Trades with a total of 100,000 members, and after World War I, the total membership rose to 250,000. Because of its effective leadership, the Jewish laboring group, which was a small minority within the American Jewish population, won a major degree of security by the 1920s. Several of their leaders deserve special mention. Sidney Hillman, founder and first president of the Amalgamated Clothing Workers of America (1914), procured notable workers' benefits. The International Ladies Garment Workers (ILGWU) numbered 10,000 members by 1903 and was the largest of the UHT units. Under its energetic leader, David Dubinsky, the ILGWU rejected strikes whenever possible, concentrating more on collective bargaining. A daring strike leader was the Russian immigrant, Joseph Barondess, who was a force among Jewish workingmen and especially those in the garment trade until his death in 1928. He was unique in that he fused socialism and Zionism into a Jewish Zionist Labor party. Two other socialists, journalist and novelist Abraham Cahan and attorney Morris Hillquit, were able to appeal directly to Yiddish-speaking workers and also represent them to the English-speaking Americans because of their mastery of both tongues. These men helped further the cause of trade unionism which became important not only in helping the East European Jews adjust to the new ways of their adopted country, but also in improving their mode of living. Through these unions, just as through their synagogues and lodges, they learned how to accommodate more comfortably to what had once been a strange land. Another aspect of Jewish accommodation was the change that occurred in organized religious institutions. According to classical Reform theology, Judaism was a religion with a universal message. Hence the political aspects of Zionism, which so absorbed the attention of the East European immigrant, simply appalled the older German Jewry. The great organizer of American reform, Dr. Isaac M. Wise, in his presidential address to the Central Conference of American Rabbis (the organization of Reform rabbis), claimed that Zionism in America was sponsored by refugees who had been persecuted in Europe, and he loudly proclaimed that the United States was the only homeland for American Jews. Through the Reform press—the *American Israelite*, founded by Isaac Wise, and the *Reform Advocate*, edited by Dr. Emil G. Hirsch, widespread opposition was aroused against Zionism. From the point of view of the children of East European immigrants, Zionism was an outlet for their nonobservant variety of Judaism. This second generation group was uncertain of its place in American culture, baffled by problems of social and economic adjustment, and fearful of anti-Semitism. Just as the influence of the German-Jew was waning, these people came forward to give Zionism its greatest impetus.

Succeeding Wise as President of the Hebrew Union College (founded to train Reform rabbis in 1885) was Kaufmann Kohler, a distinguished theologian and proponent of extreme reform. Not only did East European immigrants originally disdain Reform, but within their own ranks, Stephen S. Wise founded the Free Synagogue (New York), which, while following Reform ritual, was even less doctrinaire and decidedly more Zionist.

The Conservative movement, a compromise between

Reform and Orthodoxy, sought to harmonize tradition and modernism. Within the Conservative fold, the great leader in the early twentieth century was Solomon Schechter, who in 1902 assumed the presidency of the organization to train Conservative rabbis, the Jewish Theological Seminary. Under his dynamic leadership, that institution was regenerated and attempted to reorient Judaism into an all-embracing faith—a "Catholic Israel"—a religion with great flexibility and yet concerned with tradition. By 1913, he had established the United Synagogue of America and the Rabbinical Assembly of America, organizations of Conservative congregations and rabbis respectively, testimony to the growth of this middle-of-the-road approach to Judaism.

It has been estimated that in 1877 there were over two hundred congregations in the United States, nearly all of which were Reform. By the turn of the century, there were over a thousand, most of them Orthodox. This change, caused by the influx of a half-million immigrants, obviously affected the entire nature of American Judaism.

Despite their very real and often successful efforts at adjustment, East European Jews experienced problems of acceptance. Having heard about the liberty and justice of America, the immigrant Jew did not expect to encounter the social and economic prejudice that he found. In particular, he did not expect the condescending attitude of his own brethren. Many native and assimilated Jews were not pleased with the bulk arrival of the East European Jews. They viewed this as a threat to their already established social position. They had become part of the middle class, while the East Europeans gravitated toward the proletariat. They were the donors; the newcomers, the recipients of charity. The German Jews were in contact with American society and cultural life, while the more recent immigrants were massed together in a few large cities where the cultural milieu was more self-contained. And economic and social cleavages were hardened by ideological formulas. Thus, the German Jews could hardly remain immune to this bias, especially when recent ar-

rivals were poor, outlandish in dress and appearance, and un-
tutored in American ways. In any case, a fear swept over
American Jewry lest it be Russified.

The uptown Jews also often denied their East European
brethren membership in some of the established Jewish
cultural organizations. These older organizations were
remote and hardly receptive. B'nai B'rith, for instance,
despite the intention of its founder, Henry Jonas, became
predominantly German. Frequently Russian Jews were black-
balled because of their national origins. In addition to social
discrimination, some Jewish businesses even rejected the new
East European Jews as not good bets for employment.

While the Jew was initially rejected by those of his own
kind, the real discrimination was in the Gentile disregard for
him. At times Gentiles made their dislike obvious, and at
others they hid their feelings behind clichés and laws. The
most obvious discriminatory legislation was the passage of a
literacy test in 1897 designed to restrict immigration. Though
vetoed by President Grover Cleveland, new bills were introduced into Congress between 1906 and 1913, bills which
would have provided not only for a literacy test but also for a
character certificate from the country of origin. Obviously,
Jews could not easily receive such a certificate. Also, much
debate ensued over the use of Yiddish as an authorized
language to establish literacy.

Discrimination issued, not from primarily irrational, sub-
jective impulses, but rather from competition for status and
prestige. The Gentiles' economic fear of the Jew was great,
and so they attempted to keep him at the bottom of the social
ladder by assigning him a place of inferiority. And the more
desperately the Jew sought to escape from confinement and
move up the social ladder, the more panic-stricken others
became. While other European groups generally gained
respect as assimilation improved their status, Jews often
reaped more and more dislike as they bettered themselves.
Normally, unfavorable stereotypes have stressed the ethnic's
inferiority, but Jews often left the opposite impression of

equal or superior capacity, and their unfavorable stereotypes pictured an overbearing Jewish aggression to gain advantage in American life. Also, the impression that Jews were interested in money deepened into the conviction that they controlled the great fortunes of the world, that they were involved in an international conspiracy, the most noteworthy being the Protocols of the Elders of Zion forgery. In large part, the international anti-Semitic banker image was subscribed to by the Populists, an agrarian-labor third political party active in the 1890s. However, there are historians who feel that the Populists were no more anti-Jewish than others.

Yet the discrimination was more social than economic. The Jew was allowed to enter the economic market, encouraged to work hard, and then, once he acquired his financial empire, often barred from enjoying the luxuries which naturally should have come with his status. There had emerged in America a certain social snobbery and exclusiveness which barred Jews from elite social circles, from summer resorts, from private schools, and from some colleges. The most famous early example of social exclusion occurred in 1877 when a Saratoga Springs, New York hotel refused to admit a leading Jewish businessman. No matter what steps Jews took—economic coercion or publicity—this type of restriction continued. The *Chicago Tribune* published its first resort advertisement specifying Christian or Gentile clientele in 1913, and the frequency of such notices increased steadily thereafter. Ostracism was also evident in settlement areas. Older Brooklyn settlers took so unkindly to the newcomers that the latter established a Jewish Protective Association in 1899 to spur civil action against Jew-beating rowdies. Another sizable Jewish colony formed in Harlem, and as it expanded, many a landlord put out a sign bearing the warning, "No Jews."

There was also a pseudo-intellectual basis for prejudice. Many sociologists decided that certain groups, including Jews, were inferior. As learned a man as the author Henry

James feared that New York would become a new Jerusalem. In 1908, Alfred Schultz published *Race or Mongrel*, in which he promulgated the theory that intermarriage with "alien stock" causes nations to fall. The eugenicist, Madison Grant, in 1916, stated that the purity of the Nordic-American "race" was contaminated by Negroes, Latins, and "Semite Jews." And by World War I, there were increased references to the unique Jewish "race." Thus, to a large extent, anti-Semitism was sparked by a cult of Anglo-Saxonism.

Yet the Jews took the ostracism in stride so long as it did not infringe on their economic opportunities. However, it was not long before the Jew realized that social acceptance was necessary in the professions. Many business deals were made over a luncheon engagement or on the golf course, and how could the Jews function if they were barred from some of the prominent social gathering places? This factor became even more pronounced in the colleges. Membership in fraternities or other secret societies was mandatory to gain social prestige; and from these the Jews were barred. Older societies passed rules distinctly excluding all Hebrews, while others instituted religious tests, so that a Hebrew could not conscientiously take their vows and go through their initiation ritual. In spite of the high standing of the Jews in medical schools, the percentage of them who received hospital appointments was small. Social discrimination increased throughout the years before the First World War and affected many professions. For example, the Century Club in New York rejected the distinguished scientist Jacques Loeb because he was a Jew. Jewish lawyers were barred from the leading law firms. In an attempt to combat this social ostracism, middle-class Jews organized their own clubs and fraternities and barred Gentiles from membership. For recreational purposes, Jews converted certain areas such as parts of the Catskills into almost exclusively Jewish summertime settlements.

These hostile attitudes created a self-imposed segregation for Jews which certainly did not help the process of assimilation, but did sharpen the will to survive. In order to combat these attitudes and to protect Jewish civil rights not only in the United States but throughout the world, the American Jewish Committee (AJC) was formed in 1906 by such leaders as Rabbi Judah Magnes of Temple Emanu-El, Louis Marshall, the Sulzbergers, and Judge Julian Mack. Seven years later the venerable B'nai B'rith established its Anti-Defamation League, which still remains the Jewish community's major bulwark against discrimination, formal or informal.

Another example of organization for the common good was the New York Kehillah (a community structure), which lasted from 1908 to 1922. A false accusation by a New York police commissioner that over 50 percent of the city's crime was caused by the Jews (who composed only one fifth of the population) resulted in the establishment of the Kehillah. Despite a retraction, the Jewish community felt it needed a common defense bond. The Kehillah was primarily the creation of Judah Magnes, who despite his status as an important Reform rabbi also appreciated communitywide needs. While the Kehillah performed such important work as helping to suppress ghetto vice, its relationship with the AJC and Zionist organizations was stormy and divisiveness continued within the Jewish sector.

The Jewish refugees of 1881 had expected to find freedom and fresh air in a golden land, but America offered slums and tenements, sweatshops and pushcarts, and insecurity and tension. Yet life proved generally better and freer than in East Europe. Jewish immigrants did not give way to disillusionment or despair despite their tragic and seemingly insoluble dilemmas. They found housing and food sufficient for survival and something not available to them in the old land—opportunity. They displayed a stubborn determination to take every possible advantage of their new situation. With the vitality of its new freedoms and with unflagging perseverance, hope, and self-reliance, Jewish society re-established itself in a metropolitan environment. The mere fact that its great numbers had crowded into the cities and not dispersed throughout the countryside insured that the East European

Jewish community survived the traumas of transition. As time passed, the Jew, like other immigrant groups, became a respected ingredient in the Melting Pot. Yet the twentieth century was to prove that all forms of ethnicity had longer life than expected. Some began to speculate that America, rather than being a Melting Pot, was a gigantic tossed salad, wherein the constituents could remain identified.

2

In Defense of the Brethren: To 1920

ONE OBVIOUS RESPONSE TO the many Jewish persecutions—both subtle and overt—was the revival of the ancient ideal of a Jewish restoration, of a Jewish homeland in Palestine. While Zionism among Jews was a relatively small affair in the nineteenth century, there was such Christian Zionist interest as various colonization schemes, a Protestant vision that the millennium could come only with a Zionist restoration, and the Blackstone Memorial (1891) voicing concern over the Russian treatment of Jews. Among the Jews there were "Lovers of Zion" clubs (1884), the "Knights of Zion," the Central Organization of American Zionists (1897), and finally the Federation of American Zionists, a collection of more than one hundred Zionist clubs, organized by Rabbi Richard Gottheil who, along with Rabbi Stephen S. Wise, was its chief leader. By 1900, the federation was eight thousand strong and the number was to more than triple within five years. This is only a capsule summary of the complicated history of Zionism's origin in America.

Modern political Zionism, associated with the work of Theodor Herzl, was an attempt to achieve by diplomatic influence a Palestinian homeland. This, it was argued, would

29

not only provide Jews with tangible identification but would also serve as an escape hatch for those oppressed in Eastern Europe and elsewhere. Such was the thrust of the Basle Program adopted at the First Zionist Congress (Basle, Switzerland, 1897), the initial worldwide gathering of the Zionist enthusiasts.

In the United States, Zionism aroused much controversy and reflected the bifurcation of the Jewish community. Zionism was in direct opposition to the Pittsburgh Platform, adopted by Reform Jews in 1885, which declared that Jews were no longer a nation, but a religious community and therefore did not expect nor desire a return to the biblical homeland. In his presidential address to the 1897 Central Conference of American Rabbis, the great Reform leader, Dr. Isaac Mayer Wise, bluntly declared that the object of Judaism was not political or national, but purely spiritual. On the whole, the philosophy of Reform was utterly opposed to Zionism; its entire theology viewed the Dispersion as indispensable for the fulfillment of the "Mission of Israel." Among the exceptions were Rabbis Bernard Felsenthal of Chicago, Maximillian Heller of New Orleans, Stephen Wise and Gustave and Richard Gottheil of New York. These leaders were instrumental in calling attention to the Herzlian proposals and publicizing the latter's ideas. As a matter of fact, Reform pro-Zionists were more numerous than previously thought.

Despite the active orthodox wing of Zionism, the *Mizrachi*, many Orthodox Jews refused to adhere to Zionism. This part of the right wing placed too great a faith in the Messianic ideal to be wooed by such a secular movement as that proposed in Basle. Then, too, the Arbeiter Ring was equally opposed to Zionism. This group claimed that such a plan of restoration was reactionary and would interfere with the unity of the working classes.

But, the Basle Program greatly spurred Zionist activity in America. The multiplication of Zionist clubs and societies—the Zionist Federation, Knights of Zion, Order of the Sons of

Zion, Young Judea, Hadassah—attested to the strength the movement was assuming in the United States. A Zionist outlet offered many American Jews a release from the peculiar problems of Americanization and assimilation.

The general press showed a divided reaction. Only a minority opposed Zionism and even these were more skeptical than hostile. Events in Zionist history were reported faithfully in both the religious and secular press. The Uganda scheme, an alternate plan for a Palestinian homeland in Africa, was debated over and over in the press. Americans were kept well informed, too, of the dispute between "Orthodox" Zionists, who remained unswervingly loyal to Palestine, and the "Territorialists," who wanted an "asylum for the night"—any available Zion. The Kishinev Pogrom of April, 1903, in Russia excited beyond measure an America not yet calloused by world wars, Fascism, and Communism. President Theodore Roosevelt extended his deepest sympathy to the Jews and the press excoriated the Russian barbarity. And after Kishinev, Zionism became increasingly popular with American Jewry.

In the United States, Zionist ideology was influenced by a new influx of Russian Jews who emigrated here after the abortive Revolution of 1905. The events of 1905 disillusioned many of these Jews who had thought that their future would lie in a democratized Russia. These immigrants now wished to retain their identity as Jews and to incorporate socialist values into nascent Jewish nationalism. As already mentioned, New York garment union official Joseph Barondess synthesized Zionism and socialism into *Poale Zion* (Jewish Zionist Labor party). Thus, Zionism in the United States was represented not only by a *Mizrachi* Right wing, but by a *Poale Zion* Left flank.

Much of the impetus for the Zionist drive was thus motivated by conditions in Russia—pogroms, restrictions on where Jews could live and what trades they could pursue. Russian persecution and discrimination was obviously anathema to Americans and contradictory to the American heritage and tradition whereby United States citizens were not discriminated against on the basis of race and religion in any part of the world.

American Jews were refused passports, and with Russian-Jewish immigration increasing, some American Jews desired to return to visit relatives or to handle business matters. Also, there was the fear of renewed pogroms. While Jews applied continued pressure to both the White House and State Department, the government saw little good in threatening economic relations with Russia for a cause over which it had no control. Whether formerly Russian subjects or not, Jews could not be admitted to Russia unless they obtained special permission in advance from the Czarist government. In 1910, the American Jewish Committee, which as we have seen was created to protect Jewish rights, decided to push the matter and addressed a letter to President William Howard Taft concerning discriminatory conditions and urging the abrogation of the 1832 Russo-American Commercial Treaty. A successful abrogation resolution was introduced in 1911 by Representative William Sulzer of New York, the chairman of the House Committee on Foreign Affairs. Russia refused to soften its discrimination, and while Taft believed that Jewish demands for civil rights were reasonable when applied to American Jews residing in Russia, the treaty was in effect ended when key Russian exports to the United States were removed from "most favored nation" status.

On another level, one of the first major achievements of the American Jewish Committee was to influence the New York State Legislature to enact a law making it a misdemeanor for any public accommodation to advertise a policy of excluding anyone because of race, creed, or color. This measure, which became law on the eve of World War I, fell short of more modern equal-accommodation bills because it punished not the act itself, but merely the advertising of an intent to commit it. Similar legislation was passed by other states under the pressure of the Anti-Defamation League of B'nai B'rith. Although such laws contained more bark than bite, the American Jewish Committee found them to be quite useful instruments in combating discriminatory advertising practices during the war.

At home, religious intolerance persisted in America's attitude toward immigration. An attempt to stem the so-called surge of "undesirables" was the Burnett Bill, which eventually succeeded in imposing a literacy test on immigrants. Following its passage in the House, President Woodrow Wilson and members of Congress were besieged with a flurry of memoranda from various Jewish organizations objecting strenuously to the literacy clause. Like Cleveland and McKinley before him, Wilson vetoed the Literacy Act but it was passed over his veto. The test was particularly hard on Jews because many were highly intelligent, but by force of circumstances were only marginally literate in Yiddish.

During the war years, anti-Semitism abated considerably either because there was a shortage of labor and Jews were essential to the war effort, or possibly because a feeling of solidarity and good fellowship came through fighting a common enemy. However, such euphoria was only surface deep. Some Masonic lodges still excluded Jews, and the better prep schools, social clubs and college fraternities were also closed to them. Social discrimination was greater in the large cities east of the Mississippi and north of the Mason and Dixon line. The smaller towns, where the Jews were longer established and better integrated into the life of the community, were less hostile. Yet it was in the South that a particularly ugly anti-Semitic incident occurred. In 1915, Leo Frank, a northern Jew and a resident of Atlanta, was convicted of the murder of a young girl in his employ. Frank was innocent but nevertheless, even when his sentence of death was commuted by the governor, he was lynched and hanged by some of the angry townspeople. And the revived Ku Klux Klan (1915), in addition to an anti-Catholic and anti-black posture, also preached discrimination against Jews.

Despite the powerful Jewish role in motion pictures, that industry also had its anti-Semitic features. Whenever a pro-

ducer wished to depict a betrayer of public trust, a hard-
boiled, usurious money lender, a crooked gambler, a grafter,
a depraved firebug, a white slaver, or other villains of one
kind or another, the character was often represented as a
Jew. The Anti-Defamation League attempted to persuade the
industry-sponsored National Board of Censorship to eliminate films that portrayed American Jews as Shylocks. The
Board, however, was preoccupied with barring films that
it considered lascivious or obscene and took no action.
When one of the many theatres owned by Jews boycotted a
movie with the usual stereotypes, *Rebecca's Wedding Day*
(Chicago, 1916), Hollywood got the message and agreed to
cease producing anti-Semitic films.

Under President Wilson the philo-Semitic policies of
Theodore Roosevelt were continued and amplified. Henry
Morgenthau, Sr., was appointed Ambassador to Turkey, a
strategic spot since from the Jewish point of view, the Ot-
toman Empire misruled Palestine and oppressed a large
population of Jews and other non-Moslem minority peoples.
Later, Morgenthau undertook a mission with another Jew,
Professor Felix Frankfurter of the Harvard Law School, to
convince Turkey to leave the war and to ameliorate Jewish
conditions in Palestine. Bernard M. Baruch was placed in
charge of the War Industrial Board, which mobilized
American industry for war, and Wilson broke precedent by
naming the brilliant attorney Louis Dembitz Brandeis as the
first Jew to the Supreme Court. His confirmation by the
Senate, however, ran into unusual difficulties before assent
was given to the appointment.

In the elective sphere, Jews were also becoming politically
active. In New York State, which contained over half the
Jewish population of the United States and which was a
special area of concentration for Jews of Russian and East
European origin, nine of the sixteen Jews elected to the
Assembly were Democrats against only five Republicans and
two Socialists. Socialist inroads into the recently arrived
American Jewish vote were meager, for as long as religious

traditions and the desire to succeed under capitalism remained substantially intact, the socialist doctrine lacked mass appeal.

But by 1912 there were 125,826 members of the Socialist party—an all-time peak. The party drew its membership from rural and mining areas in the West and Southwest, but by 1920, the party's geographic and ethnic base had shifted to the urban and industrialized East, where it developed an attraction for the foreign-born, particularly Jewish workers. The strong anti-war stance of the Socialist party eventually brought in new elements, and the composition of the party changed drastically. The foreign-language sections, which amounted to less than twelve percent of the pre-war Socialist membership, climbed to a majority. Of these, the predominantly East European Jewish federations would later constitute the nucleus of the Communist party. Conditions resulting from the Industrial Revolution were terrible in New York City, where Jews labored untold hours for meager wages, often sleeping only a few hours beside their machines. Such exploitation is one of the reasons for the growth of New York City radicalism, radical party membership, and the strength of the Socialist party.

Jewish interest in militant socialism developed rapidly following the Russian Revolutions of 1917. Meyer London, a Jewish Socialist, had won an easy election to the House of Representatives in 1914 and 1916 from New York. At its 1919 convention, the Socialist party was split asunder by its left wing, which was composed of nearly 70,000 members. When the showdown came, they either joined one of the two rival revolutionary organizations—the Communist party and the Communist Labor party—or else, disillusioned by factional bickering, dropped out of the extreme left-wing movements. And the raids against "radicals" led by the Department of Justice under the leadership of Attorney General A. Mitchell Palmer reduced the membership of the Communist party by more than 50 percent between 1919 and 1920. Many Jews clung to the belief that Socialist or Communist movements would create a world in which all men would live in peace and anti-Semitism would vanish. As historic evidence controverting this expectation accumulated, American Jews reluctantly began to abandon the secular collectivist faith, but the illusion that equality and fraternity would be promoted by the victory of the left died slowly.

Another plan proposed in 1915 to ameliorate the condition of worldwide Jewry and one which received support from a large segment of American Jews was the idea of an American Jewish Congress. In essence, it was a liberal, activist, pro-Zionist counterweight to the more anti-Zionist elite American Jewish Committee. Essentially, the concept of a congress grew out of an earlier idea of Rabbi Judah L. Magnes of Temple Emanu-El in New York City (the New York Kehillah Council). The executive-secretary of the Jewish Congress Organization Committee, Bernard G. Richards, reported that twenty-three national and central organizations boasting a membership of over 900,000 had endorsed the idea. Enthusiastic support of the movement was expressed in January 1916 by more than 3,000 persons attending a mass meeting in Carnegie Hall in New York City. When the First Jewish Congress, composed of 400 delegates, convened in Philadelphia in 1918 it did not know its own mind and hardly had a common purpose. It was a loose aggregation of mutually distrustful delegates and tiny, pugnacious factions, bent much more resolutely on suppressing and discrediting one another than on achieving any common end. Yet within a three day session, the congress surprisingly achieved much. Julian Mack, Louis Marshall, and Jacob Schiff emerged as leaders, and the Congress addressed itself to the questions of pogroms and boycotts in Poland, the unfulfilled treaty obligations of the Russian government to grant civil rights to its Jewish population, the future of the starving and homeless in Eastern Europe, and the final disposition of Palestine.

Among the many other types of organizations which proliferated in the Jewish community (in 1918, there were over 3,600 in New York City alone) were those that attempted to systematize philanthropy. Each major city eventually had its Federation of Jewish Charities whereby separate appeals could be eliminated, and in 1900 the National Conference of Jewish Charities was founded. Local federations were concerned with old age homes, orphanages, hospitals, YMHAs and YWHAs, educational institutions, and family service agencies.

With the outbreak of war, the American Jewish community found itself confronted with the monumental task of providing the essentials of life for millions of its coreligionists. The war had halted the hordes of immigrants, and now American Jews directed their energies outward and across the sea. Accordingly, at its meeting in August 1914, the Executive Board of the American Jewish Committee took the first steps for the relief of the Jews in the warring countries. The problem and remedy were easily definable, but the mechanics of alleviating the misery of European Jewry were time-consuming. Relief work had to be streamlined, dissension had to be minimized, and relief coordinated and highly centralized.

Because of the need for a centralized disbursement agency, several groups organized to provide aid and united to form the Joint Distribution Committee of the American Friends of Jewish War Sufferers (referred to as the Joint Distribution Committee or JDC) in November 1914. The JDC, the major American Jewish overseas relief agency, was a nonpartisan, international organization headed by Felix M. Warburg of the premier American Jewish banking family. Its seat was in New York City though it sponsored fund-raising campaigns in each community with sizable Jewish populations. It also collected moneys from Canada and Cuba for disbursement. Within a year, $1.5 million was collected, and in 1916, a goal of $5 million was almost reached. From 1914 to 1924, about $59 million was raised, the heaviest amounts coming after the war had lifted American Jewry to a new affluence.

While this nation was neutral, the JDC could aid both sides but because the war in Eastern Europe was so terrible, most of the support went to assist Jewish communities there. Another prime area for American relief was the Holy Land, cut off by the war from necessary imports and profitable exports. As soon as Turkey cast her lot with the Central Powers, Palestinian Jews were subjected to repeated oppression, and the American press regularly publicized reports of the suffering. So intense was the problem that Ambassador Henry Morgenthau, Sr. cabled for immediate financial help from American Jews.

The Turkish generalissimo in the Palestine sector expelled those Jews branded as Zionists, confiscated their land, and rejected their naturalization applications. In 1915, foreign Jews of allied citizenship were given the alternative of either becoming Turkish subjects or leaving the country. Secretary of State William Jennings Bryan ordered Ambassador Morgenthau to hold the Turkish officials responsible for the lives and property of American Christians or Jews in case of looting or massacres.

American Jewish help was forthcoming, for in late August 1914 a conference of Zionists had organized the Provisional Executive Committee for General Zionist Affairs. This conference marked the appearance of a new Zionist leader in the person of Louis D. Brandeis, who assumed the chairmanship of the committee. He arranged through the State Department to have the American consulate in Alexandria act as a depository and distribution agency for supplies and succor to Palestinian refugees. The Jewish community in Palestine had to be saved if a Zionist goal was to be a reality.

Several American vessels, such as the *Vulcan*, laden with food and medical supplies were dispatched in 1915, and a medical unit sponsored by Hadassah, the Woman's Zionist Organization, was shipped to the Holy Land the next year. Thus, with the critical situation in the Middle East, American help—both official and nonofficial—was of tremendous importance in ameliorating conditions and in giving Jews a foothold in the Holy Land.

One interesting footnote to the involvement of Palestine

and Jews in the First World War was the impact of the hostilities on a small group of Palestinians, one of whom was David Ben Gurion, later to be the chief architect of modern Israel. This band of refugees took sail for America instead of sitting out the war in Alexandria. In the New World they toured Jewish communities as "missionaries," propagandizing the cause of Palestine as a Jewish homeland. One "convert" was the Milwaukee school teacher, Golda Myerson (Meir), who was to become prime minister of Israel. The tour was not an overwhelming success; in fact, the travelers did not understand the American mentality, nor even the ambivalent nature of American Zionism.

Since much of the American-Jewish community had firsthand experience with persecution, one would think they would have been more inclined toward intervention in the war long before an aroused American public became decidedly pro-Ally as the result of Germany's policy of attacking neutral shipping by submarine attacks. American Jewry found itself in a delicate position. Russia was the arch antagonist but she was also the ally of England with whom traditional American sympathies resided. Thus, much of American Jewry chose the path of neutrality. But, during the neutrality period, influential German Jews were often pro-German, in part out of Fatherland loyalties, in part because of Russian pogroms. Jewish socialists were against both sides since they considered war the supreme curse of capitalism. But, as April 6, 1917, neared, most Jews with the exception of the Marxists became prowar. Occupied by their own climb up the ladder of success, recent Jewish immigrants were also often uninformed of the events taking place across the Atlantic. Generally, the vanguard championing the European Jewish cause seemed to be the affluent. Louis Marshall, speaking at a meeting on January 13, 1915, deplored what he termed the failure of the American Jews to realize the terrible calamity that had overtaken the millions of Jews whose homes were in the eastern theater of the European war. Marshall, as head of the American Jewish War Relief Committee, announced that since December 1914 the Committee had sent $200,000 to Europe and Palestine.

With the Jewish cry for freedom from religious and political persecution becoming increasingly vocal, the Jewish relief effort was able gradually to free itself from the restraining elements which had retarded the centralization of authority and hence became able to channel its desires more effectively. Even President Wilson promised that when there was peace, he would use his best efforts to secure the rights of the Jews in Russia and Rumania.

Although assurances for postwar Jewry were all well and good, their needs were immediate. According to many communal leaders, Jewish relief organizations, although doing an admirable job, were felt to be unequal to the occasion. Mass appeals seemed to be inadequate, a belief reflecting the divisiveness within the American Jewish community. Therefore, in the fall of 1915, a new committee to raise funds for the Jewish War Sufferers was organized—the Peoples Relief Committee, of which the Socialist, Meyer London, was chairman. In the course of a few weeks, this body, which made its appeal chiefly to the Jewish laboring masses, succeeded in raising considerable funds. By mid-summer 1917 it had turned over to the treasury of the Joint Distribution Committee more than $800,000. Perhaps the most noteworthy and dramatic of all relief gestures was that of the Sears, Roebuck magnate, Julius Rosenwald, who promised $1 million if the other $9 million of a proposed $10 million goal could be raised. The Peoples Relief Committee was not intended to rival existing agencies. Rather, it was to work with them. The American Jewish Committee directed its efforts among the more prosperous Jews; another group, the Central Relief Committee, worked among the orthodox element; and the Peoples Committee, with the more radical, laboring and professional elements.

The great communal leader, Rabbi Judah L. Magnes, went to the German-occupied portions of Poland and Lithuania to study first-hand the conditions of the Jews there and to guide the distribution of relief from America. He told a graphic story to representatives from the American Jewish Relief Committee and the Peoples Relief Committee. He predicted that if the war continued a year longer it would be bad enough, but if it lasted for two or more years, all world Jewry would be seriously endangered.

Appeals beyond the Jewish community were also made. A Senate resolution requested President Wilson to designate a day as Jewish Relief Day, on which contributions would be raised for the 9 million suffering Jews in the war zone. Wilson eventually proclaimed January 27, 1916, as Jewish War Sufferers Relief Day. Through the good offices of Louis Marshall and the American Jewish Committee, an appeal was also directed to Pope Benedict XV, pleading for his intercession in alleviating Jewish persecution.

Of all the proposed schemes for aid to Jews or for a Jewish Palestine in which the government of the United States became involved, the only one to bear fruit was the Balfour Declaration (1917). With a vacuum created by a Europe at war, the American Zionists under the direction of Brandeis had now assumed global leadership. It was Brandeis and Rabbi Stephen S. Wise who were to exert the greatest influence on Wilson for an endorsement of the Zionist program. Brandeis's influence was especially important, for as one of the president's trusted advisors, he had provided much of the intellectual stimulation for Wilson's domestic policies.

As early as 1914 Brandeis had explained Zionist goals to Wilson and had received verbal assurances and encouragement of American support. London, eager to win more Jewish support in the United States and Russia, sought Wilson's views on an early draft of what was later to be the famous declaration.

Colonel Edward M. House, Wilson's aide, cautioned the president to be "chary" about committing himself to the Zionists. On September 19, 1917, the great English Zionist, Dr. Chaim Weizmann, cabled the tentative text of the declaration to Brandeis, urging the jurist to secure Wilson's approbation. Five days later, Brandeis reported progress to the English Zionist. Meanwhile, the president, on October 13, had written House that he had read the latter's earlier memorandum but that he approved of the English formula. When the declaration was announced, it was naturally hailed by the Jews the world over. One interesting source of opposition came, however, from the Department of State, which had been bypassed in the negotiations leading to Wilson's approval of the Balfour Declaration. Secretary of State Robert Lansing's letter to Wilson on December 13, 1917, was the beginning of a long policy of anti-Zionism in the State Department. Lansing argued that America should not publicly endorse the declaration for three reasons: the Jews themselves were divided, the United States was not at war with Turkey, and many Christians would oppose a Palestine controlled by the "murderers of Jesus." Thus, the president had to contend with both Lansing and House in his espousal of the British policy.

The story of the creation of the Jewish Welfare Board is still another example of how the Jewish community and the American government cooperated to enhance relief efforts. The United States government, recognizing the morale factor in warfare, set up a special commission on training-camp activities charged with making life there and in the communities adjoining the camps as normal as wartime conditions would allow. This commission, headed by the famous clergyman Harry E. Fosdick, utilized the services of both the Young Men's Christian Association and the Knights of Columbus.

The choice of the YMCA and the Knights of Columbus was a relatively simple selection, since they were the predominant organizations within Protestantism and Catholicism. The task which confronted American Jewry, however, assumed much greater dimensions. The fissures within Jewish ranks prevented the easy designation of a single group. It was a sad commentary upon Jewish life in America, and particularly upon its work of national organization and management, that no single agency could be selected as truly representative. Eventually, representatives of some ten or more national Jewish organizations met and decided that each group should delegate certain powers to a new agency. In this fashion the Jewish Welfare Board (JWB) was created, and it was this organization which obtained official recognition from the American government. The JWB was charged with the selection of chaplains and Jewish welfare workers in the camps and cantonments of this country and in the hospitals and rest camps abroad. The board placed almost two hundred workers in the American camps and dispatched countless other volunteers, who preached the message of religion, assisted at religious services, visited the sick, and entertained the servicemen.

Specifically, the member bodies who cooperated to create the Jewish Welfare Board undertook many varied activities:

1. The Rabbinical groups—cooperated in the arrangement of an abridged prayer book, Bible, and Haggadah for the use of soldiers and sailors.
2. The Federation of Orthodox Rabbis—tried to supply the demand for kosher food by Jewish men in the camps.
3. The Jewish Publication Society—acted as publishing agency of the Board and placed orders for 180,000 copies of the Abridged Prayer Book and 160,000 copies of Readings From the Holy Scripture.
4. Jewish Chautauqua Society—gave lecture courses to servicemen.
5. Independent Order of B'nai B'rith—made substantial contributions to town and community programs.
6. Council of Young Men's Hebrew and Kindred Associations—acted as special advisory body wherever the Jewish Welfare Board needed the viewpoint of the specialist in the inauguration of soldier activities in conjunction with YMCA work.

With the American Library Association, the Jewish Welfare Board also cooperated in supplying Yiddish books and other reading matter to Yiddish-speaking servicemen. It also prepared for distribution pamphlets in Yiddish on Government benefits and on problems of social hygiene. The JWB, unlike the Knights of Columbus and the YMCA, was also unique in the incorporation into its program of activities centered in towns and cities as well as in camps. The American Jewish Relief Committee, by relieving the JWB of the responsibility of fund raising, allowed it to concentrate exclusively on ancillary morale work.

Although American Jewry had responded rather liberally during the war, the end of hostilities signaled the dawn of a new era in relief, one which would in time eclipse the efforts and accomplishments of the past. The American people, Jews and non-Jews alike, were asked to lend or contribute the larger part of a fund to help in the reconstruction of world Jewry. The appeal was made by Felix Warburg of the JDC. The money for the project, thus far the largest humanitarian undertaking of its kind, would embrace both contributions and loans, and would be accepted from non-Jews as well as from Jews. Warburg assumed that the financial burden would fall upon the United States, Canada, and England.

The nearly $21 million collected and disbursed by the Joint Distribution Committee represented a per capita contribution of nearly $7 from American Jews, the largest per capita contribution that had been made to any single war relief by any people. This did not take into account the contribution of American Jewry to the Red Cross and to the other general relief agencies.

Herbert C. Hoover, chairman of the Supreme Economic Council from 1919–1921 and, as such, head of American relief activities, had generous praise for Jewish relief work: "I am indeed glad to see the effort being made by the American Jewish Relief Committee for sufferers from the war to raise further funds for its work in Europe. As you know, your organization has cooperated with us wonderfully in relief work at the most critical centers of Europe. I cannot speak too highly of the spirit and effectiveness of the Joint Distribution Committee in Europe, nor can I emphasize too strongly the critical necessity for its continuation. The broad nonsectarian spirit shown by the Joint Distribution Committee although primarily devoted to Jewish work, and their willing cooperation which my own administration has enjoyed, place me under an obligation to the committee'' (*New York Times*, September 20, 1919).

Another aspect of the war effort in which Jewish-Americans distinguished themselves was in actual combat. The Jewish manpower contribution to the fighting effort was sizable, certainly more than would be expected given the overall number of Jews in America. The American Jewish Committee reported that although there were fewer than 3 million Jews in this country, nearly 200,000 fought on the battlefields of Europe. Approximately 40,000 Jews who served were volunteers. Four percent of the army personnel was Jewish, while Jews made up only three percent of the total population. Close to 2,800 died, 10,000 were wounded, and over 1,000 were cited for valor. And interestingly enough, some of the Jewish servicemen had not even been in the United States long enough to take out their final citizenship papers. Nevertheless, anti-semites accused Jews of evading military responsibilities.

As early as January 1915, prominent Jews began formulating plans to insure their representation at the peace conference which would conclude the hostilities. Less than a month later, the secretary of war, while not endorsing any specific plan, stated that Jews living in the various countries affected by the war would have the same right as others to bring grievances before such a body. Thus, at the 1919 Versailles Peace Conference, Jewish problems were among the many raised by various ethnic and nationality groups. The American Jewish Congress was empowered to select delegates to petition the conference on behalf of Jewish minorities in Eastern Europe and for a Palestinian homeland. The delegation was composed of Louis Marshall of the American Jewish Committee, Judge Julian W. Mack of the American Jewish Congress, and Rabbi Stephen S. Wise. The congress, essentially the creation of Rabbi Wise, was pro-Zionist and supported by American Jews who felt that the American Jewish Committee representing the cult of the arrived did not reflect their interests.

On August 31, 1918, in a celebrated Rosh Hashanah letter to Dr. Wise, President Wilson expressed his sympathy with the Zionist cause. Such a statement naturally raised Jewish hopes again, and their sights were set high for the peace conference. The Wise Letter led to an Arab counterattack and at Paris, the American delegation was subjected to all sorts of conflicting pressures on the entire Near Eastern question. American Protestant missionaries espoused the cause of a greater Syria and Arab independence as opposed to a Zionist state. On March 28, 1919, Julian W. Mack informed Secretary Lansing that the president had allowed himself to be quoted as saying that in Palestine there should be laid the foundations of a Jewish commonwealth. The secretary asked Wilson to confirm or repudiate this statement to which the president, physically exhausted and preoccupied with more pressing problems, answered that while he did say it, the language went too far!

The Zionist case was destined to suffer further blows. The American negotiators ruled that Jewish aims in Palestine conflicted with Point Five of Wilson's famous Fourteen, which declared in favor of the self-determination of colonial peoples. Point Twelve, too, was a stumbling block, for it promised security to the non-Turkish nationalities residing under the Sultan's control.

All these pressures resulted in the dispatch of an American Commission headed by Henry King and Charles C. Crane to Palestine for the purpose of determining the wishes of the population. Ten days after they arrived, the "rapid-fire" observers learned enough to denouce Zionism and laud the missionary plan for an enlarged Syria. William Yale, a member of the commission's technical staff, prepared what he considered a minority report. Though agreeing with much of the majority view, he did reveal the machinations of Arab propaganda and reaffirmed the ideas of Balfour. Later, during World War II, Yale became bitterly anti-Zionist and violently pro-Arab.

Meanwhile President Wilson, disappointed over the larger failure of his peace ideals in the United States, suffered a breakdown, and for all practical purposes this country was eliminated from the Palestinian picture. At the San Remo Conference (April 25, 1920), the Palestinian mandate was assigned to Great Britain and three months later the land came under British civil administration.

Thus, because of conditions arising from the First World War, the United States became seriously interested in the Palestinian problem. This concern grew slowly in the days before the guns of August exploded in 1914. The First World War brought the Zionists their first real opportunity in America and though some historians feel that Wilson's interest was superficial, without him, the Zionists probably would have received less in London in 1917 and at San Remo in 1920. And at Versailles where the peace treaty was negotiated, Jewish lobbyists were divided between the American Jewish Committee group who wanted minority rights and the Zionists who advocated implementation of the Balfour Declaration. The fact that minority guarantees were unsuccessful in such countries as Poland convinced many of the logic of an Herzlian solution during the Axis crisis of a later era. Certainly, it was during the war period when the foundation was being laid for the appearance of the Palestinian question in the headlines of American newspapers and at the forefront of the diplomatic problems which were to vex the Republic in future days.

During this period, American Jewish organizational life took firm root, and much of the work of these groups involved aid for less fortunate co-religionists. Though the dogs of war had been leashed, a great portion of Europe remained in ruins and the Jewish position overseas remained serious and chaotic. The various American Jewish relief organizations had only mitigated the situation of European Jewry during the war and the Peace Conference did not ameliorate conditions. Ahead lay the major task. The relief programs produced some beneficial side effects. By providing a central focal point, these programs not only brought about a convergence of American Jewry but also exemplified their finest attributes in the eyes of the American populace. Relief work evolved into a highly refined and effective instrument which would prove to be of immeasurable value in coping with the even more catastrophic problems which were to beset Jewry in the years ahead.

3

Consolidation, Comfort, and Challenge: 1920–1929

BY THE THIRD DECADE OF the twentieth century, the Jews of the United States had come to enjoy material prosperity, acceptance by much of American society, and active participation in the business structure of the nation. On the other hand, they faced discrimination and unjust and incorrect accusations. Throughout the 1920s, Jews found their religion slurred, and especially those who lived in large cities saw their children being barred from colleges, medical schools, and other probable areas for advancement. To many, the Jew was the Christ-Killer, the international manipulator of finance, or the cliquish city dweller. Eventually, conditions improved and retractions and corrections came, but not before prejudice had been solidified in the minds of millions of Americans.

Anti-Semitism struck most obviously in a social boycott of Jews. A Jewish name was seldom found in the Social Register, in society columns, in country clubs, or even in some resort hotel registers. Discrimination against Jews was on the rise in schools, social clubs, fraternal lodges, and housing. This sort of deprivation hindered businessmen from establishing a more successful clientele and, similarly, marred friendly social relationships for wives and youngsters. *Up Stream*, a novel written by Ludwig Lewisohn in 1922, carefully illustrated how deeply this discrimination penetrated into everyday living and a work by the popular Gilbert K. Chesterton, *The New Jerusalem* (1922), received a surprising amount of attention. The book frankly called Jews "aliens" in all countries at all times.

As part of the reaction against the imperfect peace which concluded World War I, the haunting fear of the effects of the communist revolution in Russia, and the failures and disappointments of the Progressive reform era in the first decade and a half of the century, Americans under their new president, Warren G. Harding, returned to what he termed "normalcy"—a conservative approach to affairs which emphasized domestic developments.

Seeking simple solutions for postwar frustrations, certain groups attacked anything that was not "Anglo-Saxon." One such organization, the fundamentalist Ku Klux Klan, reactivated in 1915 by William J. Simmons of Georgia, started slowly, but claimed a membership of four million by 1925. Masked Klansmen, encouraging white Protestant supremacy, attacked Catholics, Jews, and Negroes, and issued propaganda opposed to immigration. Politically, the Klan controlled many Southern legislators and heavily influenced elections and officials in several Northern states. Klansmen labeled Jews as "an unblendable element," and as Christ-killers, and expressed their beliefs by writing hate literature, breaking windows in Jewish stores, and placing fiery crosses on synagogue lawns. The Klan also attacked the international communist organization, the Comintern (1919), as a world conspiracy, accused Jews of membership, and claimed that they would cause revolutionary upheaval here as they did in Russia. Jewish and non-Jewish sources struck back by means of appeals and resolutions. In December 1920, the American Jewish Committee urged non-Jews to be objective and that same month, the Federal Council of Churches of Christ in America passed a resolution defending Jews against such accusations as were made by the Ku Klux Klan, although the Klan was not mentioned by name.

Even the immigration policies of the United States government encouraged and furthered discriminatory practices. In 1921, a law provided that the number of immigrants of any nationality would be limited to 3 percent of the number of foreign-born of that nationality according to the 1910 census. Aimed at further limitation of immigrants from southern and eastern Europe, the Johnson Act (1924) lowered the quota to 2 percent and used the 1890 census as a norm in order to admit even fewer of these people, since fewer were resident in the United States in 1890 than in 1910. In 1929, the total annual quota of 150,000 immigrants mandated by the Johnson Act became operative. Since the southern and eastern European quota was so low, the result of this exclusionist program was that between 1924 and 1931 about 73,000 Jews were admitted as compared to over 656,000 between 1907 and 1914.

We have already seen how the pseudo-scientific eugenicists, who discriminated on the basis of race, contributed to twentieth-century anti-Semitism. During the twenties this group found fertile soil in which to propagate their beliefs. Madison Grant's *The Passing of the Great Race* (1916) and such works of Lothrop Stoddard as *The Rising Tide of Color Against White World-Supremacy* (1920), though clearly unscientific, were quite popular. Burton J. Hendrick's thesis in *The Jews in America* (1924) was also insulting. He asserted that German and Spanish Jews were acceptable because they were of the "white race," but that since Russian Jews were descended from the Tartars, their influx menaced racial purity. The 1920s witnessed the culmination in the United States of a full-fledged racial ideology that negatively influenced the thinking of many Americans against Jews, Latins, Slavs, blacks, and all colored peoples.

However, America's most sensational anti-Semitic campaign of the twenties was a vendetta conducted by Henry Ford's newspaper, the *Dearborn Independent*. Between May 22, 1920, and January 14, 1922, the Ford-sponsored weekly

printed a prolonged series of polemics on what it labeled the
"Jewish Question." Most of the articles were eventually
assembled into a series of four little books entitled, *The International Jew: The World's Foremost Problem*. During the
two years that the series was published, the *Dearborn Independent* grew from local obscurity to a national circulation
of 700,000 copies. Many were sold by subscription, but most
were given away by Ford dealers. Ford's association with an
organized anti-Semitic campaign was especially serious,
because as an Horatio Alger-like multi-millionaire, his name,
like his car, reached the common man, who felt that such a
hero could not be wrong.

The inspiration for the *Independent*'s claim that the Jews
sought world control was a spurious European work, the
"Protocols of the Elders of Zion," already mentioned. This
was supposedly a secret plot of Jewish Elders or Wise Men of
Zion to take over the world. The Protocols were, according
to rumor, stolen from the Jews after they had been revealed
at the 1897 Zionist Conference. Historians at once challenged
the authenticity of this document, and it was soon proved a
rank and pernicious forgery in the September 4, 1921, issue
of the *New York Times*.

Even though the circumstances surrounding the discovery
of the Protocols were highly questionable, they became the
handbook of American anti-Semitism. In most editions, there
were twenty-four Protocols. The first nine described the
means that Jews would use to gain world domination, and the
others outlined plans for a new world order after Israel's international empire became reality. Specifically, Protocol One
claimed that Jews would introduce Christian youth to im-
morality and revolt, and that in time all Gentiles would be
controlled through the use of violence, the power of gold,
and the influence of liberalism. Next, Jews would employ the
press and Gentile intellectuals to confuse people's minds.
Details were then provided on Jewish plans to create vast
economic and political chaos in the world. The Protocols
claimed that Jews would use Freemasonry, civil rights

movements, diplomatic intrigue, legal subtlety, and shady politics to undermine religion and further confuse Gentiles. Even mass violence by Jews, such as blowing up cities, ,was one of the threats mentioned in the ninth Protocol.

Other protocols dealt with the means by which Jews would take over and revise specific institutions. Governments were to be dominated, and the press and public opinion would be easily controlled by distracting Gentiles with fads and amusements. Finally, the Protocols explained the financial aspects of the new regime, the choice of leaders, and the control of individuals by the blessings, security, and happiness afforded by the Kingdom of Zion.

With the Protocols, and the legacy of European anti-Semitism as its guide, the *Dearborn Independent* set out in May 1920 to prove that Jews were "The World's Foremost Problem." In its discussion of the Protocols, the *Independent* steadfastly proclaimed that it was not anti-Semitic. With recurrent convoluted reasoning Ford's paper pointed out that its purpose was not to attack Jews, but to enlighten the entire nation on the "Jewish Question." In fact, the *Independent* piously proclaimed that anti-Semitism did not exist, "since the thing so named is found among Semites too. Semites cannot be anti-Semitic." For the *Independent*, the authorship of the original Protocols was fairly unimportant. Using a typical lack of documentation and an abundance of propaganda, the Dearborn paper decreed that the "Protocols are a World Program—there is no doubt anywhere of that."

But the hordes of immigrant Jews were not the only population problem cited by the *Dearborn Independent*. The newspaper's research revealed that even the United States Census Bureau could not determine how many Jews already lived here. Jews, according to the *Independent*, wanted to stay hidden and did so by lobbying in Washington to stop the government from counting them, by referring to themselves by nationality rather than by race or religion, and by changing their names. The name-changing method was evidently so successful that the Dearborn paper dedicated the entire

November 12, 1921, installment to an article explaining why Jews did so. A list of common revisions was included so that unsuspecting Gentiles would be prepared. Not only were Jews stealing "old Christian" names, but they were also claiming credit for a number of other Anglo-Saxon-Celtic traditions such as the Bible. According to the *Independent*, Jews insisted with "nauseating superciliousness" that "they 'gave us our bible,' and 'gave us our God' and 'gave us our religion'— not a single one of these claims being true." To make matters worse, the paper claimed that Jewish authors maintained a "supercilious attitude . . . toward the stock that made America," and a Jewish comedian had gained applause with a "fifteen minute monologue 'panning' the United States, defaming Liberty, [and] heaping contempt upon the Pilgrims. . . ."

The *Dearborn Independent* undoubtedly spoke for many middle-class Americans who were profoundly disillusioned by war and resentful of the economic challenge of recent European immigration. Frequently the series changed its format and lashed out at any peoples not of old Yankee stock. If the *Independent*'s immigration reports were accurate, the Jews stood a chance of taking over the American population numerically. On June 10, 1920, the Dearborn newspaper revealed that Zionists planned to have one million Jews enter the United States that year alone. The next October, the paper claimed that "Jewish secret societies" forced immigration officials to allow Jews to emigrate from any country, regardless of quotas or health standards. Both articles, claiming that new Jewish faces meant fresh and dangerous Jewish ideas, exhibited a real fear of this supposed mass Jewish immigration. Typical hysterical warnings were that "These people are coming here regarding the Gentile as an hereditary enemy," and that incoming Jews "behave as if they own the United States."

Using the Protocols as its major source, the *Dearborn Independent* proved to its satisfaction that Jews intended to gain economic and political dominance by promoting "frequent change" in "time honored" institutions through controlling all channels of communication and creating "problems of a moral character." Theorizing that Jews were inordinately attracted by power, Ford's weekly attempted to show that they already controlled most national political institutions. The base for this political power was assumed to be New York City; according to their statistics, Jews controlled 25,000 newsstands, most major department stores, the entire legal profession, the mayor's office, all city departments, and Tammany Hall. From this power base, the newspaper speculated, Jews proposed to change political institutions further by separating New York City from the state of New York, thus creating a new and powerful Jewish state.

However, according to the *Independent*, the greatest of all Jewish threats was not political, but financial. Typical of the economic installments in the *International Jew* were: "How Jewish International Finance Functions," and "Jewish Power and America's Money Famine." Other lengthy diatribes concerned Jewish control of the Federal Reserve System, the Jewish moneylending monopoly, and the Jewish seizure of the Stock Exchange. A review of the *International Jew* revealed the news that Jews controlled between 50 and 100 percent of each of the following businesses: sugar, tobacco, meat packing, shoemaking, clothing, theater, motion pictures, music, jewelry, grain, cotton, smelting, and liquor.

Ford's tabloid also tackled American history—beginning with Columbus. The *Independent*'s research staff thus discovered that Isabella did not sponsor the explorer, but that instead he was financed by a group of three "secret Jews." In addition, five Jews traveled with Columbus, and one, Luis de Torres, was the first man ashore. Torres went on to discover the use of tobacco and thus began the Jewish tobacco monopoly, which, the *Independent* reported, still existed. Next, the Dearborn paper turned its attention to New Amsterdam. While Governor Peter Stuyvesant ordered all Jews out of the city, the Directors, noting the Jewish capital invested in the Dutch Company, allowed them to stay. From this humble beginning, Ford's paper continued, Jews made New York the "greatest center of Jewish population in the world." Because the Jews were not known as a farm people, the *Dearborn Independent* blamed their refusal to farm on laziness and a desire not to assimilate.

The popularly held theory that campus problems were Communist inspired was also a *Dearborn Independent* revelation. Student lecture courses were supposedly fine vehicles for the Bolshevik propaganda of Jewish professors. The Dearborn newspaper challenged college students either to follow their "Anglo-Saxon" fathers or else be "poisoned by Jewish subversive influence."

Jewish advances in the entertainment world presented a twofold threat to the *Dearborn Independent*. First movies, plays, and music meant more money for Jewish monopolies; and second, they gave Jews a chance to undermine America's morals. The Protocols predicted that Jews would take over the theater, and the *Independent* reported that in America many of the most popular plays were not only "Jew-written, Jew-produced, and Jew-controlled, but also Jew-played." The *Independent* presented in one of its series details on how the "big Jews" of the theater were taking over movies. In one series, "Baring the Heart of Hollywood," readers discovered that Jews had advanced from the "penny arcades" and "peep shows" to the control of the movie houses. Gentiles were warned not to attend motion pictures because Jews owned and operated all facets of the business. One reader pointed out that the movie, "The Four Horsemen of the Apocalypse," contained a scene where a monkey picked lice from a Gentile soldier's hair while a Jewish soldier read a Yiddish newspaper. The *Independent* replied that this scene was not from the original book, but illustrated "the contributions of the Jew-owned, Jew-controlled and Jew-degraded motion picture industry of the United States".

The "Jewish World Notes" section of the *Independent* also stated that American Jews had emasculated the song, "Onward Christian Soldiers." By changing a lyric from "cross of Jesus" to "flag of freedom," Jews were encouraging Gentiles to follow the "Red Flag of Bolshevism with its Jewish star." Not only were Jews revising hymns, but they had also "created jazz" and monopolized "popular music." Also, their "musical slush" had "set the young people of this generation imitating the drivel of morons." Jews were also blamed for the "abandoned sensuousness of sliding notes" and the unashamed "erotic suggestion" of Irving Berlin songs. The Dearborn newspaper informed its readers that it could not print the words of even the least offensive Jewish songs, but it tried to shock them with a list of song titles, including: "I'll Say She Does," "You Cannot Shake Your Shimmy Here," and "Can You Tame Wild Wimmen?"

The final money-making, morality-impairing Jewish monopoly mentioned by the paper was the liquor business. After asserting that Jews were the "steadiest drinkers of all," the *Independent* described the Jewish control of the vodka business which had undermined Russia. In America, where quality aged whiskey and wine were once produced, Jews were accused of brewing cheap mixtures, obviously illegally.

But Jews were not satisfied with simply controlling the country's entertainment, finances, politics, and liquor. The *Dearborn Independent* reported on September 3, 1921, that Jews were treading on America's most sacred institution— baseball. By way of introduction to a two-part article on the sport, the paper revealed that Jews were unathletic, that they were physically lethargic, they disliked unnecessary physical action, and that they could not even tolerate the YMCAs, which welcomed them. Because the Jew was not a sport but a "gangster," he was forced to conquer baseball as an observer instead of as a participant. Jewish gamblers, according to the *Independent*, had already destroyed wrestling and horse-racing and were also responsible for the White Sox gambling scandal of the 1919 World Series. Jews were not only blamed for baseball's greatest disgrace, but they also were said to have committed unpleasantries such as harassing umpires, hurling bottles, and shouting profane insults.

Because articles in the *Dearborn Independent* were often vague and rarely directed at specific individuals, little action could be taken against Ford. However, in April, 1925, the industrialist was sued by Aaron Sapiro, an attorney prominently connected with cooperative marketing organizations of farmers and fruit growers throughout the United States. Sapiro claimed he had been accused of conspiring with Jewish bankers seeking to control the food markets of the world. Reporting that he had no knowledge of any conspiracy and that he served the marketing association only where his services were requested, Sapiro sued Ford for $1 million. After a two-year legal battle, an out-of-court settlement awarded financial damages to Sapiro, and Ford publicly acknowledged inaccuracies in articles leading to erroneous conclusions which might have injured or cast unjust reflections on Sapiro and other Jews.

There were those—chiefly intellectuals—who criticized Ford for his association with the *Independent* and for his errors in judgment and lack of historical knowledge. For example, the great American author, Sinclair Lewis, asserted that if the industrialist had only read the work of the Anglo-Jewish writer Israel Zangwill, he would never have had the "hallucination" that this nation could be terrorized by Jewish bankers.

In June 1927, Ford formally apologized for *The International Jew* series in the *Independent*. His apology may have resulted from a change of heart or from the realization that subordinates were using him. Or, perhaps a more realistic explanation was that Ford suffered from libel suits and faced a decline in sales as a result of boycotts. Graceful acceptance of Ford's apology was acknowledged by the Jewish periodical, the *American Hebrew*, which stated that it "bore no grudge" and would "forgive and seek to forget." While the retraction could not erase the incalculable harm done by a seven-year campaign against Jews, the *American Hebrew* hoped that Henry Ford would make his actions square with his words.

Ford's motives inevitably met questioning and concern. It

was Ford's recent antagonist, Aaron Sapiro, who came to the auto-maker's defense against the accusation that the apology was motivated by a desire to sell more cars. Sapiro himself was then attacked for what was called a naive attitude. Finally, in December 1927, the *Dearborn Independent* suspended publication, putting to rest the sordid story of Henry Ford's flirtation with anti-Semitism.

Because of the anti-Semitic influence Ford projected and despite the weight his retraction carried, prejudicial feelings remained a pervasive force in the 1920s. There was even one instance when one man's prejudice spread to an entire community. This case involved an alleged revival of a supposed old Jewish ritual, the requirement of the blood of a Christian child for Jewish holiday observances! In September 1928, a young girl was discovered missing on the eve of the Day of Atonement in the northern New York city of Massena. The rabbi was questioned by a local police officer, who attempted to relate the girl's disappearance to Jewish ritual practice. The girl was discovered the next day but Louis Marshall of the American Jewish Committee nevertheless communicated the Jewish position in a letter to Massena's mayor. He wrote of the excitement, indignation, and mental agony the Jews of Massena suffered when they learned of the "accursed" blood accusation. Marshall criticized the failure of Massena's public officers to protect the community against acts of bigotry and fanaticism and to prevent, rather than inspire, sentiments calculated to lead to riots, violence, and possible bloodshed.

In addition, Marshall demanded an immediate and public written apology to the Jewish people and asked for the removal of the mayor from his office, threatening if necessary to press charges of official misconduct. The mayor finally apologized to the rabbi for offenses directed against him and his people, and Governor Alfred E. Smith scheduled a private hearing in Albany. Ultimately, the case ended with the removal of the police officer for lack of discretion in the exercise of his duties and for conduct unbecoming an officer.

Marshall accepted the mayor's apology and the official Jewish community commended the forthright action of Governor Smith for his prompt and fair handling of the case. Anti-Semitism, in running its absurd and unreasonable pace during the 1920s, influenced practices in many of the nation's institutions of higher education. Outright exclusion, character tests, geographic quotas, and carefully screened admission procedures were all too commonly practiced. Jewish enrollment in post-secondary schools had grown at a much faster rate than that of the total population. By 1919, almost 10 percent of the total students receiving professional education were Jewish. As expected, there was a disproportionate number of Jews in such New York City colleges as The City College (85 percent of the enrollment in 1918), Brooklyn Polytechnic Institute, Columbia University, Hunter College, and New York University. The Ivy League schools also showed a dramatic increase. Thus, in a general defense of restrictive admission of Jews, one magazine article explained that colleges sifted applicants in order to "preserve" the student body, just as the United States restricted immigration to preserve democracy!

Syracuse University was one of those schools, however, that vigorously denounced anti-Semitism on the campus and a proposal by the student government to limit enrollment of Jews to a definite number. The University felt compelled to make such an announcement after a report that students were upset by alleged circulars sent to secondary schools, advising "Come to Syracuse, the place where they treat the Jew boy right."

Speaking about alleged discrimination at New York University, one authority equivocated, asserting that there was as little discrimination against the Jew in the student activities of the University as in any other school in the country. Yet friction among the New York University students was often visible. An example of blatant anti-Semitism appeared in a poster, announcing, "Strictly Kosher are not wanted here." Perhaps in order to strike a liberal posture, Columbia

University in 1924 initiated the Student House as the center of Jewish activity on the campus. There were those, however, who questioned the validity of the separation of Jewish students and they asked whether anti-Semitism was not reinforced by segregating Jewish student activities from the rest of campus life.

The most classic instance of anti-Semitism in the academic world was that of admission restriction at Harvard University. President A. Lawrence Lowell imposed a quota system at the school for Jews and other groups in order to keep a balance of various strains. While Harvard was probably not the first American university to attempt to limit the proportion of Jews, it seemed to be the most frank. Lowell asserted that the clannishness of Jews was partly the cause of a quota, but the contention of Louis Marshall and Julian Mack, who led the fight to end the restrictions, was that only character and scholarship should determine admission. In 1922, the Harvard Overseers partly redeemed the university's reputation, declaring against the quota concept, though the actual rule remained.

Among the other Jew-baiting techniques which left a bitter taste was the harassment of professionals. For discrimination to be carried on in such educated and intellectual circles seemed inexcusable and disheartening. Several examples must suffice. Three Jewish interns from Kings' County Hospital in Brooklyn were seized in June 1927 by six alleged fellow practitioners, gagged and tied, and soaked in tubs of a black fluid. The accused were released on bail; yet the turmoil initiated an investigation which ultimately yielded nothing. However, the Alumni Association and Medical Board of the hospital officially denied any bigotry or mistreatment of Jews. But the chief criticism of the profession was the discrimination many medical schools practiced against the admission of Jewish students. Many medical college boards limited the admission of prospective physicians, calculating that if the number of Jews in medicine increased tremendously, economic problems would result. A prominent

Jewish physician commented that "Jewish applicants [to medical school] must exert greater effort and perseverance than non-Jews." He noted, too, that Jewish practitioners suffered from other injustices, such as the inability to acquire a clientele among non-Jews. Thus, it supposedly followed that if Jewish physicians had to deal mostly with fellow Jews, their practice was limited and their numbers had to be regulated because otherwise they might indulge in unethical practices in order to make a better living. Such discrimination obviously resulted in extremely competent Jewish professionals because since relatively fewer Jews were admitted to schools, those who graduated were the cream of the crop.

The twenties were not, however, solely a period of restriction and discrimination for the Jew. The era was also one of unparalleled exuberance, business expansion, and material comfort. While there were many sub-surface tensions, to many these were the "Golden Years," the "Roaring Twenties." And Jews, like so many others, reaped benefits galore.

The 1920s witnessed a push by Jews to gain respectability, to escape oppressive employer discrimination, and to obtain financial security which could be insured by entering the professions. While still a controlling force in the garment trade, Jewish workers were reluctant to see their children follow them into manual labor occupations. Becoming a white collar worker or a professional person was equated by all ethnics as a necessary adjunct to social and economic recognition. Thus, the proletarian Jew was predominantly limited to a single generation. And as the 1920s unfolded, Jews began to enter the former relatively restricted fields of teaching and science.

The first professions that the Jews entered in large numbers were those that afforded economic comfort, altruistic motivation, and prestige. Thus, despite the prejudices already mentioned, the Jewish proportion of the medical, dental, and pharmaceutical professions—"the healing arts"—was ever increasing. Jews entered the legal profession more slowly. Traditionally in Europe they were forbidden to enter that field, but in America Jews began to study law because here there were all sorts of opportunities in the twenties: real estate, banking, construction, and many other fields which required legal skills. However, Jews were rarely found in the great law firms of Washington and Wall Street.

In the nonprofessional area, Jews remained in virtual control of the garment industry. Entire families were often employed: husbands functioned as cutters, and wives and children worked as finishers in the factory. A Jew was off to a good start if he was a skilled tailor, for these men were ultimately promoted to leading positions in the garment industry. From this position the tailors branched out and became contractors, jobbers, and manufacturers.

Another occupation that Jews seemed to be entering in increasing numbers during the 1920s was that of the formal funeral director. Before the Jews came to America burial procedures were supervised by the town *Chevra Kadisha* ("Holy Society"), and people were buried in the *Bet Hayyim* ("cemeteries"). In the United States benevolent societies were established, and land was bought to insure proper burial sites for their members. Then came the Jewish funeral director in larger cities who set up a chapel from which the dead could be buried while benevolent societies cooperated in "Americanizing" the funerals. In less than a decade the funeral director more often than not became affluent and powerful, another instance of the institutionalizing of American Jewish life.

The desire for economic independence and for influence over others prompted many Jews to enter business for themselves—often on a shoestring. They all called themselves "shopkeepers," whether they sold from a pushcart or at a modern store on the main streets of cities. Thus, retail trade was the largest and probably most successful of all the Jewish occupations. The department store was, in large measure, the work of nineteenth-century German Jews who went west and south and established outlets in most sizable cities, and the East European immigrants continued the tradition. In his relationship with the gentile community, the Jewish businessman often faced problems of assimilation. He associated with the non-Jews socially and very often felt he had to de-emphasize his Jewishness in order to get along in his business world. Yet when he returned home, it was to a Jewish atmosphere, and his after-hours social contacts were with Jewish lodge brothers or congregational associates. Such an existence was often confusing and difficult on the psyche. At the worst it could produce serious identity pressures.

While the Jewish preponderance in business was clear, and their numbers were increased in the professions, their participation in finance, commerce, and industry—three areas of life that symbolized the economic boom of the decade—was slight. Some Jewish-Americans associated with these areas were the Guggenheims, the sons of Meyer, the founder of the copper industry; Julius Rosenwald, the merchant-prince of Chicago, active in the mail-order business, in Sears, Roebuck and Company, and a great benefactor of Jewish and Negro causes; and in banking, Joseph Marcus and Saul Singer, founders of the Bank of the United States, and the legendary names of Jacob H. Schiff, Paul Warburg, and the Kuhn-Loeb empire.

The question of education—both Jewish and secular—assumed new importance in the 1920s as the children of immigrants entered adolescence, often in the new suburbs then sprouting on the fringe of every city. Because of the feeling that education was the chief technique through which one could "get ahead," many Jews were concerned over the nature of public education and its effect on religion. The fear that children were being alienated from Judaism caused much alarm. One antidote to this secularization was the proposal to establish parochial, or what would be called today, "day schools." For example, in 1927, it was suggested that a Jewish high school be set up in New York. Such a school would teach Hebrew and Bible in addition to a regular high school program. Of course, the real growth of day schools came with the Hitlerian immigration after 1945.

Higher education for Jews took on tremendous importance because it served as a prime vehicle for upward mobility. Very often, the sons and daughters of struggling businessmen or laborers lived at home and worked to help defray their expenses at college. As a result the colleges located near large Jewish populations were faced with an often unwanted influx of Jewish students. Of the estimated 50,000 Jewish college students in 1927 the great majority were enrolled in preprofessional programs. And a large number of the remaining ones pursued courses in schools of business.

In many universities, Jewish students often suffered from social discrimination. In the 1920s, college fraternities generally restricted their membership. In defense, Jews who were unable to gain entry started their own groups. An incident at Brown University became a minor cause célèbre. Brown's president complained to Louis Marshall of the American Jewish Committee about the formation of secret Jewish societies. In a *New York Times* (November 12, 1928) article, Marshall defended such societies as necessary to Jewish life. Fraternities grew rapidly among Jewish students so that by 1930 there were twenty-nine fraternities and sororities with 26,000 members, or a little better than half of the students enrolled.

As more and more Jewish students enrolled in colleges, it was soon apparent that they were in need of services and assistance, especially those attending school away from their homes. Also, many Jewish students lacked knowledge of their literature, history, and traditions. In order to ease these shortcomings and to provide services, the Hillel Foundation was created in 1923 by B'nai B'rith, and the first chapter was established at the University of Illinois. Jewish education was strengthened, too, by the establishment of Jewish chairs of instruction at Harvard and Columbia Universities in 1925 and 1929 respectively, both financed, incidentally, by Jews. But the great growth of Judaic studies was to await a later day.

As with secular education, there were increased numbers of Jewish children attending religious schools sponsored by either the community as a whole or by individual congregations. By 1927, there were 2,500 such schools in the United States and approximately one-fourth of the Jewish children of school age attended them. And this was all the more significant when one realizes that this schooling was a supplementary part-time affair, usually assigned to the late afternoon hours between public school and dinner time. Not only was the time slot bad, but there was a shortage of well-trained instructors. Too few Hebrew teachers understood children and the psychology of learning.

There were also important developments in that specialized branch of Jewish education which trained rabbis and congregational teachers. Two additional seminaries were established in 1922—The Hebrew Theological College in Chicago, which soon became the western center of orthodoxy, and Stephen S. Wise's Jewish Institute of Religion in New York, which was Reform, but attempted sectarian nonpartisanship emphasizing nationalism, Palestine, and contemporary problems. Seminaries such as these as well as those already established depended on Jewish communities throughout the nation for financial support. Raising funds for these colleges became pet projects of many affluent Jews. In 1922, twenty rabbis joined to raise $1 million for the Jewish Theological Seminary, and in 1924 a gala party was held in the Hotel Astor in New York to celebrate the acquisition of the title for the site of the new Yeshiva University.

In sum, the twenties witnessed greater educational opportunities for Jews and a better organization of their efforts to gain quality public and college educations. While suffering from tremendous disadvantages, religious education was becoming more professional in its approach and conscientious in its efforts to solicit sufficient funds to transmit the Jewish heritage.

Growing bonds among Jews in the post-Armistice years were motivated in large part by discrimination and prejudice. These bonds reflected the traditional communal concern that manifested itself in changing concepts of Jewish acculturation, a growing recreational and educational program, and concern for the protection of Jewish rights here and abroad. While Zionist strength waned somewhat, a hardcore remained faithful to Herzl's ideas. From its ranks came the great Zionist leaders of a later era.

In the field of religious thought, Mordecai Kaplan's ideas were prominent. Kaplan, a professor at the Jewish Theological Seminary of America who was in charge of teacher training, was impressed with the many facets of Jewish life and began to develop a unique interpretation of the American-Jewish existence. Kaplan was opposed to the rigidities he saw in the Jewish establishment and as a result created Reconstructionism, a pragmatic synthesis of Judaism and Americanism that was both vital and practical. By 1934, he organized his ideas and published the seminal *Judaism as a Civilization.*

Kaplan's Reconstructionism was best seen in the Jewish Center movement which became phenomenally popular in the 1920s. The centers, devoted to a variety of religious, political, intellectual, cultural, and sports activities, grew out of the settlement houses and Young Men's and Women's Hebrew Associations and came under the administration of the Jewish Welfare Board, which, as we have seen, originally supervised the nonmilitary aspects of life during World War I.

In the early 1920s, the centers were the focal points of Jewish recreation and it was recommended that each one serving 50,000 people have the following areas: six club rooms, one billiard room, and a gymnasium. It was felt that ideally each center should provide services as follows: social activities—30 percent, physical—20 percent, education—10 percent, arts—10 percent, civic—5 percent, and Jewish content—25 percent.

The greater emphasis on secularism in the twenties, together with the realization that synagogues needed to provide more than religious services, accounted for the tremendous growth of synagogue-centers. Construction was at an all-time peak and temples and synagogues now contained classrooms, gymnasia, and an auditorium and offered such myriad activities as sisterhood organizations, men's clubs, youth groups, boy and girl scout troops, basketball leagues, sewing circles, and book review sessions. It was said that everything prospered in these gorgeous edifices but the Jewish religion.

Both the Jewish concern for a homeland and for the protection of all Jewish nationals overseas, which had received such an impetus during the First World War, persisted throughout the decade after the war. The Anti-Defamation League of B'nai B'rith prepared defense literature, and the American Jewish Congress became a permanent fixture in the American Jewish community. The philanthropist Nathan Straus of Macy's and Rabbi Stephen S. Wise led the reconstituted body in the 1920s. The JDC, too, remained active, collecting $40 million between 1921 and 1930 for such tasks as the prevention of famines and epidemics, and for reconstruction in those European states ravaged by the war. One other new activity of interest undertaken in the 1920s was the establishment of the American-Jewish Joint Agricultural Corporation (Agro-Joint) to help especially in the retraining of Russian Jews for industrial and agrarian pursuits and for their resettlement elsewhere. These were the Jews who had been excluded from previous occupations or "de-classed" as the new Soviet government referred to them. The Communist seizure of power had a tremendous impact on the American-Jewish community and also placed a great financial burden on it. Not only were Soviet Jews limited to certain occupations, but 2.75 million Jews were subject to arrest and/or harassment for professing Zionist beliefs or for using the Hebrew language. As can be imagined, the variety and work of the philanthropic, benevolent, and social agencies grew more professional and sophisticated under the persistent pressures from abroad.

The growth of American Zionist sentiment thrived in the 1920s. Second-generation American Jews took great pride, perhaps even to the point of salving their other frustrations, in political nationalism as it was represented by the economic and social regeneration of Palestine. Louis D. Bràndeis of the United States Supreme Court, converted to Zionism before the Great War, had emerged as its leader during the Balfour Declaration negotiations. But, in 1921, at the Cleveland Convention of the Zionist Organization of America (ZOA), the majority of the delegates repudiated Brandeis's leadership and a decade-long rupture resulted. Chaim Weizmann in England, the world leader of Zionism, differed in ideology and method from Brandeis. The American jurist envisioned Zionism as an unemotional enterprise designed to build a state chiefly by economic measures, while Weizmann thought of the movement as primarily a task of cultural and spiritual regeneration, one which grew out of Jewish suffering. Also, the schism was exacerbated by a mutual jealousy. The symbol of the break was the Palestine Foundation Fund *(Karen Hayesod)*, a financial organization to reclaim Palestine by buying land, supported by the Cleveland Convention and Weizmann against the advice of Brandeis. An American branch of the Fund was established and Emanuel Neumann became its director. The President of the ZOA, Julian W. Mack, and Brandeis resigned from the organization, and the main leadership passed to Louis Lipsky. Brandeis, however, did not completely withdraw but instead lent his prestige to advancing the economic rehabilitation of Palestine by establishing the Palestine Economic Corporation, an investment enterprise.

American business entrepreneurs such as Jacob H. Schiff, Julius Rosenwald, Felix M. Warburg, and others, chiefly anti-Zionist in earlier years, now supported Zionist projects in Palestine. All Jews, not just Zionists, were courted to implement the cause. Eventually, in 1929, the American non-Zionists joined with the Zionist organization, recognized by the Mandate as the "Jewish Agency" to represent world Jewry at large. Louis Marshall of the American Jewish Committee and Weizmann cooperated to accomplish this union against stout opposition. A Joint Palestine Survey Commission with two Americans as members was appointed to analyze Palestine's economic resources and potential, and its report (1928) heralded a union of World Zionists and American skeptics.

Politically, the American Zionist forces achieved a measure of success when a Republican Congress concurred in the Palestine mandate (1922), specifically resolving that the United States favored the establishment of a National Home for Jews in Palestine. Washington attempted to follow a neutral course with regard to Zionist developments in these pre-Hitler years. The congressional resolution of 1922, for example, meant absolutely nothing! It favored the establishment of the Jewish National Home in Palestine, but like so many instruments of the era, was free of all commitments. The House Committee on Foreign Affairs, as though fearing even such a meaningless statement, drew an even clearer picture. It declared that the resolution expressed only moral interest and bound the United States to no foreign obligations or entanglements.

Our Near Eastern policy was further enunciated in the Anglo-American Convention of 1924, by which the United States formally approved the mandate. The convention also extended to American nationals the right to establish educational, philanthropic, and religious institutions in the mandated areas. No mention was made of a Jewish national home. The Department of State, however, harbored an additional motive beyond the grant of most-favored nation status. Secretary of State Charles Evans Hughes was disturbed about Great Britain's exclusive oil leases throughout the entire Middle Eastern mandated areas. The department, continuing a long tradition of defending the rights of American businessmen overseas, was interested in obtaining "open door" oil privileges.

Throughout the 1920s, American Zionists, now organized with an efficient public relations program, besieged the Department of State with requests for official intervention by the Government on behalf of the Jewish community in

Palestine. But even the killing of some Americans in the Hebron riots of 1929 evoked little response. Washington maintained an official neutrality bordering on outright disinterest, interruped only by nice platitudes from candidates seeking office. The only positive statements that emanated from Washington concerned the protection of American citizens and their rights, two principles that had come to be inviolate in our overseas policy. It was folly to expect that Jewish demands would fall on anything but deaf ears in a country that had receded to isolation and had rejected the grand mission of Woodrow Wilson.

Despite the prejudice and discrimination already described, Jews in the twenties were becoming increasingly acculturated to the American milieu. This was especially evident in the realm of cultural pursuits—both Jewish and secular. More and more American Jews achieved prominence in such areas as journalism, the entertainment industry, and the arts. Obviously, many names could be cited in such a hall of fame, but a few examples must suffice to illustrate how American Jews enriched the cultural life of the nation.

The Yiddish press and theater, which had figured so prominently in Jewish cultural affairs from the beginnings of the East European migration, enjoyed its greatest vitality in the 1920s. Daily circulation rose to 600,000 by the mid-twenties and in 1927 alone, there were over forty newspapers printed in Yiddish. These papers, together with the more numerous Anglo-Jewish ones, continued to serve as a socializing, educational, and informational agency for the Jewish communities. As a force for Americanization, literary creativity and communication, the Yiddish press was a most significant factor.

The Yiddish Art Theatre, which was founded by the renowned actor, Maurice Schwartz, enlarged its repertory by presenting the venerable works of the Moscow Theatre. Among the notables who performed with this troupe and who went on to Broadway and Hollywood eminence was Muni Weisenfreund (Paul Muni), who excelled especially in

Sholem Aleichem roles. Jacob Ben-Ami was one of the many actors who played both on the Yiddish and English language stage. Ben-Ami, who with Schwartz had founded the Yiddish Art Theatre, insisted that serious plays be included in its offerings. He was renowned as a cultural pluralist, appearing in plays by American, Yiddish, and other playwrights during worldwide tours, and performing in both English and Yiddish. By the 1920s, Ben-Ami and Schwartz parted and both became associated with their own companies. The popular comedians Molly Picon and Menashe Skulnik also began long and popular careers in the Yiddish theater district on New York's famed Second Avenue.

Apart from the Yiddish theater, the contribution of Jews to the uptown Broadway stage was impressive. Such names as the Shuberts, Florenz Ziegfeld, Abraham Erlanger, Sam Harris, David Frohman, and Oscar Hammerstein were identified with the administrative-production aspect of theater. Possibly the greatest of all, and certainly the most versatile, was the actor, playwright and producer David Belasco. And on the stage itself the works of such playwrights as Elmer Rice, Clifford Odets, Sidney Kingsley, and George S. Kaufman accounted in large part for the creative thrust of legitimate theater in the twenties. The popular entertainment area has always boasted a preponderance of Jews. Such entertainers as the magician Harry Houdini, and song-and-dance performers like Sophie Tucker, Fanny Brice, George Jessel, Al Jolson, and Eddie Cantor were considered by many as synonymous with the phrase "show business." So numerous were Jewish performers that they even established their own theater guild. As a matter of fact, at the close of the 1923 Broadway season, it was revealed that 15 percent of all actors, 30 percent of the directors, and 40 percent of the playwrights were of the Jewish faith.

Jews were pioneers in each branch of the motion picture industry, serving as producers, distributors, writers, directors, and, of course, as performers. The first western star who played a lead in the first motion picture that had a story line

("The Great Train Robbery," 1903) was Max Aronson, better known as "Bronco Billy" Anderson. It was Al Jolson's portrayal of "The Jazz Singer," a cantor's son who turned from the family's religious tradition, which ushered in the era of sound movies. And few could disagree that the Marx Brothers were among the great comic artists of the era. Powerful movie producers who achieved preeminence in the 1920s were Adolf Zukor, Jesse Lasky, Samuel Goldwyn, Louis B. Mayer, and the Warner brothers.

Among Jews who triggered the great changes in American art was the photographer Alfred Stieglitz, whose salon at 291 Fifth Avenue in New York City was the mecca for French impressionists and for the intellectuals of the day. He demonstrated that photography was an art of its own. In American music, such Jewish composers as Jerome Kern, Sigmund Romberg, and Irving Berlin practically established the popular American musical theater. George Gershwin was in a class of his own, combining the new improvisational jazz style with serious operatic and classical techniques. His "Rhapsody in Blue" and jazz-opera "Porgy and Bess" are two examples of his versatility. Then too, there were the classical conductors-performers-composers such as Aaron Copland, Jascha Heifetz, Mischa Elman, and Artur Rubinstein.

In the fields of literature and journalism, there were a number of noteworthy contributors. Adolph S. Ochs was the outstanding spirit behind the *New York Times*, and the publisher of the *World*, Joseph Pulitzer, was linked with many areas of culture because of the awards he endowed. The number of American Jews active in writing fiction was considerable, and the direction American literature took toward greater literary freedom was due in part to the work of such luminaries as Ben Hecht, Dorothy Parker, Robert Nathan, Charles Angoff, and Gertrude Stein—to list only a few.

While Jews contributed greatly to American cultural pursuits, in most cases their achievements had little or no relationship to their religion. In later American literature, the Jewishness of authors was to be significant, but writers and other artists in the twenties followed established trends and religion per se did not count for much. Just as the post-World War II writers purposely took Jewish themes and celebrated them, those in the 1920s (Lewisohn and Cahan excepted) tried to avoid them, perhaps because they were not yet secure in their Americanism.

In sum, by the fateful year of 1929, America's Jewish population enjoyed, like so many others, more comfort and material enjoyment than ever before. They maintained and even extended those communal agencies which sought to strengthen their faith, and they became in many ways one of the forces in the American business world. Zionist interests and the continuing concern for overseas brethren provided an international outlook, while the Jewish role in cultural outlets was considerable. In a sense, the 1920s represented a watershed. Discrimination continued, but there was greater comfort and more positive adjustment. After 1924, European immigration practically halted and, as the Depression came, Hitler provided a tragic dimension to Jewish history. The story of the Jew in America took on a new direction. Without the flow from the Old World, American Jews, now second generation, faced the new challenge of continued accommodation. Henceforth, their security would be in doubt, the protection of their rights would be an even greater problem than ever before, and as a people, they faced a new ferocity in organized hatred.

4

Continued Challenge, Depression, and Political Involvement: 1929–1939

W HILE MANY OF THE difficulties faced by Jews during the Great Depression were the same as those that were encountered by others, there were some that were unique. Anti-Semitism, stemming from Nazi Germany, and discrimination in employment in a tight labor market exacerbated the Jewish situation.

At first, a great many Jews were not directly affected by the great stock market crash of October 1929, and it took little time before the indirect effects of the financial collapse began to be felt. An interesting aside to the problems of bankers during the Great Depression occurred in Philadelphia. At a meeting of the most powerful of the city's bankers, it was decided to allow the tenth largest bank to close its doors because of a run on it, exhausting its supply of ready cash. The major reason was distrust of Albert M. Greenfield, an immigrant Jew and major stockholder of Bankers Trust. It is possible that Greenfield made uncomfortable Philadelphia's blue-blooded Main Line banking establishment.

On December 10, 1930, many of those who had been weathering the storm comfortably were suddenly drawn into the vortex, for on that day there was a run at the Bank of the

United States in New York City. That bank had been founded in 1913 by two Jewish immigrants, Joseph S. Marcus and Saul Singer, and most of its 400,000 depositors were Jews. When it failed, untold numbers of individuals lost their life savings, and thousands of Jewish businesses, including garment center factories that had accounts at the bank, went bankrupt. Scores of families were faced with an unemployed breadwinner and the unpleasant prospect of joining the ever-swelling relief rolls. The damage that was done to the New York Jewish community because of this and other bank failures was quite serious and caused much suffering as the nation sank deeper into the morass of depression.

The spectacular loss of savings caused by the failure of the Bank of the United States and other banks was only one dimension of the misfortune that was beginning to descend on the Jewish community. Recently arrived immigrants who had not yet become solidly established were among the first, but by no means the only ones, to be adversely affected. Many Jews were engaged in the real estate business where values went down so far and fast that many saw their entire fortunes wiped out, often by bank foreclosures. Those who did become unemployed for one reason or another often found great difficulty in obtaining another job because of widespread discrimination practiced by non-Jewish employers, a luxury that could be practiced because of the immense labor pool.

By October 1931, teachers in many Jewish educational institutions were forced to take substantial pay cuts in order to avert school closings which would result in complete loss of income. The general scarcity of funds was felt by Jewish community centers no less than other establishments. As the ranks of the unemployed grew larger, attendance increased appreciably. Those who were out of work flocked to the centers to spend the hours in which they would normally be working. Many of those who used the facilities were able to pay their dues only in monthly installments, and for those who could not pay at all, membership charges were often waived. In order to remain in operation the centers were forced to cut operating expenses, including 'employee's salaries, to minimum levels.

The Jewish tradition of rendering private assistance to members of their community who were in need was a long and honored tradition, and because of this ingrained practice the Jews were better prepared than many other groups for the emergency precipitated by the business slump. True, a tremendous increase in effort was required to cope with an economic collapse of such vast proportions but there was a solid framework of organizations and skilled social workers on which to build. The fact that there were no real government relief programs during the early years of the depression triggered an all-out effort by Jewish welfare agencies to help their own people. They were often the only source of aid for Jewish families who had fallen victim to hard times.

By the end of 1930 the strain of the depression was being felt by the local federations, and philanthropies were often in competition for monies. In Buffalo, New York, for instance, appeals for aid received by the Jewish Family Welfare Department increased 30 percent during the year. When the local federation had exhausted all of its cash reserves, bank loans were taken out to aid needy families. Despite the deepening of the economic crisis, however, the local federations actually increased the amount of aid given during the year by almost $1 million. During the year ending in August 1931, Jews had given a total of $56,200,870 through their various organizations for the support of charities. Of this amount, $20,497,120, or more than one-third, went to entirely non-Jewish causes, such as the Metropolitan Museum of Art, the University of Chicago, and the Hoover Illiteracy Commission. In other words, while there was a great need for increased funds within the Jewish community to aid needy families, Jews also felt a responsibility to support organizations that benefited the whole of society.

The year 1931 proved to be extremely trying for Jewish philanthropic organizations. In Chicago there were more than 50,000 Jews out of work, and Jewish charities in that city indicated that welfare cases had increased by 200 percent since 1929. The Jewish Federation for Social Service of Buffalo looked forward to 1932 with trepidation. To meet the expected costs of relief administration they issued an appeal for donations representing an increase of more than $19,000 over the previous year's goal, and there were fewer people with sufficient resources to support the campaign. All over the nation the story was the same. The Orthodox Jewish Congregations of America were faced with the task of raising $1.2 million for the year 1933. While some organizations, like the Jewish Philanthropic Societies of New York City, were successful in raising enough money to meet their goals, others were not so fortunate. For example, New York City Jews alone raised more than $1.7 million to support local relief cases in 1933.

To gain a more precise view of the impact of the Depression on Jewish charities, a word is in order about the growth of these agencies. In 1936 there were 143 Jewish Federations and Welfare Funds in the United States. The Federations were ordinarily affiliated with the local community chest organizations and formed the central agencies for the collection and distribution of funds for philanthropic purposes. They were also charged with the planning and coordination of local Jewish social service programs. The Welfare Funds, on the other hand, had the responsibility of providing special services, including Jewish education, and of supporting nonlocal Jewish agencies. Of the 143 agencies, 48, or one-third, had been established after 1931, generally in response to the pressures generated by the depression.

After 1935 there began to be increasing concern for the safety of European Jews, especially for those fleeing Germany. American Jews were called upon to sacrifice even further to render aid to those unfortunate people. In the summer of 1935 Felix M. Warburg announced the formation of a relief corporation to aid refugees from Germany and other countries. A drive was started to raise $10 million to provide the initial financing for the Refugee Economic Corporation.

Many different groups in the 1920s had carried out their own programs, though there was some coordination in 1927, when several appeals joined in the United Palestine Appeal. European relief programs remained completely uncoordinated. As Palestine began to receive many refugees from Germany, additional funds were needed but domestic conditions dramatically reduced the amount of giving. Eventually in 1939 the JDC, which had emphasized relief for East European Jewry, and the American Palestine Campaign united their campaigns on a permanent basis into the United Jewish Appeal. The American Jewish Congress, an outgrowth of World War I needs as we have seen, also took on renewed vitality in the 1930s as the Zionist movement with its goal of a Palestinian homeland seemed more than ever the answer to the European Jewish plight. At last, the Congress became a prime voice against Hitlerian policy although it could never command the loyalty of all American Jews.

One of the most striking characteristics of the American-Jewish scene in the thirties was the absorption into the United States of approximately 111,000 refugees from Nazi Germany between 1933 and 1941. Those who came before World War II began (1939) were chiefly from Germany and Austria, and those who migrated later were mostly East Europeans. The German group, especially, were well educated, were members of the upper-middle class, and were quite proud of their university background. The cultural life led by this group—dubbed the "Fourth Reich"—was cosmopolitan. Kurt Weill, the composer, Emil Ludwig, the biographer, Max Reinhardt of the theater, Dr. Theodor Reik, the psychoanalyst, and, of course, Albert Einstein, originator of the theory of relativity, were all examples of the intellectual eminence that Hitler drove to these shores. So many of these immigrants were men of scholarship that the New School for Social Research in New York established a faculty of refugees, the University-in-Exile. This was the beginning of an academic exodus that continued through the war years and that contributed tremendously to American cultural creativeness.

Although the United States was the major refugee haven,

she could have absorbed more immigrants, but the quota system remained unadjusted. The Great Depression and the anti-Semitism of an emotionally charged period combined to prevent the entrance of additional refugee newcomers—potential rivals with Americans for jobs. The Roosevelt Administration, while it refused to expel 15,000 refugees here on visitors' visas, could not easily challenge congressional prerogatives. Refugee issues were left almost entirely to the State Department, and the assistant secretary in charge, Breckenridge Long, was quite suspicious of foreigners, especially those who might turn out to be spies or Communist agents. At any rate, no asylum was found for many refugees who had fled Nazi-held territories. Some American Jews were distrustful of immigrants too. Representative Sol Bloom (New York), and the House Foreign Affairs Committee which he headed, opposed bills to create a commission to "effectuate the rescue of the Jewish people of Europe" (*New York Times*, Dec. 11, 1943).

During the Depression, President Hoover had reduced immigrant quotas in order to lower competition with American labor. Roosevelt restored the combined German-Austrian quotas and in order to assist Jews raised the quotas back to their original numbers.

One example of the refugee plight was the dramatic episode of the Hamburg American Line's *St. Louis*, which arrived at Havana, Cuba, in May 1939 from Germany carrying over nine hundred Jews. This group was rejected by the Cuban government despite the intervention of the American Joint Distribution Committee. The JDC was powerless since the State Department took no action. And the White House refused to intervene since the matter was a State Department one. Also, it was explained that the United States could not interfere in an internal Cuban affair. This country also made it clear that the refugees would not be permitted to land on American soil. The ship cruised aimlessly in circles, steaming close to Miami to alert the Jews there in the hope they would pressure Washington. After a renewed effort at negotiations with Cuba failed, the *St. Louis* headed back to Germany and ultimate death for the passengers. The Cubans had required a bond for each refugee and while the JDC was ultimately successful in raising the money, Cuba would not reconsider her decision. Roosevelt had instructed the American ambassador to stress the humanitarian aspect of the situation with the Cuban president. It was indeed ironic, however, that the United States, insisting it could not violate its own immigration laws, could ask other nations to accept the Jews. It was quite obvious that despite presidential pronouncements, the State Department was anti-refugee.

There was, during the Depression, a minor but rather exciting movement among some Jews to "return to the soil." Most of this farm activity took place under the auspices of the Jewish Agricultural Society, which was chiefly responsible for what success the undertaking had. Perhaps the most incredible aspect of the movement was that it occurred during one of the blackest periods in the history of American farming. While drought, dust storms, mortgage foreclosures, and a host of other calamities drove unprecedented numbers of farmers from their land, the Jews not only held on but actually increased their numbers engaged in farming.

The Jewish Agricultural Society provided aid to Jewish farmers in the form of loans, information on reducing operating costs, farm management programs, improved production and marketing methods, new outlets for farm products, and reorganized farmers' cooperatives. The end result of this comprehensive program was that fewer Jews were driven off their farms during the Depression than out of city jobs, city businesses, and city homes. The movement proved to be so successful, in fact, that the Central Commission for Jewish Colonization issued an appeal to the "Jewish masses" in 1933 to unite in agricultural groups and return to farms as a way of fighting the unemployment and deprivation caused by the Depression.

In 1900 there were only 216 Jewish families on farms in the United States; by 1931 that figure had risen to 80,000. But the real impact of the Depression can be seen in figures reflecting the work of the Jewish Agricultural Society. In 1929 the Society made 477 loans totaling over $300,000, while in 1930, with the first effects of the Depression already apparent, the loan figure jumped to over $6.5 million.

On the farms, as in other areas of American life, the Jews weathered the Depression because of their ability to co-operate and work together as a group. The secret of their success was a capacity to organize effectively to combat a common problem and a willingness to sacrifice to help others of their kind.

The relationship between Jews and the Roosevelt Administration was direct. In essence, the Jewish community's experience in dealing with the Depression foreshadowed New Deal policies. When members of the National Conference of Jewish Social Services met in Minneapolis in June 1931, they petitioned President Hoover and Congress to take steps in the form of federal emergency relief on a large enough scale to alleviate existing and future suffering, to sponsor the construction of public works to stimulate and revive industry, and to formulate a comprehensive program of social security insurance. In essence, the Conference proposed the very same measures that would take shape as the New Deal under the leadership of Franklin D. Roosevelt. Their foresight in anticipating Roosevelt's domestic policies by nearly two years was actually a natural outgrowth of the American-Jewish tradition. During the 1920s, for instance, Jewish leadership in the garment unions had been responsible for developing unemployment and pension funds to which employees were forced to contribute. Both the International Ladies Garment Workers Union, under the direction of David Dubinsky, and the Amalgamated Clothing Workers, with Sidney Hillman in control, had also persuaded employers to contribute to pension and unemployment funds for their workers. In addition to this innovation the Amalgamated Clothing Workers opened their own cooperative low-income housing project in the Bronx in 1929. One clothing union showed responsibility by even lending Hart, Schaffner and Marx enough money to keep in operation.

Once in office, Roosevelt conducted his administration in a manner that won the approval of a majority of the Jewish community. The unions were especially in debt to the president for the National Recovery Administration. Before the NRA codes went into effect, workers in the women's garment trades commonly worked fifty to sixty hours per week. After the codes were instituted, 90 percent of the workers in the needle trades had a thirty-five hour work week and an increase in wages ranging from 20 to 50 percent. Much of the success achieved by the Jewish union leaders was, of course, due to their own efforts but there was also the stability afforded by a friendly national administration. The garment trades not only won "bread and butter" victories, but also sponsored educational, camping, and theatrical programs.

On the national scene, Sidney Hillman was brought to Washington to work on the National Recovery Administration's National Labor Advisory Board, and David Dubinsky was a master strategist in planning negotiations on NRA codes for his garment workers. He made certain that each trade under his control had a well-organized and fully researched case before going to the NRA for settlement. When the NRA was struck down by the Supreme Court in 1935, Dubinsky increased his organizational efforts to avoid losing such gains that had been made. As a result of his work most of the NRA benefits were retained and some were extended, union membership increased slightly, and industrial standards were kept at a high level. Later, during the war years, Jewish labor leaders cooperated with the president in accelerating the war effort, showing the effectiveness of the partnership that had been formed during the New Deal years. Hillman, for instance, was active in several agencies and largely instrumental in the increased production of American factories. This increase in the power and prestige of the Jewish union leaders won wide support for Roosevelt not only among union members, but among others in the Jewish community as well. As James Yaffe has pointed out, "Jews have been in favor of unionism from the beginning: even Jewish businessmen, as most union leaders agree, are easier to deal with on this matter than gentile businessmen" (*The American Jews*, p. 245).

Prior to 1932, a great number of Jews, if not a majority, were affiliated Republicans. Many were businessmen who recalled the hard times under Cleveland in the 1890s when they arrived in the United States. They shared the phobia against free silver and thought the William Jennings Bryan faction in the Democratic Party dangerously radical. But the shift to the Democrats began with Jewish support of Al Smith in 1928, and by 1932, Franklin D. Roosevelt received generous encouragement from American Jews because they felt he championed causes to which they were firmly committed. The Jewish community in general advocated the proposition that the federal government was responsible for the welfare of all Americans and believed in social security, unemployment insurance, favorable labor legislation, and progressive taxation. Initial Jewish support for Roosevelt and the New Deal can best be explained by the liberal identity of the program. Jewish experience in America had clearly indicated that friends were to be found in liberal quarters. This liberal orientation, nurtured by early experiences in America, was also reinforced by traditional Jewish religious ethics. The ideals of charity and brotherhood were deeply embedded in the ethical teachings of Judaism. Because Roosevelt identified with the ideals cherished by Jews, they gave him their overwhelming support. This nearly universal backing was true of Jews not only in low income groups but also of those who were well off. Nathaniel Weyl has shown that this liberal idealism is the only logical explanation for the widespread Jewish support given to Roosevelt in 1932. While suffering induced by the Depression was certainly part of the explanation for the switch to the New Deal party, it does not provide the entire answer. Many other ethnic groups, who were not as economically successful as the Jews, suffered greater hardships but did not give Roosevelt the measure of support that he received from American Jews.

By the time of the New Deal, many Jewish shopkeepers, union members, and intellectuals affiliated with the Democrats. Roosevelt on the national scene and Herbert H. Lehman, first Jewish governor of New York, were activist leaders who were largely responsible for the close alliance between Jews and the Democratic party. The programs of both president and governor in fighting the Depression appealed greatly to Jews as well as to other minority groups. And, those Jews who still resisted major party affiliation were active in organizing the American Labor party in 1936. They could support Roosevelt as well as more radical candidates for Congress not nominated by the Democrats. A crisis ensued in the 1940s when Communists infiltrated the American Labor party and resulted in the creation of the non-Marxist Liberal party.

The Jewish support for the president was later augmented as the image of Roosevelt as war leader in the crusade against Nazi Germany materialized. The extent to which this warrior image aided Roosevelt in capturing the Jewish vote has been documented by James Yaffe: "In 1932 and 1936 the Jewish vote for Roosevelt paralleled that of the country. But in 1940 and 1944, when other minority groups and the working classes were beginning to have doubts about FDR, the Jews gave him 90 percent of their vote."

At least some of the support given Roosevelt by Jews can be accounted for by the success they experienced under his administrations as well as by their faith in the doctrine of liberalism. Also, like others, Jews were drawn to Roosevelt by the usual desire for aid from the Depression and from discrimination as well. He promised them action in solving their problems and they believed him. At the very least, he tried one program after another in the hope of lifting the Depression.

The ideological identity between traditional Jewish beliefs and liberal policies coupled with the enthusiastic support of many Jews for Franklin Roosevelt gave rise to some bitter accusations that Jews were overrepresented in the new administration. "The Jew Deal" became a cliché. While it is true that the number of Jews in government increased during the 1930s, charges that they controlled the Roosevelt administration are groundless. To be sure, there were a number of influential Jews in or near White House circles who worked willingly for the president. After all, FDR knew many Jews from New York State politics. There were men like Representative Adolph J. Sabath of Chicago, for example, who fostered much of the New Deal legislation. Sabath was a member of the important House Rules Committee and he often used his influence there to assist the president. Representative Sol Bloom of New York was a trusted Roosevelt advisor, a party wheelhorse in the House of Representatives and, after 1939, chairman of the House Committee on Foreign Affairs. Herbert H. Lehman succeeded FDR as governor of New York in 1932 and served with distinction for a decade. A close friend of the president, Lehman remained throughout the thirties and forties a valued associate.

Bernard M. Baruch, the financier and head of the War Industries Board during World War I, was by this time known as advisor to presidents. Louis D. Brandeis, appointed to the Supreme Court in 1916, was affectionately referred to by Roosevelt as "Isaiah," a reflection of the Judge's love of justice and judicial liberalism. There is no doubt that just as he stimulated Wilson, he did the same for FDR. Brandeis was always concerned about ruthless business practices and favored the New Deal position on control of the stock market and banks, collective bargaining, and protection of investors and consumers. In 1932 another Jew, Benjamin N. Cordozo, joined Brandeis on the high court. A gentle, scholarly, and wise man, he died in 1939, the same year Brandeis retired. FDR appointed in his place his longtime friend and advisor, Felix M. Frankfurter, who had a distinguished career as lawyer, government attorney, and Harvard professor. These three justices, together with Irving Lehman, who was elected chief judge of the New York State Court of Appeals in 1939, regarded law in a social context, evolving and sensitive to changing needs.

There were still other Jews who had important New Deal positions. Henry Morgenthau, FDR's Hyde Park neighbor, for instance, served as secretary of the treasury from 1934 to 1945. David K. Niles was an important labor advisor and, later, the unofficial liaison between the Truman Administration and Jews. Jesse Isidor Straus served as America's ambassador to France during the early Roosevelt years. Two special advisors to the president were Benjamin V. Cohen, a vital figure in the famous group of intellectuals who sparked the early New Deal, and Judge Samuel I. Rosenman, FDR's chief legal counselor and important presidential speech writer. There was also David Lilienthal, director and chairman of the Tennessee Valley Authority. He later became the first chairman of the Atomic Energy Commission. Anna Rosenberg, an expert in labor and personnel relations, held several positions in New Deal Washington and later was an assistant secretary of defense in the Truman Administration.

While the Jews were vital to the unfolding of the New Deal program, it is an exaggeration to say that Jews controlled the administration. A study by W. M. Kiplinger indicated that the number of Jews in government did not exceed the proportion by which they were represented in the population. In 1942, when the study was conducted, that figure was only 4 percent. Kiplinger speculated that perhaps the reason there seemed to be an inordinate number of Jews in the federal government was that they were often in highly publicized and visible "friction agencies," which dealt directly with the public, like the Securities and Exchange Commission, the Department of Labor, the National Labor Relations Board, or the Social Security Board. At any rate, one measure of Jewish influence in the Roosevelt years was the number of judicial appointments they received: of the 197 federal judges appointed by the president, only 7 were Jews.

The Jews who were the most seriously affected by

discrimination during the Depression were those in the white-collar administrative and clerical occupations. Typists, stenographers, and private secretaries all encountered grave difficulties in obtaining positions, as did those who sought employment in banks, insurance companies, railroads, and public service corporations. Jewish teachers who tried to find jobs in small towns and rural areas also found that many doors were closed to them. Women were especially prone to suffer from discriminatory practices. In 1930 there were ten thousand unemployed Jewish girls in New York City, while the figure in Chicago rose above eight thousand in that year.

In order to dramatize the plight of qualified Jews who could not find jobs in public utility companies, Samuel Leibowitz, a famous trial lawyer from New York City, threatened to organize a one-night-a-week boycott of gas, electric, and telephone companies if they did not halt their discriminatory hiring practices. Other prominent Jews conducted investigations of various companies and published the results. One such study revealed prejudicial behavior by a number of employment agencies. Of ninety agencies investigated thirty-four admitted placing advertisements specifying "Christians only."

American Jews have traditionally held high aspirations for their offspring and they have generally looked to education as a means of fulfilling these aspirations. The Depression did not lessen this Jewish desire to further the education of their young; if anything the desire was intensified by the poverty induced by economic collapse. When Yeshiva University was faced with the prospect of closing its doors for lack of funds, and the faculty was forced to go without salary for several months, small neighborhood grocers kept the institution alive by extending credit to its professors.

With fierce devotion to education as part of their heritage, it is little wonder that Jews became incensed when their children experienced difficulties in entering colleges and universities. In the years before the Depression, when costs were not so prohibitive, many parents even sent their children to medical schools abroad as a way of circumventing American restrictions on Jewish students. But, with the increasing hardships caused by the Depression, they often had to settle for less prestigious medical schools in remote areas of the American South and West.

Despite the problems, however, Jews continued to send their students in ever-increasing numbers to colleges and universities. Statistics in the 1937–1938 edition of the *American Jewish Yearbook* indicate that whereas Jews were only 3.5 percent of the population, Jewish students made up 9.1 percent of all those enrolled in American institutions of higher learning. Similar figures, however, were used by some to refute charges of discrimination against Jews. During the 1930s, Jews whenever possible kept attending schools of higher education and thus were in a position to take important jobs when the great takeoff came after the Second World War. Also, during the hard-scrabble Depression days, many Jews entered government work and teaching because all were looking forward to steady salaries without layoffs.

In addition to the more passive forms of discrimination against Jews already discussed, there was a general rise in overt anti-Semitic activity. As the pall of the Depression enveloped the country, people looked about them for the traditional scapegoat, and all too often Jews were chosen to fill this role. Even more influential in arousing latent anti-Semitism were the activities of the Nazis in Germany. By 1935 antagonism to Jews in the United States had assumed the proportions of a movement. Part of this movement was, predictably, centered among recent German immigrants. There was, in addition, a "native American" anti-Jewish movement supported by those who opposed the social and economic policies of the New Deal. As we have seen, some critics charged that there were too many Jews in the Roosevelt Administration, and that many Jews claimed to be non-Jews to avoid arousing suspicion. An anti-Semitic organization, the Sentinels of the Republic, claimed that Secretary of Labor Frances Perkins was actually a Jew. Miss Perkins denied the allegation, but such stories persisted. (Indeed, some even claimed that FDR was really Rosenfeld, a Jew!)

During the period 1933 to 1940 there were over one hundred organizations spreading anti-Semitic propaganda in the United States. Two of the largest such groups were the Christian Front, led by Father Charles Coughlin of Royal Oak, Michigan, and William Dudley Pelley's Silver Shirts. The Silver Shirts alone were responsible for distributing three and one-half tons of anti-Jewish material in a nineteen-month period beginning in 1937.

Coughlin abandoned his earlier policy of "social justice" and liberal reform for Jew-baiting. He envisioned the Christian Front as a necessity to preserve American liberty and fight the monied interests and the Communists. Coughlin challenged the Jews to adopt the Christian view of "love thy neighbor as thyself," which actually is from the Book of Leviticus, in place of the old Hebrew law which he erroneously described as "an eye for an eye." Despite his denial of anti-Semitism, Coughlin continued to attack the Jews, the Communists, Roosevelt, and the New Deal. While he espoused theories on many issues and lashed out at the world around him, his anti-Semitism overshadowed all else. At first, Coughlin championed FDR and warned in 1932 that it was "Roosevelt or Ruin." Yet, two years later he broke with him and vented his spleen against Jews who, he thought, controlled international monetary affairs. Coughlin was an inflationist and among other things thought that Jews were bound up with gold. He became extremely dangerous after 1938, even using Nazi propaganda written in Goebbels's headquarters. The Jew, for Coughlin, became the scapegoat for all ills, at home and abroad.

The anti-Semitic furor in the United States drew inspiration from the fount in Germany, and Nazi tactics and methods were put into practice here on a minor scale. Secret Nazi agents came to America and coached Pelley and others in the art of anti-Semitic propaganda. The German-American Bund headed by Fritz Kuhn served as a model and voice to other groups such as the Silver Shirts, the Black Legion, and the Knights of the Camellia, to name only a few of several hundred such organizations of the radical right in the United States in the 1930s. The New Deal was pictured by these groups as being of Jewish origin, and proof of this accusation was substantiated, they said, by the fact that Jews predominated as Roosevelt's advisors. The Bund's reasoning can be easily catalogued: the economic collapse of 1929 was the responsibility of the Jews, for they controlled American finance and the general economy as well as the international money marts.

Crank charges and anti-Semitic utterances extended even into the United States House of Representatives. In May 1933, Congressman Louis T. McFadden of Pennsylvania stated that Jews were responsible for the Depression because they controlled American finance and the economy of the country. He went on to charge that the gold clause repeal was the work of Jewish international money-changers and that the result was that non-Jews had the slips of paper while the Jews had the gold and the lawful money. Inflamatory statements coming from a congressman were certainly ominous and occasioned much concern and heated dialogue.

As this type of outrageous activity began to spread, the American Jewish Committee, the American Jewish Congress, and the Anti-Defamation League of the B'nai B'rith stepped up their campaign to expose anti-Semitic organizations. For example, in July 1934, a list of thirty-two such outfits, with memberships in the hundreds of thousands, was made public.

One of the most telling defenses of the Jew in America which exposed the folly of much anti-Semitic literature was a report in *Fortune* magazine on the commercial activities of American Jews (February 1936). This survey exploded the myth that Jews controlled the American economy. There were very few Jews in commercial, investment, or international banking despite the hysterical charges that they controlled these operations. Only 16 percent of the members of the New York Stock Exchange were Jews and only 55 of the

637 firms listed by the Exchange were owned by Jews. Twenty-four others were found to be half-Jewish, and an additional 39 had significant Jewish influence within the firms. Jews in the coal, rubber, petroleum, metallurgy, mining, chemical and transportation industries were shown to be almost nonexistent. An investigation of the automobile industry turned up only three Jews in prominent positions. There were only two outstanding Jews in heavy industry, leading the editors of *Fortune* to the conclusion that "The only exception to the rule that steel is not a Jewish industry is the scrap business." Similar observations were recorded about Jews in the insurance business. In fact, there were only three sectors of the economy where Jews had any appreciable influence. One of these was the liquor business. About half of the important distilling concerns in the United States were Jewish, including Seagrams and Schenley. In the textile industry there were a number of Jews; however, only a few of these were involved in the manufacturing process. Most were distributors. Half the woolen sales agents, three-quarters of the silk converters, and 75 percent of the cotton converters were Jewish. Similarly, 85 percent of men's clothing dealers and 95 percent of dealers in the women's garment trade were Jews, most from New York City. The only other commercial activity dominated by Jews was the motion picture industry. While some people complained that Jews influenced public opinion and manipulated American society through their control of the movie business, *Fortune* pointed out that Jews had little influence in other media such as newspapers and magazines.

The election campaign of 1936 brought the anti-Semitic issue into sharp focus on a national scale. Believing that rumors of a "Jew Deal" could be used to defeat Roosevelt, a whispering campaign spread the word that a vote for the Republican candidate, Alf Landon, would be a vote against Jews. Many of these rumors indicated that Landon was an outright anti-Semite and could be counted on to "put the Jews in their place" if he was elected President. The Kansas governor went on record stoutly denying all of these rumors and denounced those that spread them, but the stories persisted.

In 1937–1938 there was increased evidence of anti-Semitism because of the unsettled conditions stemming from the severe economic recession, plus the growing power of Hitler and the real fear that war was around the corner and that American Jews were interventionists.

In 1938 there was another outbreak of hate propaganda. There appeared to be a direct connection between the increased tempo of atrocities against Jews in Nazi Germany and the renewed strength of American anti-Semitism. Gerald Winrod, who claimed that an "international Jewish conspiracy" was to blame for the threat of worldwide communism, polled 53,000 votes in the Republican senatorial primary in Kansas. Shortly after this, in February 1938, the German-American Bund held a mass meeting in Madison Square Garden attended by more than 22,000 people. As the agitation reached an intensity that began to frighten many, there were warnings from the nervous of the possibility of widespread persecutions similar to those occurring in Germany. Others recognized the inherent danger to the safety of all Americans should the basic foundations of democratic liberty yield to mob rule. The newspapers of the day were filled with reports documenting the reign of terror that Hitler had instituted in Germany, and there was genuine concern that it could be transplanted to American soil. This concern was shared by non-Jews as well as Jews.

Formally organized in 1940, the America First organization was the main isolationist pressure group. One of its prominent supporters was the famed aviator, Charles A. Lindbergh, whose isolationist feelings were quite sincere. However, Lindbergh began to embroider his isolationism, asserting that the British, the Jews, and FDR were propelling the country toward war. Lindbergh felt that the greatest danger from Jews was in their "large ownership and influence in our motion pictures, our press, our radio, and our government." It was this type of reasoning which led Joseph P. Kennedy, the American ambassador to Great Britain, to warn the heavily Jewish motion-picture industry to avoid producing anti-Nazi films. Kennedy, together with such isolationists as Lindbergh and Senator Gerald Nye, accused the movie moguls of trying to push the United States into war with Germany.

There was an attempt on the part of some writers to provide rational explanations for the irrational feelings against American Jews. One reason that was advanced related to the supposed unwillingness of Jews to become entirely absorbed in the American cultural stream, because they insisted on preserving their "group solidarity." James Yaffe explains the American anti-Semitic phenomenon in terms of the difference between it and its European counterpart. European governments made anti-Semitism an instrument of state policy as a means of diverting the attention of the people from internal problems. In the case of Hitler he used it in the name of cultural and racial purity. In America, because anti-Semitism never had any legal sanction, it has usually been sporadic, impulsive, and many times the outburst of hate fanatics and unstable individuals. Nevertheless, anti-Semitism continued in the thirties and was certainly one of the least attractive features of the Depression Era.

As we have seen, the flourishing of Jewish cultural activity as well as the role of Jews in the development of American culture was one of the outstanding features of the American Jewish epic. However, despite the real accomplishments, there were a number of disappointments, especially in the fields of Jewish education and Yiddish culture.

As noted previously, Jewish education was not tremendously successful in its mission. All over the land, the numbers of elementary and secondary school age children enrolled in Jewish schools in the 1930s dropped appreciably. Bureaus of Jewish education and congregational school systems made valiant but futile efforts to make viable a part-time supplementary system. Nevertheless, Jewish education continued to flounder and to be one of the most vulnerable aspects of Jewish life in America.

The Jewish collegiate scene was more positive. Like other children of the Depression, Jewish collegians were generally quite serious and appreciative of the advantages of an education. They were library patrons, eager to discover new ideas from the books they borrowed. Education was one avenue to improvement, to a profession and a better job. The Jewish heritage of learning, combined with the tangible rewards afforded by a secular education, created a unique spirit among American Jewish youth. The Jewish poet and anthologist Louis Untermeyer, and the novelist Ludwig Lewisohn, were revered names and even became "cult-heroes" to this youthful intelligentsia. Many Jewish youngsters who enrolled in New York City universities, while respectful of education, were also among the chief radicals and protesters. They were in the leadership circle of several student leagues which professed Marxist leanings. While their numbers were small, they had an impact on college life out of all proportion to their numerical strength. Like so many members of the Old Left, the younger people eventually became disenchanted with the excesses of Russian communism. Their doubts were finally confirmed by the Nazi-Soviet Pact of August 23, 1939 and thereafter, most Jews who were in the Communist party of America left it.

Another phase of Jewish life that suffered was the Yiddish heritage, because of the fast assimilation of immigrant groups. From a peak period in the 1920s, the Yiddish press dropped in circulation by 50 percent. This type of newspaper was a prime instrument of Americanization and assimilation, and by the thirties, its task was basically completed. More appealing to the Jewish-American was the Anglo-Jewish weekly that provided national and international information of importance to Jews and, often, the more absorbing news and gossip of the local community.

The decline of Yiddish theater was also a direct result of the virtual end of immigration. This type of drama was of little concern to the Americanized second generation, who could not understand the dialogue. Of more importance was the continuing Jewish-American participation and leadership in both the motion-picture industry and the Broadway stage. Jewish themes accounted for very few stories to come from Hollywood and New York, but there were stereotypes of Jews portrayed over and over. For example, in the works of Clifford Odets or the ILGWU production of *Pins and Needles*, the Jewish prototype was clearly recognizable.

Jews were among the major participants in the Group Theater (1931), the Government's Works Progress Administration Federal Theater (1935), the ILGWU-sponsored theater, and several other small groups. These theaters not only served as a place where the unemployed could find work, but also allowed ethnic minorities to express themselves on the stage in social-protest productions and plays of social significance. The federal theater program was eventually killed by the House Un-American Activities Committee because of its leftist leanings.

The greats of the stage, screen, and radio, some of whom were already mentioned, retained their popularity. Such stars as Fanny Brice, Eddie Cantor, George Jessel, Al Jolson, the Marx Brothers, Ed Wynn, Jack Benny, George Burns, Milton Berle, and Gertrude Berg (creator and chief character of a Jewish-oriented radio serial, "The Goldbergs") were arbiters of American entertainment. And younger performers such as John Garfield, Phil Silvers, Danny Kaye, and writers and producers like Moss Hart, Dore Schary, George S. Kaufman and many others, were making their early reputations. Such directors as Ernst Lubitsch, William Wyler, and Billy Wilder, together with the well-known leaders of the industry—Louis B. Mayer, David Selznick, Adolph Zukor, Samuel B. Goldwyn, the Warner Brothers, and Irving Thalberg—became synonymous with the contributions Hollywood was making to help alleviate depression woes.

In American literature, a number of Jews began to receive notice. Judd Teller has stated that the writers of the thirties wrote fiction which had "documentary significance," and broke with immigrant stereotypes. The Jew was most often portrayed as a victim of social ills and the class struggle. Michael Gold's *Jews Without Money* is an example of this type of proletarian writing.

Within Judaism itself, there were a number of significant developments. As an institution, the synagogue attracted only a minority of America's 4.77 million Jews—only about 1.5 million or between 25 and 33 percent of all Jews. In the 1920s, synagogues were being built in record numbers. However, the 1930s witnessed a general construction retrenchment and even cases of threatened foreclosure on bank-held synagogue mortgages. In addition, many temples merged in the name of economy.

By the thirties, the Conservative branch of Judaism faced such challenges and disagreements over how to relate God's laws with the less observant practices of the laity. One formula of accommodation was that evolved by Professor Mordecai Kaplan. For Kaplan, one could be an observant Jew even while rejecting certain traditional beliefs. What was new in his approach was the categorization of Judaism as a civilization. Whether Judaism conformed to accepted revelation or emphasized the divine law was not basic; the crucial question was whether Jewish practice enriched Jewish life. As Nathan Glazer put it, "Kaplan provided a rationale for those Jews who no longer believed in the divine origin of Jewish religious law but who nevertheless wanted to keep on living as Jews." By 1935, Kaplan founded the Reconstructionist branch of Judaism to propagate his philosophy that theology was only one part of Jewish life, that it could be stripped of the supernatural and still be a dynamic religious experience. While Kaplan had great influence among all sectors of Jewry, his movement in its purity was accepted by only a handful of synagogues.

The Reform wing of Judaism was the wealthiest and boasted the greatest number of congregations. Strangely, Reform, which helped Jews adjust to secular life, was changing its orientation. The Hitler menace directed Reform Jews more and more toward Zionism. It was no longer Reform credo that Judaism was only a religion. Rather, it reaffirmed the common bonds of Jewish tradition—history, faith and, at least by inference, concern with a Jewish homeland. The Central Conference of American Rabbis even formally repudiated the anti-Zionist Pittsburgh Platform. This resulted in part from the heavy influx of East European Jews into Reform, especially the rabbinate. The traditional philanthropy of German Reform Jews toward their East European co-religionists brought the two often antagonistic groups closer together, and this relationship was enhanced by their mutual hatred of Hitler. Lastly, Reform moved more and more to the center and even to the right, modifying its leftist, antitraditional position. For example, Reform services began to emphasize the use of Hebrew, Jewish singers in the service, and more rituals such as Sabbath candle lighting, the use of the *shofar* (ram's horn sounded in the synagogue, particularly during the High Holiday services), more home observances, and the recital of the *Kiddish* (prayer for sanctification of the Sabbath and holidays).

Centuries of persecution and discrimination had developed by the thirties a sense of community spirit among the Jews that made each member of the group responsible for the other members. This social morality was enforced and strengthened by lingering traditional religious beliefs. The Jewish experience in America carried on and further developed this commitment to social solidarity. Jewish unions developed unemployment insurance plans long before the Social Security Act was enacted, and as already noted, Jewish welfare groups had been caring for members of their community for as long as there had been Jews in America. Thus, when Franklin Roosevelt began to move in this direction he received support, advisement, and the votes of the Jewish community.

The fact that the Jews continued to suffer from the effects of discrimination while at the same time they faced the extreme hardships of the Depression made the situation even more critical. Many Jews lost their jobs for no better reason than the fact that they were Jewish, and Jewish students continued to face collegiate admissions quotas. The hardships caused by discrimination served to increase the load on welfare agencies that were already overburdened. Anti-Semitism was also a serious problem during the 1930s. The economic decline accounted for some increase in the irrational attacks on Jews, but the rise of Nazism in Germany seemed to be even more closely related to this unfortunate occurrence. Most of these attacks were related to completely false reports that the Jews controlled the American economy through some sort of insidious "conspiracy" and were, therefore, entirely to blame for the Depression.

As the tension between the Roosevelt administration and the primary source of attacks on Jews, Nazi Germany, increased, Jewish support for the president grew rapidly. Roosevelt's domestic programs aimed at providing increased social justice for all groups had already captured the sentiments of most Jews. When this feeling was heightened by the administration's public disapproval of Hitler's treatment of the Jews in Germany, the American Jewish community lined up almost solidly behind the president for the duration.

By the thirties, it was apparent that the American Jews had solidified their role and identity in the United States. Accommodation had come full circle. In the realm of cultural life—art, music, theater, motion pictures, education, government—Jews remained prime contributors. In the next era, that of the Second World War and the emergence of the modern state of Israel, there would be a new consciousness and pride in Jewish ethnicity and, hence, still a new dimension in the history of the Jews in the United States.

5

War, Zionism, and Israel: 1939-1948

FROM SEPTEMBER 1939 TO May 1948, two events reshaped the modern history of the Jewish people—the Second World War and the reestablishment of the State of Israel. The war was obviously one of survival for the United States because of Hitler's resolve to destroy the free world. While Jews shared a common concern with all other Americans, their anxiety was especially heightened. In a world dominated by Nazis, American Jews would undoubtedly share the fate of their European brethren.

The German blueprint for the destruction of European Jewry was revealed by the end of 1942, but it was only after victory that the enormity of the Nazi murder of six million European Jews among others was clearly understood. The concentration camps of Auschwitz, Dachau, Buchenwald, and many others were locations where the Nazis attempted to put into effect what they called the "final solution." For the Jewish people, this dark period of their long history is known as the Holocaust. While legislatures passed resolutions and demonstrations and prayer days were held, the government of the United States did painfully little to save those that still could be saved. The Roosevelt administration withheld the news of the Holocaust for months while investigating its authenticity. There was conscious suppression of information about the Hitler policy of exterminating Jews. Walter Laqueur in his book *The Terrible Secret, Suppression of the Truth About Hitler's "Final Solution"* (1981) has shown that State Department officials concealed such information from Zionist leader Rabbi Stephen Wise in 1942.

While there was some knowledge about the Holocaust, it remains a mystery why there was such widespread ignorance. Possible explanations include skepticism and the feeling that these stories might be rumor or propaganda and that the military necessities of waging war made such incidents of low priority. Disbelief of anything so incredible, together with apathy, explain in part American policy, or rather, non-policy.

Secretary of the Treasury Henry Morgenthau, Jr. appealed directly to FDR, accusing the State Department of apathy, of non-co-operation with private organizations, and of suppressing reports of Nazi plans. There was a conference convened in Bermuda (1943) under Anglo-American auspices on the refugee problem, and FDR established the War Refugee Board in 1944, small but positive steps taken to rescue the remaining victims of Hitler's butchery. Historians are prone to place the chief blame for this humanitarian lapse on the State Department and especially on Assistant Secretary Breckenridge Long, who as head of the Visa Division allowed administrative red tape to slow the flow of refugees to America. His belief was that radicals, saboteurs, and spies might enter this country as Jewish refugees.

Secretary of State Cordell Hull, who was married to a Jewish woman, chose not to override his subordinates. Rigid and of constricted vision, he also took a dim view of liberalizing American immigration laws. Undersecretary of State Sumner Welles, long held to be the great friend of Jews in the State Department, was in reality not consistently favorable. The International Red Cross, too, failed in the face of Axis policy. It held that it could not intervene in the case of persecuted minorities since its greater task of ministering to prisoners of war might be jeopardized. Apathetic public opinion in 1939 had led Congress to reject a plan to bring ten thousand refugee children to the United States outside the quota system. Non-Jewish refugee children from Britain were admitted, however.

On all levels—including that of American Jewry—there was apathy and delay, but, according to such writers as Arthur Morse and Henry L. Feingold, the ultimate responşibility rested upon President Roosevelt, who chose to acquiesce rather than use his position to arouse a nation to some action. Already mentioned was the ineffective American pressure on Cuba to secure a solution for the *St. Louis* refugees, and a camp was established at Oswego, New York, to provide shelter for some German victims. (Less than a thousand found a haven there.) Henrietta Szold, the great American Zionist and founder of Hadassah (the women's Zionist organization), had in 1934 established the Youth Aliyah, which sought out and saved many Jewish children by sending them to safety in Palestine. This work continued for two decades and while valuable had but limited effects.

There were many opportunities for governmental action. The president could have rescinded the orders limiting immigration quotas (Other countries were far more hospitable). While FDR did liberalize immigration quotas, he could not do more without Congress, and it would not budge on immigration. The sad fact is that Congress wanted FDR to push Britain on Palestine and the president wanted Congress to act on liberalizing immigration, a political impossibility, and the result was that little was done. Jewish organizations suggested two plans: to conceal Jews in Axis-controlled areas with the aid of local undergrounds and to apply pressure on neutral nations to admit refugees, the JDC bearing the costs. Morse maintains that had the United States displayed the same determination to save European Jewry as Hitler displayed in destroying it, the toll of human life would have been lessened. For example, some say the American military rejected the offer of the Czech underground to furnish intelligence to the allies allowing them to bomb rail lines linking Hungary with the Polish gas chambers.

All this suggests a lapse of the American conscience. The Holocaust, upon reflection, was aided by missed opportunities to save German Jews—especially the lackadaisical attitude of president and Congress, the feeling that there was not enough shipping space to take the refugees to asylums, the ever-present anti-Semitism, disunity within the ranks of American Jewry and, most important, the overall war effort which our leaders felt must be given first priority.

Another sad aspect of the refugee story was the number of Jewish children who were weaned from the faith and from their parents. The Finaly Affair became the best known of these cases. The two Finaly boys were entrusted to a Catholic institution in Grenoble, France, by their parents, who were deported by the Nazis and never heard from thereafter. Beginning in 1945, relatives tried to recover the boys but it took eight years before they were brought to Israel and then only after protracted court actions, negotiations, and arrests. The boys' custodian, in violation of assurances given to the parents, had them baptized. The American Jewish Committee petitioned the State Department, and the World Jewish Congress was involved in the recovery of the children.

Those refugees that did settle in the United States presented an interesting sociological challenge to the Jewish establishment. The American Immigration Department estimated that approximately 244,000 refugees entered this country in the period, 1938–1944, and of these, 67 percent were Jews. The refugees who came during the Axis nightmare were quite different from the waves of immigrants who had come previously. A larger percentage were married women, over forty-five years of age; many were from the middle or upper classes, had white-collar occupations, and were generally more educated than earlier immigrants. According to official immigration statistics, an unusually large proportion of the refugees were engaged in professional and commercial fields.

When the refugees arrived, they faced severe adjustment problems. In addition to language difficulties, many lacked friends and families. Then too there was the question of earning a living. Though well educated and perhaps even professionals, they found proper connections hard to come by. In fact, the refugees were often forced to accept menial employment. There was resentment toward them on the part of American laborers who feared unemployment would result from the new influx. As a matter of fact, refugees often actually created new job opportunities by setting up small workshops and factories of their own. These businessmen started by employing two or three workers and, their factories often grew to a size where it was necessary to hire fifty or sixty. Thus, instead of creating an adverse effect on the economy, the refugees actually offered new opportunities to many American workers.

Of all the occupations, medicine proved to be a special problem. American physicians often resented their new refugee colleagues because of possible competition. Medical journals exaggerated the actual number of refugee physicians who came and these miscalculations, coupled with the unfounded cries of inferior ability and lower standards of European training, exacerbated an already difficult adjustment problem.

While refugee physicians were facing difficulties because of their failure to be accepted by their American counterparts, the refugee lawyers were experiencing hardships of a different nature. Since a much smaller percentage of refugees were lawyers as compared to the number in medicine, the lawyers were not faced with the unfounded allegations which stemmed from fear of competition. Instead, the problems of lawyers were mainly centered on the very nature of their profession. Since each country's laws and legal systems were so different, and since the refugee lawyers were trained in Roman law, they faced a real occupational dilemma. In fact, some even left the profession because they could not comprehend English law. In order to make ends meet, refugee lawyers often performed menial jobs. Once in the United States, these lawyers turned their hands to many kinds of work. They were not lazy and did not disdain manual labor; they were bottle washers, firemen, mechanics, and unskilled workmen of all sorts. A fortunate few found white-collar jobs—selling insurance, translating documents, handling real estate, or teaching school.

The Jewish role in the war undoubtedly was their finest hour and, incidentally, the most effective antidote to anti-Semitism. Aside from the men and women in combat, Jewish physicians and rabbis served with distinction. The number of physicians in service was quite high—approximately 60 percent of those under forty-five and over three hundred of the rabbinate joined the chaplaincy. The most famous of these was Abraham Goode, who died in June 1943, along with three Christian colleagues, because they gave their life preservers to men on board a torpedoed ship.

The National Jewish Welfare Board's Bureau of War Records was responsible for compiling the facts and figures of Jewish participation in the war, and the results were published in 1947 under the title, *American Jews in World War II: The Story of 550,000 Fighters for Freedom*. The proportion of Jews in the armed forces was, as in the case of World War I, higher than their proportion in the overall population. Approximately 3.6 percent of the population was Jewish in 1945, while 4.8 percent or 550,000 of those who served were of the Jewish faith. Thousands of Jewish-Americans died or were wounded during the hostilities. The approximate figures were at least 10,000 dead and 35,000 wounded. For their heroic efforts, they received over 50,000 medals and awards.

One of the most famous of all Jewish-American war heroes was Sergeant Meyer Levin, a bombardier flight mate of the equally famous Colin Kelly. Levin enlisted in 1939 before the attack on Pearl Harbor. His career had a tragic, yet heroic ending. After over sixty combat flights, Levin engaged in his last mission in January 1943. It was a Flying Fortress reconnaissance flight for which Levin had volunteered. On the return to New Guinea, following the air battle, Levin's plane encountered a violent storm. As the aircraft was about to plunge into the rough sea, Levin climbed out of the bomb bay and successfully unhooked the life rafts. Unfortunately, he failed to free himself before the plane crashed into the sea. Levin went down with his plane, but through his heroic efforts, the remainder of the crew was able to scramble onto the rafts and subsequent safety.

Barney Ross, one-time lightweight and welterweight world champion, was awarded the Silver Star for his heroic activities in the battle of Guadalcanal on November 20, 1942. While on a patrol with three other comrades, Ross's contingent was ambushed by a group of Japanese infantrymen. Except for Ross, the others were incapacitated. Ross quickly dragged the men into a nearby foxhole and held back the Japanese machine gunners with a lone rifle.

Sergeant Robert Kessler from McKeesport, Pennsylvania, distinguished himself for heroics in the European theater of action. Kessler, who directed the *Black Maria*, a B-24 Liberator, accumulated 349 combat hours, which included thirty-five bombing missions. The Kessler story was all the more fantastic because he stood only five feet tall and weighed only 108 pounds. In fact, his parachute was specially made for his minute body because the regulation parachute fell directly to the ground after being placed on his shoulders. This twenty-one-year-old man was the recipient of such honors as the Silver Star, the Air Medal, the Distinguished Flying Cross, and an Oak Leaf Cluster.

There were two Jewish-American Congressional Medal of Honor winners. One was Sergeant Isadore S. Jachman, a paratrooper from Baltimore, Maryland. Jachman, while involved in a fierce battle at Flamièrge, Belgium, ran through a volley of enemy fire in order to stave off the enemy offensive single-handedly and, as a result, saved his company from certain massacre. He accomplished this heroic feat by seizing a bazooka and, in full view of the enemy, rendering both tanks *hors de combat*. However, while halting the enemy offensive,

Jachman sustained wounds which soon after proved fatal. Isadore S. Jachman was a German Jew who immigrated to this country from Berlin at the age of two. He gave his life for a cause which he believed was worthy.

The other Jewish-American recipient of the Congressional Medal of Honor was Second Lieutenant Raymond Zussman of Detroit, Michigan. Zussman was a tank officer, stationed in the Rhone Valley of France. While engaged in battle, his tank broke down. Young Zussman grabbed a carbine, killing seventeen enemy soldiers and captured over ninety prisoners. Most important of all, he freed a village from the Nazis. A few days later, on September 21, 1944, Zussman was killed by enemy fire.

The highest ranking American-Jewish hero was Major General Maurice Rose, an armored-division officer and son of a rabbi. His life was snuffed out at Paderborn, Germany, during the final stage of his victory march, but previously Rose had commanded the Third Armored Division in the Normandy breakthrough and had pushed his division into the forefront of the fighting. He was the hero of several important battles, cracking the last German resistance at the Belgian frontier and finally reconquering Cologne.

During the war years, the issue of a Jewish state had not been moribund. Indeed the tragic events of those years had made the need for statehood even more imperative. Before 1939, the Zionist aim had been simply stated as that of a Jewish national home, but in that year Great Britain issued a White Paper which limited Jewish immigration to Palestine subject to Arab approval. Because of the White Paper, and later, Pearl Harbor, this aim was changed. Neutrality and isolationism were dead, and the destruction of the Axis was openly espoused. American Jews called outright for a Jewish state in Palestine as the only answer to the problem and a just reward for Jewish trials and tribulations at the hands of the Axis.

President Roosevelt responded to Great Britain's White Paper by privately calling it unjust. Ambassador Joseph P.

Jewish children orphaned by the Kishinev pogrom in Russia in 1903 are received by the Hebrew Immigrant Aid Society (HIAS).

Religious News Service Photo

Jewish immigrants working in a
Boston garment factory ca. 1910.

*Courtesy, American Jewish Historical
Society, Waltham, Mass.*

Eastern European immigrants wait in line for food on Ellis Island ca. 1914. The group had been refused entry to the United States and was to be compelled to return to its port of embarkation in Germany.

From the YIVO Archives

Young Jewish peddler with his pack in Easton, Pennsylvania in 1890.

American Jewish Archives of the Hebrew Union College (Cincinnati)

AMERICA FOR THE AMERICANS

American Bulletin

THE WHITE MAN'S VIEWPOINT

Box 4, 1308 First Avenue, New York City

Vol. II No. 25   September 29, 1936.   Price 5 Cts.

CONTENTS:

This copy has been compiled with the intent to illustrate the unity existing among the Jews as a PEOPLE, not a religion; their part in Communism and High Finance, and the devastating influence of their nature in all countries.

K O L   N I D R E

Sundown on September 25th marked the beginning of YOM KIPPUR, Jewish Day of Atonement. On this day the "Kol Nidre" meaning "All Vows" was recited by Jews throughout the world as they were gathered in their synagogues:

"All vows, obligations, oaths or anathemas, pledges of all names, which we have vowed, sworn, devoted, or bound ourselves to, from this day of atonement, until the next day of atonement (whose arrival we hope for in happiness), we repent, aforehand, of them all, they shall all be deemed absolved, forgiven, annulled, void and made of no effect; they shall not be binding, nor have any power; the vows shall not be reckoned vows, the obligations shall not be obligatory, nor the oaths considered as oaths."

Whoever assists the Jew in his work, is bound to become besmirched.

One of many anti-Semitic periodicals printed during the Great Depression of the 1930s.

Courtesy, American Jewish Historical Society, Waltham, Mass.

Abraham Cahan, socialist leader, novelist, and editor of the *Jewish Daily Forward*.

From the YIVO Archives

Rabbi Stephen S. Wise, Zionist leader and fighter for Jewish rights.

Courtesy, American Jewish Historical Society, Waltham, Mass.

Justice Louis D. Brandeis, associate justice of the United States Supreme Court and American Zionist leader.

Courtesy, American Jewish Historical Society, Waltham, Mass.

Isaac Mayer Wise, pioneer of reform in America and founder of the Union of American Hebrew Congregations, Central Conference of American Rabbis, and the Hebrew Union College.

American Jewish Archives of the Hebrew Union College (Cincinnati)

Leo Frank, victim of anti-Semitism
in Atlanta, Georgia, in 1915.

*American Jewish Archives of the
Hebrew Union College (Cincinnati)*

Adolph Ochs, journalist who acquired control
of the *New York Times* in 1896.

*American Jewish Archives of the
Hebrew Union College (Cincinnati)*

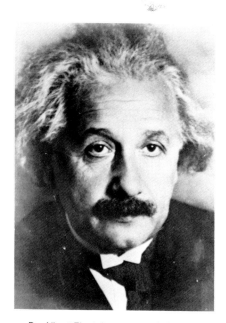

Dr. Albert Einstein, renowned physicist
who formulated the Theory of Relativity.

Religious News Service Photo

Dr. Mordecai M. Kaplan, faculty member at
New York's Jewish Theological Seminary
and founder of Reconstructionism.

Religious News Service Photo

Dr. Jonas Salk, discoverer of the polio vaccine.

Religious News Service Photo

Nobel Prize-winning author
Isaac Bashevis Singer.

Courtesy of Buffalo Jewish Review

Boris Thomachefsky, one of the
giants of the Yiddish stage.

From the YIVO Archives

Bernard Baruch, financier and ''unofficial''
adviser to presidents.

Religious News Service Photo

Milton Berle, vaudeville, radio, and movie star better known as "Mr. Television" during its early days.

George Burns, vaudeville, burlesque, radio, movie, and television star.

Al Jolson, legendary entertainer who starred in "The Jazz Singer," which brought sound to the screen.

Jack Benny, star of vaudeville, movies, radio, and television.

Singer Sophie Tucker, popular in various entertainment media, especially nightclubs.

American Jewish Archives of the Hebrew Union College (Cincinnati)

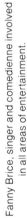

Fanny Brice, singer and comedienne involved in all areas of entertainment.

American Jewish Archives of the Hebrew Union College (Cincinnati)

Carmel Myers, vamp-siren star in silent movies.

Eddie Cantor, movie, stage, radio, and television comic. Photograph is taken from one of his most successful movies, "Ali Baba Goes to Town."

© 1937 by 20th Century-Fox Film Corp.

The Marx Brothers, comic stars of vaudeville and movies who were famous for their antiestablishment buffoonery.

Sandy Koufax, ace pitcher for the Brooklyn (and Los Angeles) Dodgers.

American Jewish Archives of the Hebrew Union College (Cincinnati)

Dory Schary, successor to Louis B. Mayer at Metro-Goldwyn-Mayer and liberal spokesman for Jewish causes.

Jan Peerce, operatic tenor and star of the Metropolitan Opera Company.

George Gershwin, composer associated with the development of jazz and such shows as "Of Thee I Sing" (Pulitzer Prize winner) and "Porgy and Bess."

Louis B. Mayer, president of Metro-Goldwyn-Mayer studio.

Zionist activist Rabbi Abba Hillel Silver.

Religious News Service Photo

Former U.S. senator Jacob Javits of New York.

Religious News Service Photo

Herbert H. Lehman, governor of New York
and U.S. senator.

*American Jewish Archives of the
Hebrew Union College (Cincinnati)*

Henry A. Kissinger, secretary of state during
the Nixon and Ford administrations.

Religious News Service Photo

Zionist leader Dr. Abba Hillel Silver and American United Nations representative Warren R. Austin discuss U.N. plans for Palestine in 1948.

Courtesy Zionist Archives and Library

The *Exodus,* an American-manned ship carrying more than 4500 Jewish refugees from Europe after World War II, was turned away from Palestine and forced to return to Europe. The incident profoundly influenced world opinion, reinforced Britain's decision to give up her mandate, and pointed up the need for a Jewish state.

Courtesy Zionist Archives and Library

President Harry Truman receives the Holy Scroll from
Chaim Weizmann at the White House on May 15, 1948.

Courtest Zionist Archives and Library

Egyptian president Anwar Sadat, U.S. president Jimmy Carter,
and Israeli prime minister Menachem Begin clasp hands
after signing the peace treaty between Egypt and Israel.

Religious News Service Photo

Rabbi Sally Priesand (center), ordained in 1972 as the
first female rabbi in the United States, congratulates
Marcia S. Bernstein, (left), the second female rabbi, and
Barbara Herman, the first female cantor.

Religious News Service Photo
By John Lei

Russian Jewish immigrants take part in
a Passover seder in Buffalo, N.Y.

Courtesy Bureau of Jewish Education
of Greater Buffalo

The faculty and graduates of the Jewish Theological Seminary (New York) ca. the 1930s.
Selected faculty include: (seated) Professor Louis Finkelstein (fourth from left); President
Cyrus Adler (fifth from left); and Professor Alexander Marx (seventh from left).

From the YIVO Archives

Dinner at a Jewish urban commune in Cleveland, Ohio.

Religious News Service Photo

Rabbi Manachem M. Schneerson, the Lubavitcher Rebbe, broadcasts his message to Lubavitch centers around the world.

Religious News Service Photo

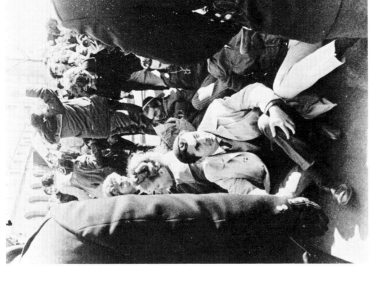

Rabbi Meir Kahane (seated, center) of the Jewish Defense League participates in a sit-in held near the Soviet Embassy in Washington, D.C. to protect the plight of Soviet Jews.

Religious News Service Photo

Jerry Rubin, and Abbie Hoffman, Jewish radicals who were arrested on charges of trying to incite a riot at the 1968 Democratic National Convention in Chicago.

Religious News Service Photo
By Ronald L. Mrowiec

Brandeis University's famous three chapels (Jewish, Catholic, and Protestant).

*Courtesy of Brandeis University
Public Affairs*

The Jewish Center of Greater Buffalo suburban building, built in 1974,
is representative of the move of vital services out of the central city.

Photo by Mickey Osterreicher

Temple Beth Zion, rebuilt in 1967, exemplifies modern synagogue
architecture with its famous Ben Shahn stained glass windows.

Photo by Mickey Osterreicher

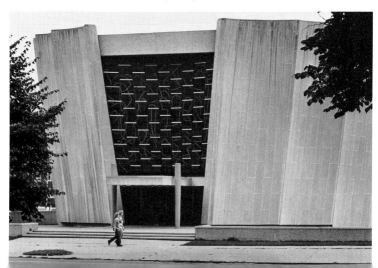

Kennedy did informally relay the disappointment of the American Government to the British Foreign Office. Lack of further action or protest simply reflected the times: America was still relatively isolationist and American Jews were primarily concerned with their status as Americans. The president, following the cue of the State Department, contended that Palestine was a British matter and, in essence, his policy was to view the Palestine situation as a problem which could be solved only after victory. Also, it was important to keep the Axis from overrunning the Middle East by not upsetting the neutrality of the Arab world with pro-Zionist declarations.

In 1941, the Middle East war was deteriorating, and the State Department was concerned with Rommel's army reaching Palestine. If this occurred, it was certain that the Arabs would probably attack the Jewish settlement there. Thus, attempts were made to persuade Zionist leaders to reduce their political claims on Palestine. For example, Assistant Secretary of State Adolph A. Berle, Jr. suggested that in exchange for withdrawing political claims to Palestine, Jews could be evacuated to Kenya or even, ironically enough, to Saudi Arabia under King Ibn Saud's protection. Such plans were typical of the long-standing anti-Zionist position of the State Department. High officials like Cordell Hull and Sumner Welles offered token gestures of sympathy but too many middle-echelon career officials were probably not only anti-Zionist and perhaps even anti-Semitic, but also honestly felt that it was in America's national interest to keep the Arabs out of the Axis camp.

The Arabs in general and King Ibn Saud in particular were important cogs in FDR's ideas on settlement. As early as 1940, Chaim Weizmann had told FDR of a British plan developed by H. St. John Philby, British advisor to Ibn Saud, in which Palestine would become a Jewish state while the Arabs would be settled elsewhere. The Jews would pay $20 million to the king, the Arab nations would become independent, and the United States and Britain would jointly guarantee implementation. Three years later, Colonel Halford L. Hoskins of the State Department, a well-known anti-Zionist, was sent as an envoy to Ibn Saud. The king rejected the idea with indignation, but FDR still did not give up hope of an Arab role in an eventual settlement. Roosevelt assured Ibn Saud in April 1943 that there would be no decision on Palestine without consulting both Arabs and Jews. With this pledge, then, American involvement in the Middle East became a reality. It must have been obvious, however, that no solution to which the Zionists would agree could have been acceptable to Arabs.

On the domestic scene, the American Zionists were quite energetic. By 1942 they realized that Britain would not aid in the fulfillment of their aims, and they turned their efforts toward the United States government. The Zionist Emergency Council called for a conference at the Biltmore Hotel in New York City on May 6–11, 1942, to publicize their postwar aims, the most important of which was that the White Paper should be rescinded and the Balfour Declaration recognized as having had as its goal the creation of a Jewish Commonwealth in Palestine. With the Biltmore Conference, American Jews became the most vociferous community supporting the creation of a Jewish state. America, it was assumed, would become the dominant power after the war and, hence, Zionist political and diplomatic activity was transferred to the United States.

On August 29, 1943, the American Jewish Conference, representing 65 Jewish organizations, convened with the authority to speak for all of American Jewry. Rather than merely calling for free immigration, the conference followed the stand of the militant Cleveland, Ohio, rabbi, Abba Hillel Silver, and adopted a Palestine resolution that incorporated the Biltmore program. Rabbis Stephen S. Wise and Silver cochaired what was called the American Zionist Emergency Council (AZEC), the organ for mobilizing American opinion in support of the repeal of the White Paper. With local branches in every major community, and totaling over 400, an active propaganda campaign was launched. The powerful Zionist lobby influenced all levels of government, and other governments and overseas business organizations as well. The Zionists indulged in heavy pressure activity, but American Jewry never allowed their emotionalism for a homeland to interfere with their essential loyalty as Americans. The AZEC sought to win the support of apathetic and uncommitted Americans, Jewish and non-Jewish. The Yiddish press proved a valuable ally because it linked Zionism with the old country and tradition, thus appealing to a large segment of American Jewry. The American press was also generally favorable. Pamphlets were distributed to public libraries, clergy, community centers, educators, writers, and other leaders of civic thought. Rabbi Silver was a master at the technique of mass meetings and protest rallies. The council purchased radio time and during a thirty-nine week series of fifteen-minute programs, Americans heard such stars as Gene Kelly, Joseph Cotton, Eddie Cantor, and Edward G. Robinson in professionally produced dramatizations. Finally, there were the fund-raising activities which benefitted the Jewish National Fund and other agencies. The United States Palestine Appeal raised $14.5 million in 1945, over $32 million in 1946, and close to $43 million the next year.

Winning American-Christian support was one of the more crucial aims of the AZEC. Aid from the non-Jewish community was channeled through the American-Palestine Committee, headed by Senator Robert F. Wagner of New York. Eventually, that group merged with the Christian Council on Palestine to form the American-Christian Palestine Committee, whose purpose was to serve as the major vehicle for the expression of Christian support for the establishment of a Jewish national home in Palestine.

Of all the activities undertaken during this period by the Emergency Council, the attempt to win congressional support for Zionist aims was given highest priority. AZEC lobbying in Washington and locally had, by the end of 1943, been sufficiently effective to win enough support in Congress so that in early 1944 resolutions were introduced into the House of Representatives, and Senators Robert F. Wagner and Robert A. Taft sponsored one in the Senate calling for American support in opening the ports of Palestine for immigration, for colonization, and for the reconstitution of the land as a Jewish commonwealth. Testifying before the House Committee on Foreign Affairs, Dr. Emanuel Neumann gave assurance that a Jewish Palestine would be achieved through mass immigration and not through the eviction of the Arab community. Non-Zionist witnesses presented strong evidence against the case. For example, the radically anti-Zionist American Council for Judaism agreed to provisions for settlement, but not those favoring a commonwealth. Its president, Lessing J. Rosenwald, even described a Jewish state as based on Hitlerian concepts of racism. Though a small part of the American population, Arabs also staged an efficient campaign. Speaking for them was Princeton Professor Philip K. Hitti. Arab pressure on the State Department brought repeated assurances that the president was not bound by any congressional action.

The fate of the resolution in the House was sealed, when on March 17, 1944, the committee chairman, Sol Bloom, received from Secretary of War Henry L. Stimson a brief note advising against an affirmative vote since it might adversely affect the war effort. The House committee subsequently voted not to act on the resolution.

In the Senate, meanwhile, the Committee on Foreign Relations held closed-session hearings. Secretary of State Cordell Hull advised that a pro-Zionist resolution would disturb oil pipeline talks which were already going badly and might create a conflict necessitating the diversion of troops to the area. The Senate committee also shelved the resolution.

During the presidential election year of 1944, neither party could afford to disregard Jewish support. Both parties adopted strong pro-Zionist planks, and once again the Zionists attempted to push through Congress pro-Zionist resolutions. After 411 out of 535 members of Congress had in

October 1944, endorsed the Zionist call for immediate action to approve a Jewish commonwealth in Palestine, and after the secretary of war had removed the objections of the military, the hearings on the resolutions were reopened. Responding at least in part to the Jewish voting bloc, politicians everywhere endorsed the American Zionist Emergency Council proposals. Secretary Hull warned, however, that to avoid upsetting the Arabs or the balance of power in the Middle East, Palestine should not be made an issue by either party. Despite the expected Arab reaction, both parties included planks calling for unrestricted immigration and the establishment of a democratic commonwealth in Palestine. The efforts of Rabbi Wise at the Democratic and Rabbi Silver at the Republican convention were significant in attaining this goal, as the Zionists pushed the idea and importance of the strategically located "Jewish vote".

To carry the electoral votes of his home state of New York, Thomas E. Dewey, the Republican presidential candidate, tried to lure the Jews away from the Democrats. Roosevelt matched this bid in a letter to Senator Wagner to be read at a Zionist Organization of America meeting. The president pledged, if reelected, to work for the establishment of a Jewish commonwealth in Palestine. In the November, 1944 elections, FDR captured 92 percent of the Jewish vote at a time when some other ethnic blocs had deserted him. Postelection actions were another matter, however, as the president reverted to his previous policy of straddling the issue. Following the November Democratic victory, the Zionists worked for the fulfillment of campaign pledges. Despite the Democratic espousal of a Jewish commonwealth and Roosevelt's reiteration of the platform on October 15, the president was still reluctant to act. He informed Wise and Silver that it would be unwise to reconsider the congressional resolutions.

As the war was ending, American Zionists differed over President Roosevelt's pledges on Palestine. Rabbi Stephen S. Wise's faction—the majority—had faith in FDR's promise for a Jewish commonwealth, but Rabbi Abba Hillel Silver spoke for a minority who did not trust the president. Dr. Silver was especially incensed at the British policy, accomplished with American contrivance, of keeping refugees out of Palestine. Roosevelt seemed especially disingenuous because on the very day (March 9, 1944) that he asserted a national home was, in the face of Nazi genocide, more urgent than ever, he had congratulated Speaker of the House Sam Rayburn for holding the line against such a pro-Zionist resolution.

Presidential declarations of sympathy with the Zionist cause were generally matched by State Department dispatches of promises to the Arabs. On three occasions, FDR approved a projected Anglo-American statement freezing the Holy Land status quo. And with the revelation of Roosevelt's meeting with King Ibn Saud of Saudi Arabia while enroute home from the Yalta Conference came further Zionist disenchantment. American oil company concessions were of greater political importance than Zionist aspirations. But, despite Arab feelings about a Jewish state, FDR gambled one last time on uniting the two sides. However, the meeting between president and king in the wake of the Yalta Conference resulted only in a stalemate. Roosevelt evidently talked separately to Zionists and Arabs and when faced with insoluable questions for which there was no easy response, he flitted from plan to plan. To Dr. Chaim Weizmann, grand old man of Zionism, and to Zionist sympathizers, he dismissed Arab objections to Jewish settlement as impediments which could be overcome with financial aid. But, FDR was never very concrete about his thinking, flirting continuously with plans for a Jewish haven in regions far from Palestine. He toyed with the idea, too, of a semi-autonomous Jewish Palestine united into a federation to include Syria, Lebanon, and Transjordan. Such a scheme was consonant with the plan of the *Ihud* (Union) party of Palestinian Jewry which called for unity with Arabs along binational lines.

But FDR's health intervened and his death in April 1945 precluded any solution. His Palestinian diplomacy had been a failure. But, in fairness to him, he had as first priority the overall war effort. This seemingly necessitated a pro-Arab sentiment which would insure open supply routes to Russia and hence the reversal of the German eastward push. Also, there was always the prejudice of the State Department. Wallace Murray, chief of the Division of Near Eastern Affairs, was a long-standing anti-Zionist. He constantly warned that forcing Britain's hand on easing entry of Jews into Palestine would bind the United States to the area at a time when we were already overcommitted elsewere. And Secretary of the Navy James V. Forrestal (later secretary of defense), was anti-Zionist. As a former president of a Wall Street company with close Arab connections, the Secretary felt that these relationships were a necessity because of the future Russian threat. He believed that Middle Eastern oil was an absolutely essential ingredient for American security. All in all, despite FDR's feelings, more influential was the widely held belief that increased immigration to the Holy Land and the creation of a Zionist state there would delay the Axis defeat. Communist antagonism to Zionism must also have played on Roosevelt's mind and perhaps softened any pangs of conscience as he helped keep Palestine shut to the Hitlerian victims. Certainly, it now appears that the great Zionist faith in the Rooseveltian pronouncements was misplaced. Roosevelt, traditional friend of Jewry and lionized in the pantheon of liberalism, in truth, presents a quite different picture.

Roosevelt's equivocal stand on the Palestine issue was insufficiently clear to American Jews who sincerely mourned his death in April 1945. They had believed that he could eventually have brought the British to agree to Zionist goals. The new president, Harry S. Truman, soon discovered FDR's contradictory promises and lack of a coherent policy. Although aware of the Arab opposition to Jewish settlement, Truman was sincerely concerned about the refugees, perhaps failing to realize that such sympathy played into Zionist hands as a strategy for achieving a political state. Yet the new president also repeated assurances to the Arabs that there would be no changes without consultation. At the same time, he also assured Rabbi Wise that he would continue FDR's policy! This equivocating pattern was encouraged by the State Department, which did not want the Palestine question brought up during the Potsdam summit meeting in midsummer of 1945. In a memo to Prime Minister Churchill, Truman recorded the "passionate protests" in America against restrictions imposed on Jewish immigration by the White Paper of 1939.

At the San Francisco Conference called to set up the United Nations in April 1945, Zionists sought representation in order to counteract any possible concessions given to the Arabs. Despite the fact that other "non-recognized" entities were allowed to attend, Jews, representing various national organizations, were given only "consultant" status. The Arabs, who had not fought against Hitler, were allowed five delegations. Zionist propaganda activities were in full operation but they failed to alter the representational situation.

The results of the conference, however, favored the Zionists. Although they could not extract at San Francisco any guarantee of an eventual Jewish state in Palestine, they did thwart Arab attempts to undo the Balfour Declaration. The Arabs had tried to end the power of the Jewish agency as provided in the Mandate, but the Trusteeship Committee draft included a provision disallowing the alteration of the rights of people in a territory that were assigned by previous agreements.

Late in June 1945, after the German surrender, Truman dispatched Earl G. Harrison, former United States commissioner of immigration, on a fact-finding mission to Europe to investigate the Displaced Persons (DP) problem, paying particular attention to the Jews who did not wish to return to their original homes. Harrison's report described barbed wire camps with poor sanitation, high mortality, and low morale, and the report implied creation of a Palestinian Jewish state. Truman forwarded the report to Prime Minister Clement

Attlee, asking that as many as possible of the displaced persons be allowed to emigrate to Palestine. Attlee agreed, on the condition that the United States would assume joint responsibility. This the president would not agree to, since he was still not ready to link the refugee problem to a political solution in Palestine. As a compromise, Britain suggested that the two countries undertake a joint investigation of the Jewish problem. The resultant committee's feeling was that the White Paper was a mistake, that land and immigration restriction should be lifted, that Palestine was the only place available for the DPs, that 100,000 immigration certificates should be issued, and that the UN should still govern Palestine as a trusteeship.

Great Britain had made its support of the recommendations contingent upon American financial assistance, the disarming of the Palestine population, and the unanimous agreement of the committee members. The opinion offered to the president by the Joint Chiefs of Staff was that the use of force in implementing the report would only hurt American and British interests in the Middle East and allow Russia to penetrate the area. Britain delayed once again on the ground that the United States would not commit its troops to aid in the entry of 100,000 refugees. The committee had made a conscientious attempt to appraise fairly the Arab and Zionist cases but in making recommendations, its hands had been tied from the start by the conditions imposed by British Foreign Secretary Ernest Bevin that Palestine be converted into a trusteeship.

The president still sought to implement some of the recommendations and on June 11, 1946, appointed the secretaries of war, state, and treasury to a special cabinet committee to advise on Palestine policy and negotiate with the British. In turn, the secretaries appointed their own working force, headed by Henry F. Grady. He concluded that 100,000 refugees be admitted within a year after implementation of the plan and that Palestine be divided into three parts, the British controlling the trusteeship.

Truman accepted the plan, assuming that the Jews would approve partition in order to admit the refugees. However, opposition became so great that on August 12, the president informed Attlee that he had changed his mind. There are several possible reasons for Truman's action. One is that the government knew of the intentions of the Jewish agency to support a different partition plan. A second is that Truman had to counter what he predicted would be the pro-Zionist remarks of the Republican Thomas E. Dewey in his new reelection bid as governor of New York. On Yom Kippur Eve (October 4, 1946), the president called for the immediate entry of 100,000 refugees and partition along the lines suggested by the Jewish agency, even though American Zionists were against any such abandonment of the Biltmore program. The fact that this was only a month before the congressional elections appeared significant to contemporary observers.

Failing to reach any type of agreement with the United States, Great Britain at last handed the Palestine issue over to the UN in April, 1947. A special session of the General Assembly was called to establish a committee of inquiry on Palestine (UNSCOP). The United States and Britain agreed that Arabs ought not to have a vote on Palestinian independence to the exclusion of Jews. Another procedural battle involved American delegate Warren R. Austin, who objected to an invitation allowing the Jewish agency to speak, claiming that nongovernmental bodies were excluded by the charter from appearing before the General Assembly. And yet, at another meeting, the United States and Britain favored the idea of allowing the Arab Higher Committee, a nongovernmental body, to be heard. In the end it was decided that the Jewish agency should be heard, since the Arab case would appear only before a smaller committee and not before the entire Assembly.

Final terms of the United Nations' designation of a special committee on Palestine entrusted the committee with wide powers to record all the facts and investigate all issues concerning the Palestine question, including the religious interests of Islam, Christianity, and Judaism. The future of the troubled land now depended on how well the Zionists and their Arab foes were able to present their respective cases to the world: everything was now up to persuasion and propaganda. The Zionists were ready with a new approach. Since the UN, unlike the League of Nations, had not committed itself to a pro-Zionist solution, the Zionists pressed for a return to the Mandate, allowing for unlimited immigration while toning down political goals. The United States had an important role in the new strategy. Knowing that the American government would be more susceptible than the UN to pressure during any negotiations, the Zionists vied to include the United States in Near East policymaking. Still another tactic was to represent the Palestinian Jews as the last bastion of democracy in a totalitarian Middle East.

The final UNSCOP report on August 31, 1947, concluded that independence would have to be granted and the mandate end, that the political structures be democratic, that there be economic unity, that the holy places should be accessible to all, and that the General Assembly should act to settle the refugee problem in Europe. But beyond this, the committee was divided between minority support for federalism and majority approval of partition. By this time, the great majority of American Jews favored partition.

In contrast to official reticence, American public opinion gave strong bipartisan support to the partition scheme. Zionists regarded it as the best they were likely to get. Britain rejected the report and refused to have any part in its implementation, while the American position was still equivocal since the government did not wish to alienate the Arabs. Nor could it envision a US-USSR force to implement partition once Britain's rejection had been made public. But, finally, American support was announced by UN delegate Herschel Johnson on October 11, forty days after the report was released.

The announcement of the American position included several reservations. The United States feared incurring the wrath of the Arabs or the Soviet Union, and therefore Western Galilee and Jaffa would be parts of an Arab state. The American delegation had been instructed to exclude the Negev from a Jewish state, or at least the area surrounding the Gulf of Aqaba. But, as a result of a Truman-Weizmann interview on November 19, and Zionist lobbying, the importance of the area for the Jewish state was impressed upon the president, who instructed the delegation to support a "Jewish Negev."

During the UNSCOP debate, the threat of USSR intervention increased as Moscow announced that the Soviets would be responsible for maintaining the UN decision. Herschel Johnson therefore suggested a shortened transitional period and the movement of the date of independence from September 1947 to July 1, 1948, without the trusteeship in which the USSR would have participated. A compromise was reached on November 10, the British to end their occupation by May and the Arab and Jewish states to be established no later than July, and a commission of three to five of the smaller propartition nations to administer the area during the transition.

The problem of how to implement a UN decision still had not been resolved. America would not commit its troops, knowing that to do so would be to invite Russia into the Middle East. And Great Britain was loathe to administer Palestine during the transition. With approval of the partition plan by the full UN committee on Palestine, the question was referred to the General Assembly. There, with American and last-minute Zionist lobbying, the support of the uncommitted smaller states had been secured, and on November 29, 1947, the resolution for partition passed by a vote of 33–13, after a futile effort by the Arabs to offer a plan calling for a unitary state with local autonomy for the Jewish minority.

That pressure was brought to bear on the uncommitted is evident, but there is disagreement over the specific role of President Truman. In the end, his support of partition might well have been a purely political move, since Truman counted on heavy Jewish support in the upcoming presidential election. The State Department was finally instructed by the president to contact the committed delegations to gain pledges of support for partition. These delegations were probably pressured by the veiled threat of losing various assistance programs.

The Arab nations, not about to accept partition, were armed and massed on the borders, and Palestine's Arabs indulged in a wave of terrorism. The Security Council was to assist in implementing the partition decision and to devise measures to keep the peace, but at the same time, no force or authority was proposed. Former Under-Secretary of State Sumner Welles claimed that this country was responsible for the lack of sufficient foresight, since it naively believed that both sides would peacefully abide by the decision. What was established was a "Committee of 5," which was to work to transfer power from Britain, an illusive goal because she refused to cooperate with the commission. In fact, at one point they had to appeal to the Security Council for arms.

An indication of a shift in American policy was the December 5 arms embargo to all Middle East belligerents. An effort at neutrality, this move really hurt the Jewish defense efforts, for it was known that the British were supplying the Arabs with arms. Many sources point to the influence of the secretary of defense, James V. Forrestal, in influencing American policies early in 1948. Always opposed to American support of the Zionists, the secretary reported to the House Armed Forces Committee in January that the partition vote was harmful to American interests. In fact, Forrestal's diaries accuse Truman of selling out the American position in the Middle East in order to gain the Jewish vote. Incidentally, Dean Acheson, future secretary of state, opposed Truman's program. Military strategists felt that the Jews could never stand on their own in a war and that an international force would be necessary, allowing the Russians to participate and thus projecting them into the Suez Canal region and the rich Middle Eastern oil fields.

At the same time, by effective lobbying, the oil interests were reinforcing the military's views. The Arab nations were not allowing the American companies to lay their pipelines, and the oil representatives stated that the United States would not have access to Middle East oil if she persisted in advocating partition. Such a stand would obviously endanger the European Recovery Program and the Truman Doctrine, two aid programs that were bulwarks of America's early Cold War diplomacy. The Truman administration was obviously confused over whether partition was that basic to our interests and also whether the policy of advocating the reconstitution of Palestine as a free and democratic Jewish commonwealth was viable.

The public comments of the president and the secretary of state in February would indicate that they were still propartition. Yet on February 24, the American delegate to the UN, Warren Austin, announced in favor of a trusteeship, stating that the Security Council did not have the power to enforce a political settlement, but only to keep the peace; Britain, as the mandatory, was the only one who could act to implement the decision.

Meanwhile, the Zionist propaganda machine had been mobilized to offset the newest opposition to partition. Zionists fervently wooed clergy, civic leaders, and politicians by a massive campaign of telegrams, letters, and nationwide rallies. In fact, the combined pressure of all these activities became so strong in Washington that the President gave instructions that he did not want to be approached by any more spokesmen for the extreme Zionist case. And it was only because of the efforts of Truman's good friend and World War I crony, Eddie Jacobson, that Dr. Weizmann was allowed to see the president and, even then, he was shuttled in through a back door to the White House. Another assurance of support for partition was then apparently given to the Zionist leader. This supposedly marked the turn in Truman's attitude in favor of a Jewish state.

But on March 19, 1948, Warren Austin suprisingly announced to the Security Council an American proposal for a temporary trusteeship, since partition was obviously unworkable. Reaction to "Black Friday," as the Zionists called the day of Austin's proposal, was quick. The Jewish Agency, on March 22, rejected the proposal and said that a provisional government would be established by May, even if the UN did not implement the partition decision. In what *Time* (April 5, 1948) called a "comic-opera performance," the president replied to criticism in a press conference on March 25. Since troops could not be used to effect partition, trusteeship would be a temporary arrangement to fill the void created by British withdrawal, until proper conditions would allow the two states to be established. In other words, according to Truman, this was a step toward partition.

The question surrounding this reversal is whether Truman authorized the switch. According to a high State Department official, the proposal was cleared by the president after the memorandum had first been initialed by Secretary of State George C. Marshall, since Truman had been in Key West, Florida. And yet there is the contention that Truman was unaware of the events beforehand. Apparently realizing that the United States was indeed cornered and that the American delegation was unable to offer anything affirmative without a firm commitment to send troops into Palestine, the delegation temporized. America offered four more resolutions during the next two months, each one further removed from the trusteeship idea and probably intended to allow the United States gradually to return to its original position in favor of a Jewish state.

Back in Palestine, statehood plans gathered momentum, despite State Department pressure against this move. Even an American proposal to extend the Mandate until May 25 was refused. The British insisted on withdrawing, leaving a power vacuum.

After receiving a letter from Dr. Weizmann on May 12 stating the intent to declare independence two days later, President Truman met with Secretary Marshall, Robert

Lovett, and David Niles of the White House staff. Marshall's opposition to recognition of the new state prevailed, only to be reversed on May 13, after Lovett and the Middle East Division of the State Department advised the president in favor of recognition. As a result, Marshall was not informed of the decision until 3:00 P.M. on May 14. Acting, therefore, without the State Department's knowledge, the president opted for recognition as the only alternative. Trusteeship was bogged down in the General Assembly, and Truman was displeased with the UN's vacillations. Military operations indicated that the Arabs and Jews were willing to go to any lengths to fight over Palestine. It was also an election year, but most important, recognition was undoubtedly a maneuver hastily devised to beat the Russians in diplomatic gamemanship because of Truman's fear of driving Arabs into their camp. Thus, Harry Truman, while he came to office unprepared on the Palestine-Zionism issue, listened to all comers, did his homework, and weighed the conflicting advice from Jews and Gentiles. The climax was his typically independent and courageous decision to recognize Israel against the advice of his own State Department and after he himself had refused to make a pro-Zionist statement.

The new State of Israel was born at 6:01 P.M. Washington time, May 14, 1948. De facto recognition was granted at 6:11 P.M., while at the UN the trusteeship plan was still under discussion. At the moment the Declaration of Independence was being issued, Egyptian aircraft were dropping their first bombs on the outskirts of Tel Aviv. After de facto recognition of the provisional government, diplomatic representatives were exchanged. James G. McDonald served first as American envoy, but by February 1949, he was made a full-fledged ambassador.

Along with Great Britain, the United States had originally supported the so-called Bernadotte plan, which proposed a federal union with Trans-Jordan and the exclusion of the Negev from the Jewish state. However, since Truman realized that Israel was going to create its own boundaries regardless of the plan, and probably because the presidential election campaign was going poorly, he ignored the previously endorsed UN plan. At a rally at Madison Square Garden in New York City on October 28, he committed himself to supporting the November 29, 1947, boundaries. By February 1949, the War of Independence had ended with a modus vivendi in which all of the Negev but the Gaza Strip, and the Galilee section had been added to Israel. Israel's first elections had been held in January, and after her first application for admission had been turned down, the State of Israel was finally admitted to the UN on May 11, 1949.

Certainly the Arab-Jewish relationship has been fascinating and, at the same time, tragic. Out of the ashes of the Second World War emerged the State of Israel, the first Jewish state in modern times. When World War II broke out in 1939, the situation looked all but hopeless for a Jewish Palestine. It was true that physically the Palestinian Jewish community had come into being, but this phenomenal growth had taken place in an uneasy and unfriendly atmosphere. The British and Arabs had cooperated in cruelly limiting Jewish immigration into Palestine to a pitifully small number. The course of world events completely changed America's foreign policy toward the Middle East. After Pearl Harbor catapulted us into a Second World War, the United States was drawn swiftly and completely into the entire Middle Eastern region in a very real sense. By 1942, Washington was a sponsor of the vital Middle East Supply Center, and American military personnel were stationed in the Eastern Mediterranean. But our prime consideration in the Fertile Crecent during the days of war revolved around oil, the supplies of which were elsewhere fast being depleted, like a prophecy of the events of the 1970s and 1980s.

With these interests, it was obvious that the United States could not avoid entanglement in the approaching Palestinian crisis. As we have seen, President Franklin D. Roosevelt, who, in his long political career was addicted to promising all things to all men, attempted to straddle the issue of Arab-Zionist relations. It was Roosevelt's hope to resolve the Palestinian problem after the war as part of a general Middle Eastern settlement. After his death, and after the war was over, it was apparent that the need for domiciling homeless European refugees was most urgent. To many of these unfortunates, their treatment in DP camps resembled the Nazi policy, except they were not exterminated. Partition of Palestine was rejected in favor of a temporary trusteeship arrangement under the United Nations. However, UN action amounted only to many well-meaning words because Britain made American financial and military assistance in Palestine a prerequisite for acceptance of the UN plan.

In the meantime the situation had deteriorated. Illegal immigration of Jewish refugees had commenced, and Jewish terrorists, impatient with Great Britain, had declared open defiance of the established authority. Finally, on February 14, 1947, Great Britain announced that it could find no solution to the Palestinian problem and would turn the entire issue over to the UN. Despite the fact that the United States had originally supported partition, our policy became so evasive that within four short months we were to reverse our attitude completely. American prestige and Truman's popularity were at their lowest ebb. At the UN, the United States still argued for a trusteeship, urging that partition be abandoned. The Soviet Union insisted upon partition and used America's vacillating policy and unsure opinion as an effective weapon in the Cold War, then already in progress.

On May 14, the Israeli Jews declared their independence and, on the next day, war came. The United States again made an about-face, for Truman extended to Israel de facto recognition. The United States had now assumed full responsibility for the Palestine problem. The cycle was complete—from total lack of concern to complete leadership. By January 1949, the United States had extended to Israel de jure recognition, arranged a $100 million loan from the Export-Import Bank, and urged Israel's admittance to the United Nations. After two thousand years of hopes and wishes, a Jewish state took its place among the nations of the earth. In this fait accompli, the United States and American Jewry played a role of supreme importance.

6

Post-World War II American Jewry: The Political Equation

T HE POLITICAL INTERESTS of American Jews evolved
from certain historical and sociological roots. The
liberating ideas of the Enlightenment and the French Revolution broke with full force upon Eastern European Jewry late
in the nineteenth century. In contrast to the situation in
Western Europe, where the leaven of new thoughts worked
gradually for many decades, the ferment in Eastern Europe
developed rapidly. Since Jews did not benefit from the
political status quo, they naturally allied themselves with
those interests urging change, and because parties of the
political right were not only conservative but also Christian,
the parties of the left were the only ones to whom the Jews
could turn. Even in those blocs of the moderate left the
distinctions of religion remained. However, in the emerging
factions of the more radical left, there was supposedly neither
Jew nor Christian.

Against this political background the alien Eastern European Jews migrated to the strange and often hostile United
States. Despite anti-Semitic stereotypes, most Jews did not
get off the boat with Marx and Engel's *Das Kapital* in one
hand and a bomb in the other. They came to this country

with relatively little political knowledge or concern and often with a deep orthodoxy. While the American political structure incorporated classical biblical concepts, these were not part of recent Jewish political thought. Other aspects of American government were either alien to, or made suspect by, the Jewish experience in Europe. Since Old World Jews were more likely to have received fair treatment at the hands of the central government, they tended to appreciate national rather than state or local agencies. And the often avaricious and corrupt bosses they encountered in the big cities did not improve their opinion of municipal government.

As we have seen, even if American free enterprise had its weaknesses, basic democratic ideals and the freedom to live without undue outside interference attracted Jews to the United States. Certainly, there could be no comparison with the European picture. As Jews were being integrated into American society economically, they were also being brought into the political system. Since the nation's ethical idealism alone did not guarantee security from discrimination, Jews felt that only a truly liberal sociopolitical milieu would grant them an equal opportunity for success in life.

In the twentieth century the labels "liberal" and "Jew" were often considered synonymous. All Jews, of course, had not been liberal-oriented, but as has been seen, those that were, were conspicuous by their disproportionate representation within liberal/radical blocs. Such movements as trade unionism, socialism, the Progressive reform era, anti-World War I agitation, the early Communist party, the New Deal, the anti-McCarthy feeling of the 1950s, and the Civil Rights and the New Left activities of the 1960s and 1970s all owe much to American Jewry's dedication to the principles of liberalism.

There are several possible explanations for the Jewish link with liberalism. Jewish minority group status created what sociologists have called the "Marginal Man," one who is poised in psychological uncertainty between two or more social worlds and reflects the discords and the harmonies of this existence. In America the psychological manifestations of marginality become most evident in the second generation immigrant who attempted to reject his foreignness but was hindered in his efforts to become a completely assimilated American. Many Jews chose to escape the problems of marginality by becoming involved in radical/liberal politics in the hope that the success of liberalism would guarantee equality of opportunity and hence eliminate their marginal status. The fact that vast numbers of Americans would never fully accept Jews as social equals meant the continuance of a certain degree of marginality and hence the continued advocacy of radical/liberal solutions.

Further complicating Jewish status as the marginal man was the desire to maintain Jewish identity. Of all white ethnic groups only the Jews and the Pennsylvania Dutch have resisted complete assimilation. The perpetuation of a Jewish identity was tremendously influential in forcing Jews to evaluate and re-evaluate both American and Jewish ideals. The result was an increased dedication to an ethical idealism which not only advocated equality of opportunity, but also guaranteed freedom of religion and the right to be different. Needless to say Jews found their beliefs best espoused by liberal philosophy and political action.

As the twentieth century passed its halfway mark Jews found their situation in America greatly altered. They were no longer a truly "foreign" element of the population. Their successful acculturation had reduced much of the social tension connected with marginality, but Jews had maintained their identity. Assimilation, by and large, had been resisted, and Jews remained conscious of their continued status as a minority group. In the 1940s and 1950s a sociological phenomenon—the reawakening of ethnic consciousness—began among third generation Jews. According to the sociological theory known as "Hansen's Law," whenever an immigrant group reaches the third generation stage in its development, a spontaneous and almost irresistible impulse arises—to interest themselves in their common heritage, the heritage of blood. What the son wishes to forget the grandson wishes to remember. For Jewish Americans, as Will Herberg has noted, this "law" appears to be unusually applicable. The crisis of world Jewry created by Nazism, and the pride in Jewishness instilled by the creation of the state of Israel contributed to this upsurge in group consciousness. Jews rededicated themselves to Judaic ethical idealism and seemed to strengthen their ties to American liberalism. Synagogue membership mushroomed, especially in the suburbs, where loss of identity was more probable away from Jewish neighborhoods that kept one Jewish without conscious effort. In fact, the phenomenon of the third generation identity resurgence was quite likely extended to the fourth and fifth generations because of the traumatic events of the Nazi era, the threats to the security of Israel, and the reactionary Red scare of the postwar years. These events underlined the unique identity of Jews and perhaps served to perpetuate the Jewish commitment to the radical/liberal philosophy.

The background for understanding the contemporary American Jewish political scene is rooted in the interwar decades. As the Republican party became increasingly the party of big business, and inasmuch as anti-immigration sentiment, prohibition, isolationism, and the Ku Klux Klan spirit typified the twenties, the politically oriented progressive Jewish electorate sought a place within the developing liberal coalition of the Democratic Party. By 1928, Democratic candidate Alfred E. Smith had swung the urban Jews into the Democrat camp, and part of his success was due to one of his advisors, the reformer Belle Moscowitz. The economic chaos generated by the stock market crash, and the lack of significant action on the part of the Republican administration to restore economic stability assured Jewish support for the Democratic presidential candidate in 1932.

With the election of FDR in 1932, the Jewish association with the Democratic party became solidified and continues to the present. Roosevelt seemed to be nearer than any other politician to the liberal ideal which so many Jews held. The

New Deal promised economic and social reform and, moreover, Roosevelt's opposition to Hitler and his evolving internationalist foreign policy attracted Jews who for familial as well as ideological reasons advocated a strong anti-axis stand rather than historic nonentanglement.

The radical Jewish labor movement of the thirties was one of the most solid supportive elements behind New Deal social action programs. In 1935 all three of the major Jewish unions—the International Ladies Garment Workers, the Amalgamated Clothing Workers, and the Hat, Cap, and Millinery Workers—were instrumental in the establishment of the militant Congress of Industrial Organization (CIO). In the struggle that was to divide the American Federation of Labor, Sidney Hillman and David Dubinsky were highly influential supporters of the C.I.O. Hillman abandoned the doctrinaire type of socialism he had brought with him from Russia, but he remained a passionate seeker after increased economic, social, and political justice. Dubinsky, who rose in the ranks of the International Ladies Garment Workers Union, was always in the anti-communist wing. Both men provide dramatic examples of American Jewry's newfound willingness to operate within the more traditional channels of the liberal movement. Also, Roosevelt's political success owed much to organized labor's political agencies, such as the AFL's Labor League for Political Action, the CIO's Political Action Committee, and the American Labor party of New York State.

Symbolic of the increasing Jewish involvement in liberal Democratic party politics, there were three men who in 1932 achieved high governmental positions: Henry Horner was elected governor of Illinois, Herbert H. Lehman won the same office in New York, and, though appointed by a Republican president, Benjamin N. Cardozo began his service on the Supreme Court. During his six years on the High Bench, Cardozo was a constant supporter of F.D.R. and the New Deal. His death in 1938 was a blow to American liberalism but during his short tenure, he had helped create a tradition of progressive jurisprudence. Both Brandeis and Cardozo were no longer on the Supreme Court by 1940, but their presence during the crucial decade of the 1930s was of invaluable aid in forwarding the cause of American liberal reform.

The New Deal reform era was perhaps the shining example of the relationship between liberal government and the Jewish people. By the time the New Deal domestic program was coming to an end, the president was becoming more and more preoccupied by foreign events. Reconstructionist leader Mordecai Kaplan appealed eloquently for continued Jewish support of liberal idealism. He felt that Jews should strive for the establishment of a social order that combined the maximum of human cooperation with the maximum of human freedom. Jewish organizations and institutions, Kaplan asserted, ought to make Jews sensitive to those social evils that impeded the attainment of this goal. Jews were admonished to cooperate with the general population in furthering all movements which had as their purpose the eradication of poverty, exploitation, violence, and war. And, at the conclusion of World War II, Jews were among the leading advocates of the United Nations formula to insure peace through collective security. A resolution of the Central Conference of American Rabbis characteristically warned against the pitfalls and evils of a system of continued militarism.

The Jews were different from the other minority groups within the Democratic coalition in that they were generally of a higher socio-economic position. Despite the paradox of a minority group of such status supporting increased government economic and social controls, the Jewish vote for Roosevelt had increased each time he ran for re-election. In contrast, Roosevelt's support from other minority groups tended gradually to decrease. And in the 1948 election, Jews continued to back liberal candidates, over 90 percent of the Jewish electorate choosing either Harry S. Truman (Democrat) or Henry A. Wallace (Progressive). Despite General

Dwight D. Eisenhower's wartime reputation as the savior of Europe, Jews overwhelmingly supported the Democrat-liberal Adlai E. Stevenson in both his tries for the White House (1952, 1956). During the 1950s, there was a conservative reaction in the nation often associated with Senator Joseph McCarthy of Wisconsin. His unreasoned and prejudicial attack on what he termed Communism and disloyalty in government was negatively received by the liberals in the Jewish community. The attempt to stifle dissent seemed a direct attack on basic Jewish ethical ideals, though McCarthy never attacked Jews directly and even had two Jewish aides. Jews equated "McCarthyism" with the demagoguery of past authoritarians who sought power by sowing the seeds of suspicion and fear. As one Jew commented, one thousand years before the birth of Senator McCarthy, Jews were fighting "McCarthyism," and in the Senate, one of McCarthy's chief antagonists was Herbert H. Lehman.

In 1952, before the Senate censured McCarthy, a Gallup Poll demonstrated that 56 percent of Catholics and 45 percent of Protestants approved of McCarthy and his tactics, but that 98 percent of the Jews considered him a menace to the country. The McCarthy era seemed to have pricked at Jewish conscience, for early in 1953, The Union of American Hebrew Congregations and the Central Conference of American Rabbis began campaigns to organize "social action" committees in every reform synagogue in America. By 1954 the conservative Jewish congregations joined the movement, and a Joint Committee on Social Action was established.

As the South began its campaign of massive resistance to desegregation and the Civil Rights movement gathered momentum, Jews became conspicuous within the ranks of the white liberal group that championed such causes. It has been said that Jews, even when rich, still tended to identify with the poor, with the powerless and persecuted, since they had been but recently poor, powerless, and persecuted. Early in the century, Rabbi Stephen S. Wise had been one of the founders of the National Association for the Advancement of Colored People, and the Julius Rosenwald Fund, begun in 1917, had aided thousands of young Negroes in their pursuit of higher education. These efforts and many others had established a tradition of supporting the demands for equality of America's most oppressed minority. Many rabbis were ardent supporters of the civil rights movement of the 1960s. Jewish congregations throughout the South spoke out in favor of ending segregation and, as a consequence, Jewish Centers, synagogues, and homes were bombed or threatened with destruction. Jews refused to be intimidated, and young and old alike continued to be the most consistent white allies of the blacks. They preached the justice of desegregation in the South, many suffering physical abuse and some even death at the hands of southern segregationists. The Civil Rights movement, with its failures and its successes, was to serve as both an example and a training ground for yet another generation of young American Jews who out of frustration and idealism would embrace even more radical ideals and movements in the years to come.

In 1960 the young, dynamic presidential candidate from Massachusetts, John F. Kennedy, captured the imagination of the Jewish community and he was able to claim 91 percent of their vote. No other group, not even the Negro or Catholic, gave the young senator such support. Though the Kennedy "New Frontier" version of Camelot became bogged down in the halls of Congress and ended in November 1963 with an assassin's bullet, American Jewry continued to support the new president, Lyndon B. Johnson, and in 1964 he received nearly the same percentage of the Jewish vote as had Kennedy in 1960, significantly against Barry Goldwater, whose paternal ancestors were Jewish.

The Johnson administration's escalation of the war in Viet Nam, the limited success of school desegregation in the South even after ten years, the riots in the northern ghettoes, and the restlessness on college campuses began to create a climate susceptible to radical social and political movements. A large portion of the Jewish youth embraced "radical" solutions, while many less militant Jewish youth enrolled in the Peace Corps. Perhaps fully 50 percent of the revolutionary Students for a Democratic Society and as many as 50 to 75 percent of those in campus radical activities in the late 1960s were Jewish. Jewish youth, too, were often the leaders in organizing Marxist or Socialist groups on college campuses and were prominent on the editorial staffs of radical or revolutionary newspapers from the junior high school to the college level. Examples of this type of campus activist were Mark Rudd, Jerry Rubin, and Abby Hoffman.

Thus, one cannot accuse American youth in the sixties of a lack of either fervor or activism. Whatever the specific causes students in the sixties played a far more decisive role in shaping the social and political course of contemporary American life than had any previous generation. Within the group of young Americans who set the tone of political movements in which their peers participated, Jewish students seemed disproportionately represented as leaders. But despite this heavy representation, the Jewish leadership comprised a small proportion of the entire Jewish student population.

Yet it is the radical student whose action received the most publicity, whose opinions attracted the most attention, and whose influence seemed to be the strongest with his fellow students. The radical stance of many young Jews is not difficult to understand. Contemporary Jewish radical youth are often the offspring of affluent, successful parents, but those same parents did not allow prosperity or a move to the suburbs to destroy their idealism. And as a matter of fact, many of them were considered the radicals of an earlier day. The children of these liberal families existed in a world permeated by the mass media, and thus injustices were much more readily exposed than in the days of their parents. The reality of day-to-day prejudice, discrimination, poverty, and war were in direct contrast to the vision of America propagated by school and parents, despite the fact that the latter were often of a liberal persuasion. The youth became impatient with the slow progress of liberal reform in an age when one could literally watch a human being starve, suffer, or die on the nightly news program. Thirty years of basically liberal government on the national level seemed to have accomplished little in the area of meaningful social reform for millions of Americans. Young Jews, like other youth, thus demanded more dynamic change, but in other ways than their grandfathers had sought it at the beginning of the century.

Even several years before the student unrest of the 1960s, a study made of Jewish young people in the deteriorating Brownsville section of Brooklyn found that a "consciousness of discrimination in our society constitutes the initial factor in the cultural consciousness of Jewish youth." But, although discrimination was the initial factor in cultural consciousness, it was not the primary one for Jewish young people; rather, it was emotional nationalism (or ethnic consciousness) and the supposed "return of the third generation." On the basis of the Brownsville study, it was concluded that about one-fourth of the youths were "frustrated escapists," with a pervading sense of anxiety because social justice seemed neither feasible nor attainable. The emphasis which Jewish youth put on social action to achieve social justice was thus thwarted. Hence, even before the upheaval of student revolt, Jewish youth demonstrated those concerns associated with a later time.

Other distinctive features characterized many Jewish radical students. A large proportion of them had working-class grandparents and thus a familial link with an older radical tradition. Their parents were generally successful middle-class liberals who fostered a consciously intellectual, politically articulate atmosphere in the home. Many fathers were self-employed professionals and businessmen, anti-organizational types. Despite the fact that most of the Jewish students identified themselves as Jews in some sense, they were not conscious of being specifically Jewish radicals. Their Jewishness or the recent travail of European Jewry seems not to have shaped their radicalism.

While Jewish youth captured the liberal-radical spotlight in the years since 1964, their parents had not abandoned liberalism. Most Jews did not desert the Democratic party even though increasing numbers of them opposed the Vietnam War on the grounds that it violated Jewish ethical teachings. As a matter of fact, in 1968 Jews gave 85 percent of their vote to Hubert H. Humphrey.

Jewish participation in the liberal coalition is expected to continue but there may be developing a breakdown in the old political consensus. During the 1972 presidential campaign, many seasoned political experts predicted a Jewish defection to the Republican party because of concern over Democratic candidate George McGovern's stand on Israeli issues, and over his job-favoritism program for other minorities which threatened Jewish teachers and civil servants whose numbers in these occupations exceeded their proportion in the general population, and basic Jewish confidence in President Richard Nixon's support for Israel. Also, McGovern made little effort to win over the Jewish vote. When the returns were analyzed it was discovered that while Jewish-Americans were still mostly Democrats, the number was decreasing. Disaffection with the Democrats was seen chiefly in Jewish political absenteeism from the polls. In 1968, Nixon received about 17 percent of the Jewish vote, while four years later, that figure climbed to 35 percent, the largest ever received by a Republican candidate up to that time.

In 1976, Gerald Ford got about 30 percent of the Jewish vote compared to Jimmy Carter's 68 percent. Certainly, while most Jewish voters still supported Democrats, a trend seemed observable—more Jews are voting Republican and, as one writer put it, "It is no longer *trayf* (nonkosher) to vote for the GOP."

Jews have had no special reason to be fond of Carter. He made his share of blunders in trying to walk a tightrope between the Arab and Israeli positions. In likening the Palestinian problem to the Civil Rights movement in the United States in a July 1979 interview, he provoked anger and dismay from American Jewish leaders, especially in possibly giving the Palestine Liberation Organization a respectability. In March 1980, there was what the State Department called an error in communications with regard to an American vote in the United Nations protesting Israel's plans for installing Jewish settlements in the captured West Bank area. Previously, the United States had been against these settlements but always abstained, but this time, Washington ordered a negative vote. Then after a delay and removal of a paragraph impugning Israeli respect for religious freedom in Jerusalem, Ambassador Donald F. McHenry joined in a unanimous condemnation of Israel. Carter then disavowed the vote, stating there had been a failure to communicate. Israeli leaders and those of the American Jewish community were stunned and saw in the episode traditional State Department antagonism and Carter flip-flopping. Carter's Democratic party rivals were quick to pick up on the administration embarrassment. The president's admission of a mistake placated some American Jews, but others cited this fact as one more proof of an erratic policy. Carter strategists saw in this episode still another reason for Jewish suspicions.

In March 1980, New York City Mayor Edward Koch accused Carter of being the victim of Third World and Arab-oriented advisors such as American ambassadors to the United Nations, secretary of state, Cyrus Vance, and National Security advisor Zbigniew Brzezinski. Koch reminded the president that FDR and Truman overruled their State Departments in their anti-Israeli stance but that Carter had not asserted himself in the same way, and American Jews felt that in a crisis, it appeared as if this country was submitting to Arab-oil blackmail.

Despite the fact that Carter engineered Israel's first peace treaty with an Arab nation and appropriated billions to cushion the cost of the settlement, there was also the Andrew Young episode (see page 152), Jewish concern over the president's "born-again" religious background, and the allegedly anti-Semitic remarks of his brother, whose close association with Libya galled many. The paradox exists that a president who had so many Jewish associates and who began successful peace overtures in the Middle East was the most unpopular of recent chief executives in the Jewish mind. Many American Jews felt that Carter risked Israel's survival in urging greater sacrifices by the Jewish state compared to those he asked of the Arabs.

Dissatisfaction with Jimmy Carter encouraged Jewish efforts on behalf of Ronald Reagan in 1980. One poll showed that Carter received over 45 percent, Reagan about 39 percent, and Third Party candidate John Anderson 14 percent of the Jewish vote nationally. Reagan's percent represented an increase in Jewish-GOP relations compared to the 35 and 30 percentages for Nixon in 1972 and Ford in 1976. While Carter received more Jewish votes than did Reagan, his vote was the lowest for a Democrat since before FDR. In essence, neither political party could claim a Jewish vote as its own.

At any rate, there appears to be a watershed in the traditional, liberal identification with social reform, labor, and civil rights. There is no one Jewish vote—the New Deal Democratic Jew belongs to the past. Perhaps it can even be predicted that in the last decades of the twentieth century, American Jews will become centrists, and while retaining a liberal focus, they will become more moderate in their demand for change.

Since Ronald Reagan's inauguration in 1981, American Jews have expressed concern for what the president termed a reappraisal of the U.S.-Israeli connection in order to preserve a "strategic consensus" in the Middle East. A shipment of jet bombers to Israel was postponed and concern was voiced over the Israeli destruction of an Iraqi nuclear facility and the bombing of the Arab and Soviet supported Palestine Liberation Front facilities in Lebanon. However, Reagan's long-standing support for Israel has remained an advantage in his reputation with American Jewry. Israel and America are united by cultural, emotional, military, and political commitments, but there seem to be increased doubts about each other's reliability.

Actual Jewish participation in government, as appointees or as officeholders, has been significant. Little could the immigrants of 1900 imagine how effective that participation was to become or even how many Jews would actually see government service on the highest levels. For example, early in the twentieth century there was Oscar S. Straus, secretary of commerce and labor in the Theodore Roosevelt administration, and Henry Morgenthau, Sr., appointed by Wilson as ambassador to Turkey. In 1924, the first Jewish woman, Florence Prag Kahn (Republican, California), entered the House of Representatives and remained there until 1935, when she was defeated in a Roosevelt landslide. Succeeding her husband, Julius, Florence Kahn was fiercely loyal to her San Francisco area and to military preparedness. Perhaps her most noteworthy accomplishment was in securing legislation for the construction of the San Francisco-Oakland Bay Bridge.

Among the distinguished Jewish Supreme Court jurists were Louis D. Brandeis, Felix Frankfurter, Benjamin Cardozo, and Abe Fortas (although he resigned under a cloud of suspicion over "conflict of interest"). Herbert H. Lehman was the first Jew to become governor of the State of New York, winning four times, and later he served as a United States Senator.

The list of Jewish cabinet and administrative appointees is distinguished. Henry Morgenthau, Jr. served as secretary of the treasury under FDR from 1934–1945. David Lilienthal was chosen by Roosevelt to direct the Tennessee Valley Authority, an agency that virtually reshaped the role of government toward business. Later, he also was chairman of the Atomic Energy Commission. Arthur Goldberg served as John F. Kennedy's secretary of labor and was appointed by Kennedy to the Supreme Court and by Lyndon B. Johnson as American ambassador to the United Nations. Kennedy chose

Abraham A. Ribicoff as secretary of health, education, and welfare, and later Ribicoff served in the Senate. Johnson named Wilbur J. Cohen to the HEW post and in the Nixon-Ford administrations, Henry Kissinger, formerly a Harvard professor, served as secretary of state, and Edward A. Levi as attorney general. Jews Alan Greenspan and Arthur Burns were chairmen of the Council of Economic Advisors and the Federal Reserve System, respectively. In the Carter administration, there were the following cabinet officers: the secretary of defense, Harold Brown; the secretary of commerce, Philip M. Klutznick, and the secretary of transportation, Neil Goldschmidt, as well as assistant to the president for domestic affairs and policy Stuart E. Eizenstat, Robert S. Strauss, Carter's choice for almost everything and in 1980 chairman of his reelection campaign, and former Xerox Corporation chairman, Sol M. Linowitz, special Middle East envoy. Certainly, there was a large number, perhaps even a record number, of Jewish-Americans participating at the top level of the Carter administration.

Three important recent Jewish senators no longer serve in Congress. Jacob Javits (Republican, New York) won his first term in 1956 and in 1980 lost in the Republican primary but ran unsuccessfully on the Liberal party ticket. His seniority was unrivaled by any New York senator in modern times, and he was the senior member of the Senate Foreign Relations Committee. Abraham Ribicoff (Democrat, Connecticut, 1962–1981), former House member, governor, cabinet member, and judge, did not seek reelection. Richard Stone (Democrat, Florida, 1974–1981), was chairman of the Middle East subcommittee of the Senate Foreign Relations Committee and did much work to advance peace in the area. Along with Javits, he sponsored a resolution that no rolls be held on Jewish holidays.

As of this writing (1981), there are six Jews serving in the United States Senate. Howard Metzenbaum (Democrat, Ohio) was appointed to the Senate in 1974 to fill a vacancy and was elected in 1976. Edward Zorinsky (Democrat, Nebraska, 1976–) is a former Omaha mayor whose parents, unlike many other politicians' families, migrated west instead of remaining in New York. Carl Levin (Democrat, Michigan, 1978–) is a former Detroit councilman and assistant attorney general of Michigan. Rudy Boschwitz (Republican, Minnesota) was a lawyer-businessman who escaped from Hitlerian Germany. He is heavily involved in Jewish activities, especially the Minneapolis Lubavitch Center. The newest senators elected in 1980 are Republicans Arlen Specter (Pennsylvania) and Warren Rudman (New Hampshire). The senators elected before 1980, together with the departed Javits, Ribicoff, and Stone, agree with the American Jewish community on most issues; they deny there is a "Jewish position" and there is no Jewish bloc in senatorial voting. But, it seems as if they desire to retain religious identity and several have spoken about Jewish concepts of justice, objectivity, historical tradition, and Israeli interests as helping to guide them.

In 1981, in addition to the six Jews in the Senate, the Jewish contingent in the House of Representatives numbered twenty-seven. Six percent of the Congress is of Jewish origin. Among the more prominent is Sidney Yates (Democrat, Illinois), dean of Jewish members of the House. Other Jewish politicians who served as governors in the 1970s were Frank Licht (Rhode Island), Marvin Mandel (Maryland), and Milton J. Shapp (Pennsylvania).

In local public service, Robert Moses of New York City was preeminent for his creation of parks, bridges, highways, and many other types of civic improvements. Moses held such posts as advisor to Governor Alfred E. Smith on the revision of state government (1919), New York City park commissioner (1934–1960), and head of the Triborough Bridge and New York City Tunnel Authority (1946–1968). In 1973, New York City elected a Jewish mayor, Abraham Beame, and he was succeeded by another Jew, former Representative Edward Koch. San Franciscan Dianne Feinstein became the first Jewish woman chosen mayor of a major American city in 1978, succeeding the victim of an assassination, and the next year, she was elected in her own right.

Thus, though Jews constitute less than 3 percent of the population, their political influence is considerably greater. According to Stephen D. Isaacs's treatment of Jews and American politics (*Jews and American Politics*, 1974), American Jews normally contribute over 50 percent of the sizable contributions to the Democratic party and are also well represented as active workers. In states with large Jewish populations, they often determine the victor. In New York State, for example, where they make up 14 percent of the population, they cast 16 to 20 percent of the vote in national elections.

It is possible that the ever-increasing Jewish participation in government service and the traditional liberal political focus of American Jews were in part responses to those feeling that they were a people apart. Anti-Semitism was never far from Jewish thought in determining their political behavior and in part probably explains why more have not held elective office. During World War II, there was a resurgence of anti-Semitism. In the light of subsequent history, most observers interpreted this upsurge as part of a greater outburst against minority groups generally and not something directed against Jews alone, though it appeared so while Hitler lived. The wartime attitude toward Jews was reminiscent of that toward German-Americans and other hyphenated Americans during World War I. Virulent anti-Semitism abated quickly after the war in large part because of greater Jewish affluence, but this decline did not mean that Jews were free from the effects of prejudice and discrimination. Covert manipulation of the laws still denied many Jews jobs, homes, facilities, and accommodations. Often Jews could succeed in the economic world and still not be accepted as social equals. As we have seen, the new suburban class found that the Jewish-Christian interrelationship was often a nine-to-five arrangement. Jews and Christians seldom met socially even in suburbia, perhaps less so than within the cities.

One manifestation of anti-Semitic behavior was in the American private business club. Probably because many Christian business executives find it uncomfortable to relax with Jews, most of the prestigious clubs exclude Jews from membership, or perhaps accept a few "tokens." These clubs are often an essential adjunct to the conduct of business and Jews as a result are excluded from such decisions. Ludicrous discriminatory cases abound. William S. Paley of the Columbia Broadcasting System was kept out of Washington's famous F Street Club, and former U.S. ambassador to France and treasury secretary, C. Douglas Dillon, with only 25 percent Jewish ancestry, languished for years on the waiting list of Washington's Chevy Chase Club.

More important was the discrimination still felt in education, a particularly sensitive area because of the traditional Jewish regard for study and the ability of Jewish-Americans to perform well in college. The extent of actual and potential discrimination came to light when in 1949 the Anti-Defamation League of B'nai B'rith analyzed the content of application forms for undergraduate and professional schools. In the latter especially, Jews felt discrimination keenly. The survey revealed that schools were asking directly discriminatory questions about race or color, religion, nationality, and father's or mother's nationality, and indirect questions about place of birth and language spoken at home. Photographs were also often required.

There were occasional outbreaks of anti-Semitic behavior like the swastika epidemic that swept the world in the winter of 1959–1960. These incidents were generally erratic and innocuous, though highly visible. They were annoying but ultimately not indicative of a widespread upsurge in virulent anti-Semitism. Indeed, the trend in anti-Jewish feeling since World War II has been consistently downward. On the basis of most measurements and general observations of American society, the Jews are living in one of the most peaceful periods in their history.

However, some skeptics feel that this peace is relative, existing only because society as a whole is more peaceful. The traditional sores of hard-core anti-Semitism still fester. But prejudice began to stimulate a group not traditionally opposed to Jews. The Negro in the once Jewish urban ghettos of the North often vents his rage by attacking the Jews, both verbally and physically, particularly the ones with whom he is most familiar, the exploiting slum landlord, the small businessman in his neighborhood, and the teacher in the ghetto school. But, Jewish liberals, the traditional champion of the blacks, also receive abuse, often being accused of a hypocritical posture, since they preach equality but live in lily-white suburbs.

Although Negro anti-Semitism is not completely new, it gained national prominence only during the last half of the 1960s. It reached a height in 1968 and, at least overtly, diminished after that. Its most malignant outbreak occurred in the fall and winter of 1968–1969 in New York, a city that contained 1.8 million Jews and 1.5 million blacks. Three events during that period contributed to the tense, near-hysterical rancor that seized both the Negro and the Jewish communities. First and most prominent was the series of strikes that crippled the city school system in the fall of 1968. Behind the strikes lay the establishment of a school district in the once solidly Jewish Ocean Hill-Brownsville section of Brooklyn as an experiment in decentralization and closer association between the school and the local neighborhood. Teachers collaborated in plans for the new district from the beginning, but almost immediately had to contend with representatives of local parents. When the governing board of the district overstepped its authority and dismissed nineteen teachers in the spring of 1968, it set a course bound to collide with the teachers' union. When the administrators of the district had not reinstated the teachers by the opening of school in the fall of 1968, the union called a strike for the entire city school system.

Then in a series of three strikes involving disputes between the teachers and the Ocean Hill-Brownsville district, the hostility between Negro parents and the teachers, many of whom were Jewish, broke out in a war of threats, pamphlets, and sometimes bodily harm. The discord created near-hysteria, especially in some Jewish areas of the city. When the union distributed anti-Semitic pamphlets which were allegedly written by Negroes, it fanned an already heated controversy. In the midst of threat and counterthreat, charge and counter-charge, it was difficult to determine which side was at fault. A Special Committee on Racial and Religious Prejudice reported that neither side was free of blame. The blacks openly aired their bigotry, sometimes physically. The whites, no less bigoted, were more subtle in expressing anti-black sentiments. Assignment of guilt was neither possible nor desirable. Both Negroes and Jews struggled in a fracas neither to their liking nor completely of their own making.

Another fracas between the black and Jewish communities aggravated the Ocean Hill-Brownsville dispute. This one broke out because of the appointment in July 1968 of John F. Hatchett as director of the Afro-American Center of New York University. His appointment became controversial when it was disclosed that he was the author of an article in which he urged his fellow blacks to fight against the Jewish teachers, whom he accused of practicing racial and cultural genocide against Negro children. Eventually New York University ousted him when he continued to make inflamatory racial statements.

Before the mutual recriminations stopped, a third incident provided fresh ammunition for the two groups. The Metropolitan Museum of Art, which received part of its support from the city of New York, held an exhibition entitled "Harlem on My Mind." The catalogue describing it contained an essay by a teenage Negro girl which said in essence that Negroes are anti-Semitic because anti-Semitism makes them feel more completely American. Mayor John V. Lindsay tried to get the catalogue removed, and the official and unofficial representatives of the Jewish community of New York protested the overt racism, but the museum director refused to ban the offensive publication. The catalogue was quietly withdrawn less than two weeks after the opening of the exhibition, even though the young author disclaimed being a racist in reverse.

There is little agreement about the causes of Negro anti-Semitism. One opinion holds that Negroes are not anti-Semitic but anti-white and that Jews are the most visible white targets in the Negro ghettos. Many Jews feel that their leaders should not placate these Negroes, that is, appease the unappeasable. Some observers see no evidence among Negroes of the traditional racist, Anglo-Saxon variety of anti-Semitism. Rather, blacks are anti-Semitic because of their agrarian background—they dislike the big city and big business and Jews are usually associated with both of these forces. The Jewish liberal position is that while they have done more for the Negro than has any other group, Jews have still not done enough. While the Jew, almost alone in America, is freer of guilt than all others about their treatment of Negroes, he recognizes that even more can and needs to be done.

Most Jews are genuinely bewildered by black behavior. A 1969 survey found that 45 percent of Jews polled believed that Negroes wanted to tear down white society. Negroes and Jews, despite a common alliance in past wars against discrimination, have evidently gone separate ways. The Jew, using education as a leverage, has become one of the most successful minorities from the point of view of assimilation, and the ▓▓▓▓▓▓▓▓▓ blacks, the least successful. Another explanation for negative Jewish-black feelings is that even though Jews have real concern for the rights of the Negro, many disdain what they perceive as their carefree and careless life, seemingly the very antithesis of the work ethic that most

Jews cherish. And yet, a story by the noted Jewish humorist Harry Golden points up the contradictions in Jewish-black relations. In the Forest Hills area of New York City, Jews demonstrated against the construction of high-rise, low-income buildings for ghetto blacks, but one block away, they contributed heavily to the conservative-oriented National Association for the Advancement of Colored People! Although there is the understandable feeling among many that blacks do not appreciate the assistance Jews have proffered, there is continued Jewish support for Negro Civil Rights and economic betterment. The Jewish legal involvement in these causes by such attorneys as William Kuntsler is an example.

A very real Jewish response to recent anti-Semitism, increased harassment of the ghetto-dwelling poor Jews, and the growing uncertainties in the black-Jewish story, was the founding of the Jewish Defense League (JDL) by Rabbi Meir Kahane in 1968. Its stirring motto, "Never Again," has become the symbol of activist and radical methods used to protect Jews who were vulnerable to black, right, or leftist militants. Originally numbering approximately a tiny seven thousand, the JDL has adopted an action program: criticizing the Jewish Establishment as well as middle-class liberals, expressing anti-communism, portraying the Jew as aggressive and tough, and championing the Jewish poor. Kahane believes that assimilation is a self-defeating tactic and that Jews must assert their Jewishness. Orthodox in background, the JDL accuses Reform and Conservative Judaism of accommodating to the will of the stand-patters. The JDL has widened its geographic base, having established branches in most major American cities and in Israel, and attesting to the belief that fire must be fought with fire, fisticuffs, and also karate.

While Jews have traditionally led in the quest for civil rights for blacks, much of the leadership against affirmative-action programs designed to help blacks and other nonwhite minorities achieve greater educational and employment opportunities is Jewish. Such programs threaten the merit system by which poor Jews could hope to achieve middle-class status. For example, if blacks received jobs in the New York City school system because of affirmative action, Jewish teachers were often denied those positions.

In 1972, the American Jewish Committee launched an attack on quotas which, in an attempt to right wrongs of the past and liberalize minority hiring or admissions to colleges, discriminated against Jews and other whites. The climax occurred with the Marco De Funis case. De Funis was denied admission to the University of Washington Law School though his credentials were qualitatively better than those of minority students who were admitted. De Funis and such allies as the Anti-Defamation League of B'nai B'rith, among others, claimed reverse discrimination. As we have seen, Jews are on campuses out of proportion to their numbers in society and perhaps attempts to limit their continued professional study in favor of minority students and to provide more diversification exacerbated an already explosive issue. This confrontation divides not only Jews and blacks but also Jews themselves, some maintaining the importance of the historic fight for the rights of all. De Funis was ordered admitted to law school but the University of Washington nevertheless appealed and won; however, Justice William O. Douglas issued an order allowing him to continue, and he graduated in 1974. Because it was after the fact, the Supreme Court refused to render a definitive decision.

In 1978, the Supreme Court handed down a split 5-4 vote in the famous Bakke case. A California Supreme Court decision was affirmed that a special admissions program at the University of California at Davis was unlawful and that a white, Allen Bakke, should be admitted. At the same time, confusion resulted because the judgment overturned a section of the California court's ruling that barred the medical school from considering race in its admissions policy. Jewish organizations generally reacted favorably, one official hailing the decision as a milestone in the furtherance of equal rights and individual rights as well. But, while the Court stressed both ethnic diversity and race as an element in the selection process, universities could use racially nondiscriminating policies as covers for de facto quotas. Thus, the whole matter of affirmative action remains an uncertainty and its potential as a source of anti-Semitism continues as an irritant.

However, on the leadership level at least, there were efforts made at a black-Jewish accommodation. There had been a joint conference on recession problems and statements by black leaders in support of Soviet Jewry and Israel. Despite the violence of the 1960s and the conflicts over affirmative action, traditionally positive black-Jewish relationships were once again apparent. But, even with such hopeful signs, as of 1979, the black-Jewish affinity took a turn for the worse. By 1979, black anti-Semitism had flared up more dramatically than previously. A Louis Harris poll of the previous November revealed increasing bad feelings toward Jews by blacks between 1974 and 1978. It is assumed that it was motivated by antagonism over affirmative action, job quotas, black power, and economic relations. In 1979, the resignation of Andrew Young as United Nations ambassador in the wake of his unauthorized discussion with the Palestine Liberation Organization touched off controversy anew in the already strained relationship between black and Jewish Americans. Also, the PLO is for many blacks an organization sharing human rights issues with them. Blaming Jews for Young's resignation ignored the fact that Jewish organizations did not call for his ouster and Young himself pleaded that his departure not be used to fuel divisiveness. Nevertheless, black activist leader the Reverend Jesse Jackson and other articulate black spokesmen continued to speak out against Israel and in defense of the PLO stand. The old alliance in the civil rights struggle had been drifting apart for years and the Young case was the climax. These tensions reflected the fact that Jews overcame prejudice and discrimination to become in the view of some blacks a part of the establishment from which they were still mostly excluded. As blacks were becoming more assertive, especially in diplomatic matters, newer frictions became apparent in black-Jew relationships.

Another recent unfortunate episode that cast shadows over Jewish relations with Christians involved Daniel Berrigan, the liberal Jesuit priest with a prison record for his activist political involvements. Jews had been in the forefront of his movement against the Vietnam war and for draft resistance. But, in the aftermath of the 1973 Yom Kippur Arab-Israeli war, Berrigan spoke out against Jews as well as Arabs before the Association of Arab University graduates. He spent more time on the Jews, however, accusing them of militarism and imperialism, and calling Israel a "criminal Jewish community." American Jews naturally felt disappointed and were mystified, though Berrigan maintained that his one-sided portrayal was arrived at in order to focus attention on Middle Eastern tensions and the supposed unreasonableness of American Jewry.

While being anti-Israel does not mean one is anti-Semitic, many Jews feel uneasy about what has come to be called the anti-Israel lobby. Among the various elements in this group are: State Department Arabists who equate Arab oil with American self-interest, including State Department officials who feel Israel has been inflexible with regard to its security and is hence holding up "peace," and the usual anti-Semites who always felt Jews controlled American economic life.

Former Vice President Spiro Agnew turned anti-Israel (and some would say anti-Jewish) after he was forced to resign from office. Business associations with Arabs accounted in part for his anti-Semitic remarks, but there are those who feel that such behavior began when Baltimore County Jewish businessmen sought immunity by turning state's evidence against him.

In 1974, General George S. Brown, then Chairman of the Joint Chiefs of Staff, in discussing the Middle Eastern situation at the Duke University Law School, referred to the

"Jewish influence" in the Congress and to Jewish control of banks and newspapers. When these statements were publicized, Jewish groups accused him of blatant anti-Semitism and asked for his dismissal. President Ford ordered a reprimand and personally discussed the situation with the general. Brown announced his regrets, insisting that his remarks did not represent his real convictions. At any rate, such a heedless comment evoked the clichés of anti-Semitism, and American Jews were understandably upset. What exacerbated this situation was that Jewish influence on banks and newspapers is almost nonexistent and that such accusations had been disproved almost four decades earlier.

Another occurrence that shocked American Jews was the revelation that President Richard Nixon had warned aide H. R. Haldeman to eschew the arts because Jews were so much involved in them and had said that Jews were left-wingers. These remarks were among several slurs against various ethnic groups that were on the famous Nixon tapes that were publicized in the wake of the Watergate scandal. Such remarks as those of Brown, Agnew, and Nixon are examples of stereotyping that have for Jews the same effect as a synagogue marred by a swastika.

The Anti-Defamation League of B'nai B'rith reported 377 anti-Semitic episodes in 1980, a dramatic increase from the previous year. While there is no evidence of an organized campaign, these incidents, which involved graffiti, burnings, vandalism, personal harassment, and arson, caused Jewish organizations to worry. Then, too, the Ku Klux Klan and the American Nazi party, as well as new so-called patriotic and religious groups convening conferences and publishing anti-Semitic tracts have begun to spread. The Moral Majority, a combination of radically conservative forces and fundamentalist religious groups, has also caused Jews much concern. Jews do not necessarily see this group as anti-Semitic, but they feel preaching about a Christian America at this time has the same effect.

A statement made by the president of the Southern Baptist

Convention in 1980 that God does not hear the prayer of a Jew, and another by a New York leader of the Moral Majority in 1981 that referred to the Jewish "supernatural" ability to make money, aroused concern, both Jewish and non-Jewish. Senator Alfonse M. D'Amato of New York denounced this as bigotry and demanded an apology to Jews. These situations indicate to Jewish leaders that anti-Jewish feeling still exists, albeit often beneath the surface of American life.

Thus, in conclusion, it can be said that many Jews in the United States tend to the liberal political left. Jews generally support liberal candidates and causes with little regard to their own social class; middle-class and upper-middle-class Jews vote for liberals as readily as do Jews still in the working class. Jewish loyalty to liberalism arises from a persistent concern for the underdog. Jewish participation in the Civil Rights movement in particular reflects a concern with justice for all men. A broad interest for the welfare of mankind accounts for the internationalism which made Jews major supporters of the United Nations, aid programs for underdeveloped nations, and for more liberal immigration policies. This, of course, was before the Third World, with its anti-Israel orientation, captured control of the United Nations General Assembly.

And the Jewish university students are even more liberal than their parents, especially in their political thoughts and social concerns. For example, they are in the forefront of such liberal educational reforms as the de-emphasis of college athletics, the legalization of marijuana, and the institution of curricular changes. Away from the university, Jewish youth support school desegregation, ethnic and racial equality, the abolition of capital punishment, "left-of-center" political candidates, and demonstrations for alterations in American military policy.

The political role of American Jewry is another example of how successfully Jews have accommodated to the American scene. A Democratic leader has succinctly stated that Jews feel a keener interest in democracy because "they have a bigger stake in democracy than anyone else." The political interests of the Jews, then, seemed to mesh easily with the democratic Jeffersonian heritage updated to late twentieth-century needs. The ever-present evidences of anti-Semitism, as aggravating as they are, have not blunted this interest.

7

Post-World War II American Jewry: Anxiety, Affluence, and Affirmation

SINCE THE END OF WORLD War II, American Jewry has merged into the mainstream of American society. It has poured its vigor into the tide of national life, mingling its values, institutions, and self-images with those of the larger society. The Holocaust rewove Jewish life in America even as it sundered the fabric of world Jewry. Within a decade the centuries-old civilization in Central and Eastern Europe was destroyed. A fountainhead for the familial, cultural, and religious sustenance of American-Jewry ceased to flow. Yet at the very moment that one source was being destroyed, another was being created. The State of Israel came into being, as its first prime minister, David Ben Gurion, has said, by "a whirlwind of history." Although nothing could supplant the influence of the Eastern European heartland, Israel did nourish a new spirit in the institutional and often the personal lives of many American Jews. If one doubts the impact of the State of Israel on American Jewry, he need only remember its reaction to the Six-Day War. Thus, two very opposite historical events, a birth and a death, shaped the current era. Moreover, the jet era has made Israel a suburb of the American Diaspora and vice versa.

One of the most important questions asked by modern American Jews is, Who am I? That the question of identity arises so often is the inevitable consequence of the Jew's position as a member of an island minority group surrounded by a Christian sea. As long as the Jews were isolated in their own communities, there was no problem of group personality. However, with emancipation and settlement in an open society, the problem of identity became crucial. There was no longer a single model of Jewishness. The dissimilar opinions about Jewishness within the Jewish community itself are perplexing to those seeking an ideal conception of what it means to be a Jew, and many Jewish young people are seekers for this ideal. Another result of integration into a larger society is a limited arena for expressing one's identity. With the move to the suburbs and the decrease of large solidly Jewish neighborhoods, Jews are increasingly surrounded by non-Jewish influences. Schools, businesses, neighboring families are no longer exclusively Jewish. Kinship exists only within the nuclear family. Therefore, the patently Jewish acts in one's life are increasingly limited to particular times and places which one comes to identify with the Jewish aspects of one's being. Jewishness becomes something specific, an act or a ceremony rather than the general expression of one's self.

Qualms about Jewish identity are not a development of the postwar period only. Prior to World War II, Jews frequently were assimilated by the majority society. Some of them rejected everything Jewish, while secularist Jews rejected only their religion. The events of the war period and the gnawing recollections of and guilt feelings about the Holocaust reversed the previous trends. Following the war, large numbers of Jews renewed or strengthened their identification through formal affiliation with Jewish institutional life. There was increased enrollment in Jewish schools, a growth of the Jewish Community Center movement, more generous donations to Jewish causes, and the establishment of Jewish institutions such as Brandeis University, and both scholars and laymen renewed their interest in the riches of all aspects of their Jewish heritage, including the search for lessons to be learned from the Holocaust experience. All this formed new patterns in Jewish life.

Each year the *American Jewish Yearbook* lists the major national Jewish organizations, generally over three hundred. These are usually grouped under the headings: Religious and Educational (the largest number), Civic Defense, and Political, Cultural, Youth and Student, Women's, Overseas Aid, Social and Mutual Benefit, Community Relations, Professional Associations, Social Welfare, Zionist and Pro-Israel. There are also Jewish federations and community councils, which raise and allocate funds for local, national, and overseas service, and coordinate such local services as family welfare, care of the aged, child care, health, and recreation, and there are groups which deal with Jewish-Gentile relationships. The increase in the number of institutions which are directly or indirectly dedicated to the preservation of Jewish identity has not been accompanied by a tendency toward unity of plan or action. These Jewish agencies are, nevertheless, in general agreement that the Jews in the United States either are or should be a corporate social group, or to use a frequently applied misnomer, that the Jews are a "community." While close to 60 percent of all Jews (excluding those who have intermarried) are not active in Jewish organizations, the estimated figure of funds contributed during the 1975–1978 period for Jewish philanthropic purposes, domestic and foreign, was between $460 million and $475 million.

The expansion of Jewish institutional life, although partly a consequence of the trauma of the Second World War, is also an outgrowth of the spread of the Jews into the suburbs since the end of that war. Although there are some predominately Jewish suburbs, most suburban Jews live alongside Gentiles. Both groups associate in community secular activities and are generally on friendly terms; however, on the level of intimate friendship, it would seem that most Jews still choose to associate with other Jews. This preference is scarcely strange since people usually feel most at ease with those who share common interests, mutual friends, and similar philosophies and styles of life.

The most notable transformation in Jewish identity did not occur because of "secular" Jewish organizations or suburban togetherness. It occurred instead because of the much-discussed return to the synagogue which will be treated more fully later. Although the return was no doubt spiritually fruitful, its most productive harvest was an increase in Jewish identity. After the Holocaust, many Jews came to see that secular Jewishness could not insure group survival. Survival required deeper spiritual resources and, as a result, more and more Jews, especially young people, identified themselves as a religious group. Given the return to the synagogue and the increased emphasis upon Jewish education, this religious identity is not surprising. Not only the ethical and theological teachings of Judaism but also its rituals and holiday observances form a matrix in which a person's Jewish awareness develops.

The extraordinary economic heights American Jews have reached is placed in perspective if one looks back to the early years of the twentieth century when perhaps 80 percent of New York's Jews worked in sweatshops, earning less than $15 per week when they were lucky enough to find employment. Obviously the Jews did not attain their present level of affluence by remaining in the working class. As stated earlier, if the first generation labored in the sweatshop, the second generation owned a business, and the third generation usually entered such professions as medicine, law, and teaching. The pattern repeated itself in various combinations of generations and occupations, but the direction was almost consistently upward on the socio-economic scale.

The rise of Jews to middle-class status came primarily in the years before World War II. Economic consolidation and diversification in the middle and upper-middle classes marked the postwar years. During the Truman era some Jews worried about their marginal economic position. The businesses in which they specialized were becoming more vulnerable to the control of the American economy by heavy industry, which was not then and is not now dominated by Jews. The future did not look promising for the Jewish businessman nor for the professional who depended on others for his success.

Surveys have indicated that, of any other ethnic or religious group, Jews are the most numerous in business and professional occupations and have the lowest percentage of urban manual workers and farmers. About three times as many Jews are engaged in trade and commerce and twice as many in professional services as any group in the entire nation. Earlier in this century, Jews were the chief source of operatives for the ready-made clothing industry, but by the 1920s, they constituted less than half of the operatives and by mid-century less than 28 percent. In the meantime, Jews have risen to management and ownership, thus achieving almost exclusive control of the entire wearing apparel industry.

The rapid rise from factory, wage-earning occupations to those in commerce has contributed to the stereotype that Jews control the American economy. Though there is today no area of economic activity without its Jewish participants, it has never been easy for the Jew to fit into the "normal" occupational pattern, a fact due in large part to a past which compelled Jewish preoccupation with certain forms of commerce and merchandising. Even today the considerable antagonism the Jew often encounters in banking, insurance, transportation, utilities, and in many "heavy" industries helps maintain a Jewish preponderance in garment manufacturing, merchandising, trading, the service industries, and the professions. Thus, far from controlling American industry and finance, the Jews have been forced into marginal and newer industries such as electronics, plastics, computers, air conditioning, motion pictures, advertising, and radio and television.

In the new consolidated community that they are in the process of creating, Jews have started their own vocational bureaus to offer special help to fellow Jews and to advance their economic integration. In a world of commerce and rapidly proliferating automation, the American Jew seeks a white-collar job and in smaller towns he is frequently self-employed. The irony is that Jewish business success has taken place against the resistance of American industry. Of the largest 1,200 American corporations, only a few have one or two top Jewish executives, especially if "Jewish" companies such as RCA and Levi Strauss are eliminated. Although Jews account for 8 to 10 percent of American college graduates, they comprise less than 1 percent of the leading executives of major American corporations. For example, there has never been a top Jewish executive of any major automobile manufacturer. In New York City, about 50 percent of the college graduates are Jewish, but only a few Jews serve as senior management officials and not one of the twenty-two top executives of the seven largest banks is Jewish. A case in point involved Sears Roebuck. Edward Gudenan rose to become vice-president for merchandising, but the late Sears chairman, Robert Wood, forestalled his appointment as president in 1959. As of 1979, only one of Sears' corporate officers was Jewish. Fifteen percent of Harvard's Graduate School of Business are Jews, but only one-half of one percent of those enrolled in the school's Advanced Management Program where industry sends its promising managers are Jewish. Except for a few, it is virtually impossible for a qualified Jew to head a major corporation that is not already controlled by Jews. In view of the Jewish mercantile tradition, such a consistent absence of Jews is a remarkable oversight, and *Jewish Living* (November–December 1979) asserts that the corporate executive suite may well be the last frontier in the battle against American anti-Semitism.

Some Jews, however, have overcome the barriers and risen to high levels in industry. Gerard Swope was president of the General Electric Company in the 1920s, David Sarnoff became president of Radio Corporation of America in 1930, and various members of the Block family (Joseph, Philip, etc.) founded and managed the Inland Steel Company. In 1974, E. I. DuPont chose Irving Shapiro as its chief executive. Shapiro was not only Jewish, but the first non-DuPont family member to head the company. Shapiro is one of those businessmen vitally concerned with change and in improving the image of American industry by participating as activists in society and politics. For example, he has persuaded B'nai B'rith to accept a compromise American policy for dealing with the Arab boycott of Israel, and he travels constantly speaking about American technology and the need to find more jobs for blacks and Hispanics. Samuel Goldwyn and Louis B. Mayer were among the many top motion picture producers, and Nelson Morris was known as a pioneer in the meat-packing industry. The leading department stores in this country were founded by Jews—Benjamin Altman, Samuel J. Bloomingdale, Bernard Gimbel, Louis Bamberger, and the Straus family (who were also prominent in philanthropy and public service). In the construction and real estate fields, there are such giants as Webb and Knapp; the Uris Brothers; Tishman; Levitt; and Rudin and Wolfson Enterprises. In banking, the names of Schiff and Warburg have been preeminent and ironically, in 1974, the Philadelphia National Bank which had rejected Albert Greenfield named Richard Ravenscroft as president of its holding company.

Happily the anti-Semitism of an earlier time is weakening. Following an American Jewish Committee discrimination complaint in 1976, the Pennsylvania Human Relations Commission ordered the Provident Mutual Life Insurance Company to undertake a program for hiring and promoting Jews into executive positions. Many companies followed suit and active recruitment of Jews has increased.

High educational achievement undoubtedly contributed to high Jewish income, and this motivation helped to increase further the proportion of Jewish youth who attend college— some 62 percent in 1955 versus 26 percent of the general population. Jews have always had the reputation of being wealthy. Although Jews account for only about 3 percent of the population, they receive 10 percent of the total personal income. The disproportion is greatest in the highest brackets where about 20 percent of American millionaires are Jewish. There are some notable true aristocrats of the American Jewish wealthy. According to *Jewish Living* (September–October 1979), dozens of Jews have amassed tremendous fortunes, but there is no truth to the assertion that Jews control the country economically. The Chicago Pritzkers, the wealthiest Jewish family in America, are worth about $750 million as compared to the Mellons and DuPonts, each worth between $3 and $5 billion. Percentage-wise, Jews are of minimal importance among the nation's super-rich. It is also true, as already seen, that Jews have not been represented in such benchmarks of American wealth as oil, land, and banking. Of the top ten superwealthy Jews, two made money in oil but they controlled only part of the total process. Among the top Jewish wealthy and their companies are the Pritzkers (Hyatt hotels, real estate); Samuel I. Newhouse (various publications); the Bronfman family (Seagram Liquor Company); the Crown family (General Dynamics and real estate); Marvin Davis (Davis oil); the Haas family (Levi Strauss & Company); Leonard Stern (Hartz Mountain Industries, including pet foods); Walter Annenberg (publications, i.e., *TV Guide*, *Seventeen*, *Daily Racing Form*); Laurence Tisch (Loew's Corporation); the Guggenheim's (mining and metallurgy); the Lauder family (Estee Lauder cosmetics); the Sulzberger's *(New York Times)*; William S. Paley (Columbia Broadcasting System); and Lew Wasserman (MCA, Inc., motion picture and record production). In the top fifty, there is also the legendary Meyer Lansky of Miami Beach, reputed to be connected with organized crime. Certainly most Jews are far from this exalted economic class, but they are better off than most non-Jews. The Jewish median income in 1971 was $12,630 compared with $10,285 for the rest of the population, and 14 percent of Jewish families made $25,000 or more a year. While 57 percent of Jewish families have incomes of $7,000 a year or more (compared to 35 percent of the total population), it is noteworthy that 800,000 mostly elderly Jews are below the poverty level of $3,343 per year, half of them in New York City. These "Jews without hope," as they have been described, are often sickly, lonely, and frightened of their ghetto neighbors. A symbol of the economically depressed conditions, Jewish mobility, and the radically changing neighborhoods is the dwindling number of congregations in older sections of cities. In 1900, there were about 500,000 Jews and three hundred synagogues on the lower east side of New York while seventy years later, the number decreased to 15,000 Jews and six congregations.

With general economic comfort and even affluence came the inevitable move to the suburbs. Jews as well as Gentiles were on the move, but the former settled in suburbia in probably greater proportions than the latter. However, both groups moved for the same reasons: a need for adequate housing, a desire for the suburban environment of green grass and fresh air in which to raise their children, and a push outward from the crime-infested cities.

Most students of suburbia do see a kind of cultural and religious return to Judaism of which the unprecedented growth in synagogue memberships and buildings is the outward sign. Furthermore, the trend in Jewish education is more and more toward centralized Jewish education within one city or else merger of congregational schools. Many suburban Jews wish to perpetuate their Jewish identity by means of their children's Jewish education. If there is a change in the Jewish attitude toward the religious and cultural aspects of their heritage, perhaps it mirrors similar changes in American society generally. Through religious affiliation, Jews are conforming to suburban folkways and finding that such affiliation gives their children a feeling of belonging and gives adults themselves status and respect in the eyes of their neighbors.

Although most authors stress the contrast between the Jews' previous urban experience and their new experience under the pressures of suburban togetherness, there are those who maintain that Jews have in a sense returned to their old home. Symbolically they are in the *shtetl* again, except that their affluence prompted the concept of the "Golden Ghetto." According to this thesis, one's affiliation with the Jewish community is compulsive; he is subject to its claims and demands in the way the metropolitan Jew has never been. Although suburbia and the city seem far apart, they are significantly alike, especially in organizational life. Both the synagogue and the secular organizations for education and welfare bind the suburban community to a greater extent than did the informal Jewish institutions of the city. Through its communal and religious institutions the Jewish community stands on an equal footing with the non-Jewish communities.

Jewish residential patterns in the suburbs differ from those in the city. Except for a few areas around New York, the suburbs have nothing that resembles the urban ethnic neighborhood. The third-generation suburbanites generally live in largely non-Jewish areas, but such "Golden Ghettoes" as Great Neck, Larchmont, and Shaker Heights have concentrated Jewish populations. While the suburban dwellers are still preoccupied with financial success, as were their fathers, they seem to be more concerned with security and status. They often do not work in the world of business and the marginal retail trades of their fathers, but frequently choose occupations that are deemed non-Jewish, such as salaried professions. In the 1970s, big industry decentralized, often going into small towns in the West and South. By this time Jews were in such industries, and this helped to scatter them into suburbs. Unlike their fathers, Jews customarily associate in business with Gentiles with whom they share a common life-style. They join general business and professional organizations and they indulge in the same leisure activities as do Gentiles.

The criticism most frequently levelled at this generation is that they pattern their lives after the fashions of the Gentiles instead of seeking guidance from the cultural and spiritual precepts of Judaism. However, this criticism assumes a dichotomy that does not in fact exist. The American culture is not completely the creation of the Gentiles. Jews, too, have had a strong influence on shaping modern American culture. Whatever the degree of influence of Jews upon Gentiles and vice versa, the fact which even the criticism illustrates is that to a greater degree than ever before the two communities influence each other. The scene of much of this mutual influence is the suburbs.

If the Jewish suburbanites see themselves as energetic citizens, the suburban Jewish mother probably generates a large portion of this drive. A descendant of the *balebosta* (good housekeeper), she is like her predecessors—the competent, energetic, often frugal, compassionate person. Most writers believe that she plays a greater role in the family than she did previously. Whether she dominates it to a greater extent than does her Gentile counterpart is a question more discussed than studied. Reporters and analysts of the suburban scene state that she supervises her husband and family, takes great pride in the achievements of her children, sets the tone in cultural and spiritual matters, and is the chief support of the local synagogue, whose programs would cease without her assistance. Although detractors criticize her, they seldom fault the quality of the family she raises.

Neither the urban neighborhood nor status suburb has daunted the Jewish family. Its legendary stability is based not on myths but on matters of fact. The banes of so many non-Jewish families' existence—alcoholism, abandonment, unemployment—have until recently been almost completely unknown among Jews. Jews have a lower infant and maternal mortality rate, less juvenile delinquency, fewer fatherless homes, and their children stay in school longer. Also, Jews have a higher rate of marriage and of remarriage of the widowed and, above all, there is family cohesiveness. However, new negative currents are obvious which run counter to this traditional interpretation—the increase of divorce, nonmarital sex, alcoholism, drug abuse, and youth rebellion among Orthodox Jews. This was also true of Conservative and Reform families, but Orthodox Jews experienced these upsets later. At the present time (1981) four out of ten Jewish marriages dissolve, though the rate is somewhat lower among Orthodox families. The feminist movement has increased expectations among Jewish women, and the secular opportunities open to them also help explain the increase in divorce. Jewish versions of the marriage encounter, where secular interests and traditional values are discussed, have become more common. While devout Jews have generally heeded God's commandment to "be fruitful and multiply," overall, American Jewry produce fewer offspring than other Americans, indeed fewer than the replacement level of two per family. One rabbi even warned that Jews are an "endangered species." The Reform rabbinate seemingly have veered from zero population growth, and Jewish leaders are finding practical reasons to speak out against assimilation, abortion, mixed marriage, and birth control.

One basic aspect of the Jew as American is the role he played in the development of this country's culture. We have already described the importance of that contribution, and this vitality continues. Indeed, one can scarcely conceive of modern America without the contributions of Jewish artists and intellectuals. Most authorities attribute the success of Jews in scholarly and creative fields to the deep regard with which Jews traditionally hold learning. If historically Jews were always assiduous in work and study, why did the fruits of their labor ripen so obviously in the postwar years? The first two generations of Jews in America occupied themselves primarily with gaining physical necessities, although considering their burdens of adjustment and survival, they managed to be quite active culturally. The third generation, who reached their maturity in the postwar period, did not face pressing material cares. They were freer than the earlier generations to follow cultural interests. Like the economy of a developing nation, the Jewish cultural creativeness was quite obvious by the end of the war.

American Jews have made tremendous contributions in all

aspects of general culture. In the professions, in music, in literature, in painting and sculpture, in the academic world, and in the area of science, Jews are often distinguished and in many instances pre-eminent.

In the field of music Jews have made a reputation as composers and performers in both classical and popular fields. Ernest Bloch and Aaron Copland are composers who have enriched American musical life, the former in a specifically Jewish sense and the latter in a distinctly American idiom. In the field of light music and the musical theater George Gershwin, Jerome Kern, Alan Jay Lerner, Richard Rodgers, Oscar Hammerstein, and Irving Berlin, just to name a few, have become household words. As performers and conductors, such Jews as Leonard Bernstein, George Szell, Erich Leinsdorf, Artur Rubinstein, Mischa Elman, Yehudi Menuhin, Vladimir Horowitz, Jascha Heifetz, Isaac Stern, Itzhak Perlman, Pinchas Zuckerman, Robert Merrill, Roberta Peters, Beverly Sills, and Jan Peerce are pre-eminent. And for the youth, nobody spoke or sang more clearly in the 1960s and 1970s than Bob Dylan (Robert Allen Zimmerman), the folk singer. As of 1980, Dylan regards himself as a Christian.

With the exception of the creations of Ernest Bloch, the works of Jewish composers are not noted for their specifically Jewish content. Although there has been activity in liturgical composition and inspiration in folk music from the Israeli and cantorial examples, music for a wide audience has not been marked by Jewish themes.

In art as in music there is no distinctly Jewish school, although as creators of modern art Jews have been prominent. The versatile Ben Shahn, Mark Rothko, the abstract painter, and Jack Levine, a satiric artist, are especially noteworthy examples. Jo Davidson and Jacob Epstein were probably the most renowned Jewish sculptors of recent times.

Evidently beginning with the last years of the 1940s, the enormity of the European devastation and the success of the establishment of the State of Israel caused some literary intellectuals to re-examine their Jewish heritage. Many seemed alienated from the majority culture just as they were often estranged from traditional Judaism. Alienation is not without value to the Jewish writer. It grants him, an outsider, a novel prospect from which he can criticize American society. To an American nation nurtured by relatively shallow historical roots, the Jew, conscious of the history and travail of his people, can enrich their memory of mankind's development.

In order to act as critic and guide, the individual must himself come to terms with his own alienation. The Jewish intellectual, therefore, is often searching for his own identity. As a result, in much Jewish writing the major problem is self-definition in an alien secular culture, and generally the works picture Jewish adaptation to the American scene. By extension, then, the writer becomes Everyman, seeking his proper place in the world, and his search for orientation generates a concern with ethical and social realities.

Long before modern writers discussed alienation, the Jewish humorist and jokester dealt in his own way with the same problem. The marginal role in society, so often the Jew's lot in life, created an ambiguous position from which he could observe society in general as well as his own peculiar fate within it. Although only 3 percent of the population is Jewish, at least 80 percent of the comedians are Jewish. Psychologists feel that Jewish humor born of depression and alienation, accounts for the number of professional Jewish comedians. Comedy was the Jewish self-defense against hostility. It has been noted that until the 1950s, there were many Jewish comics but few Jewish jokes; the themes of changing names and the shape of noses were common. While those who worked the Catskill (New York) mountain resorts adjusted to a Jewish audience, this was an exception. Jack Benny pretended to be a typical small-town American, and the Marx Brothers were important mainly for their anarchic mocking of conventions. A psychologist who has studied Jewish humorists, Samuel Janus, feels that most were ambivalent about their Jewishness. They tended to break out of the Jewish world and gain general acceptance. The post-1950 comics, unlike their older colleagues, are better educated, have less contact with the religion, and are more likely to emphasize social or political messages rather than Jewish humor. And yet, there are Jewish comedians today who are also as popular by being Jewish as their predecessors were by denying it.

Although Jews work in all fields of creative endeavor, they especially cultivate the field of literature, where an array of distinctively Jewish novels, poetry, and criticism flourishes. That there would be a renaissance in Jewish letters was by no means obvious immediately after World War II. The growing awareness of the Jewish heritage, whether accompanied by pride or alienation, prompted intellectuals to ask about the meaning for themselves of their Jewishness. The advent of a group of talented Jews with similar backgrounds heralded the literary awakening. The critic Alfred Kazin referred to their appearance on the literary scene in the late 1940s and early 1950s as the "coming of the 'intellectuals'" and since World War II made anti-Semitism a taboo, Jewish writers came into prominence with varying degrees of Jewish self-consciousness.

Many of these authors explored their own ethnicity and, while often not religious themselves, they respected the tradition and recalled affectionately the warmth of family life, the nostalgia about the vanished life of the ghetto, and the humor in Jewish experience. These themes, together with celebrations of the glory of the new State of Israel, appeared in novels like Sholem Asch's *East River* and Leon Uris' *Exodus*. The latter, a best seller, probably had a tremendously important role in determining attitudes of Jews and Christians about the European Jewish tragedy and the founding of Israel. *Marjorie Morningstar*, Herman Wouk's all-American girl of the New York Jewish middle class, found appreciative Gentile audiences, where she was one of the first Jewish heroines to be accepted as a representative American character rather than as a quaint or romantic alien figure. To a degree unknown before World War II, Jewish writers, both popular and serious, attracted public attention. This popularity perhaps resulted from the increasingly similar life-styles of Gentiles and Jews—Jews remaining sufficiently different to arouse Gentile curiosity. Even serious writers such as Philip Roth, Saul Bellow, Norman Mailer, Bernard Malamud, and J. D. Salinger, who are generally considered the leaders of the Jewish renaissance, have enjoyed not only wide critical acclaim but enormous popularity. Bellow's initial success was *The Adventures of Augie March* (1953), a description of how a young Chicago Jew met poverty. Eleven years later, his *Herzog* portrayed a man who learned to adjust to life as it was. Bellow's messages interested more than Jews; they had meaning for the entire society. In 1976, he received the Nobel Prize for literature, the committee citing his human understanding and subtle analysis of contemporary culture. Malamud's best known work, *The Fixer* (1966), depicted an event in Czarist Russian history, but the novel really treated the whole of Jewish survival and the bigger-than-life hero defying the inevitable. Roth's *Goodbye Columbus* (1959) and *Portnoy's Complaint* (1969) are amusing but often cruelly analytical novels portraying the manners and mores of Jewish youth and suburbia, not always to the pride of American Jewry. His *My Life as a Man* (1974) is another examination of a Jewish writer-intellectual beset by family and marriage woes and his attempt to become mature or a whole man. Like the protagonists of his other works, Roth's hero is haunted by the "Jewish guilt" that was for certain Jews a consequence of "ethnic desertion."

Jewish writers who are associated mainly with non-Jewish themes have also been noteworthy. In the 1930s Nathanael West was the precursor of the postwar flowering of American-Jewish literature. His *The Day of the Locust* was a searing indictment of the movie scene. Norman Mailer's *The Naked and the Dead* is certainly one of the best of the World War II novels, and Joseph Heller's *Catch 22* has become a classic and favorite of youth, because it shows war as a struggle for individual survival in a bureaucratic world. Norman Pod-horetz, editor of *Commentary* magazine, calls Mailer a "non-Jewish Jew" but asserts that he is beset by Messianic longings and while Heller's work has not a single Jewish character, its "self-pity and self-irony" were distinctly Jewish. All of the Jewish influence in American letters does not extend from the achievements of the novelists. Of almost equal importance are the writings of the critics. The list is stellar: Paul Goodman, Alfred Kazin, Leslie Fiedler, Irving Howe, Norman Podhoretz, Harvey Swados, Robert Warshow, Lionel Trilling, Isaac Rosenfield, Lionel Abel and Philip Rahv. These men are part of the Jewish cultural establishment which influences American literary tastes through the pages of such periodicals as *Commentary*, *Judaism*, *Partisan Review*, and the *New York Review of Books*. Incidentally, *Judaism* was begun by the American Jewish Congress in the mid-1950s to counteract *Commentary*, published by the American Jewish Committee. *Judaism* was more Zionist and more concerned with Judaism as a religion.

In two other areas of American writing Jews have been active: drama and poetry. In the 1920s and 1930s, the theater was distinguished by such talents as Moss Hart, George S. Kaufman, S. N. Behrman, Elmer Rice, Lillian Hellman, Clifford Odets, and after the war by Arthur Miller and Neil Simon. Although Jews have long been prominent on the American stage in the prewar and postwar periods, Jewish writers have not projected the convincing image of Jewishnesss that the novelists have. Similarly, in poetry, the Jewishness of the Jewish authors has not been so visible although poets as diverse as Allen Ginsberg, Delmore Schwartz, and Karl Shapiro have dealt with Jewish themes.

Of special interest in American Jewish letters is Isaac Bashevis Singer, winner of the 1978 Nobel Prize for literature. His acceptance speech included remarks in Yiddish, the language in which he writes. Singer called the language "the tongue of martyrs, saints, and dreamers" and "the idiom of frightened and hopeful humanity." He has written thirty books, including *The Family Moskat* (1950), *The Manor* (1967), *The Estate* (1965), and *Sosha* (1978). Important, too, was Charles Angoff, a literary figure for over half a century and author of a series of eleven autobiographical novels. In 1925, he began an association with H. L. Mencken at *The American Mercury*, leaving the journal in 1950. Angoff was the author of thirty books, including the famous novels that centered on the figure of David Polonsky. His authenticity of material was noted by critics.

The contemporary Yiddish theater, certainly not the prolific theater of an earlier day centered on Second Avenue, still exists in New York City. The Hebrew Actors Union, which has about two hundred members, has never admitted that the Yiddish stage died. Perhaps the leading name of the modern genre is Ben Bonus, who has noted that audiences are generally young and non-Yiddish speaking. A recent disappointment was the inability of Yiddish theatrical star Ida Kaminska to found an American-Israeli-Yiddish theatrical company.

Whether in English, Hebrew, or Yiddish, on the adult or juvenile level, in fiction or works of scholarship, literary activity among Jews has been significant. The Jewish Publication Society (Philadelphia) is no longer the only publisher of books on Jewish subjects; commercial publishers and even university presses have discovered that an interested Jewish reading public exists. A disproportionate number of books are bought by Jews, which may help explain the dominance of the Jewish cultural establishment in literature.

Jews have long been active in newspaper journalism and in book publishing, although only fifty of the eighteen hundred American dailies are owned by Jews. The great American newspaper, the *New York Times*, has been a Jewish family property for almost eighty years, and Jews control a number of major book publishing houses including Random House, Simon and Schuster, Farrar, Straus and Giroux, the New American Library, Alfred Knopf, and Atheneum.

American Jews have kept pace with the quickened march

of theoretical science and its applications to the needs of war and peace. As early as 1905, Albert A. Michelson, who headed the Department of Physics at the University of Chicago, was the first American to win the Nobel Prize for physics, discovering how to measure the velocity of light. Between 1905 and 1965, sixty-seven American scientists received Nobel prizes, and eighteen of these were Jewish. Albert Einstein won the award for physics in 1921. Einstein's theory of relativity is one of the greatest scientific discoveries of the age. In 1934, he came to this country to head the prestigious Mathematics School of the Institute for Advanced Study at Princeton. Of special interest is Nobel Laureate Rosalyn Sussman Yalow, who won the prize in medicine in 1977. Her contribution was the development of a test to measure various substances in the body in order to help determine changes between normalcy and disease. Dr. Yalow's rise from secretary to research scientist focused much attention on the role of women in the professions. The scientist who played a key role in the production of the atomic bomb was J. Robert Oppenheimer, and the developers of the first hydrogen bomb and atomic-powered submarine were Edward Teller and Rear Admiral Hyman J. Rickover, respectively.

A large number of Jews made important contributions to the progress of public health and medicine in America. Jews came to the United States with a tradition of reverence for the art of healing which went back to the Middle Ages. In the New World, the tradition retained its vigor, and in the dreams of thousands of sweatshop workers the first choice of a job for their sons was that of physician. Approximately 10 percent of the more than 277,000 physicians in the United States were Jews. "My son, the doctor," became a cliché. Earlier in the century, Dr. Abraham Flexner helped to revitalize and professionalize medical education, and in the recent past, probably the most noteworthy contribution to the entire area of public health medicine was made by Dr. Jonas Salk, who in 1953 developed the first vaccine that gave almost complete immunity from poliomyelitis.

Psychoanalysis in America is a peculiarly Jewish enterprise; probably one out of five psychiatrists is Jewish. In part, the explanation for the number of Jewish psychiatrists and for the number of Jews in analysis lies in the effects of secularism on Jews. They have been more rapidly divorced from traditional religion and have accepted more enthusiastically than others the possibilities of science and the intellect. And perhaps they were attracted to Sigmund Freud, himself a Jew.

Among the outstanding American-Jewish economists are two Nobel Prize winners. In 1970, Paul A. Samuelson was honored for his work on scientific analysis in economic theory, and seven years later, Milton Friedman's contributions on the role of money and monetary systems were recognized.

In the area of the popular arts, especially the entertainment industry, Jews have long been a crucial and controlling factor, whether as producers, directors, writers, musicians, or performers. It has been estimated that one out of every seven members of the American theater and radio/television elite is Jewish. As we have seen, Hollywood has always been a largely Jewish institution, pioneered and founded by Jews. Personalities such as Adolph Zukor, Carl Laemmle, Samuel Goldwyn, Harry Cohn, the Warner Brothers, Louis B. Mayer, and Irving Thalberg were entrepreneurs, responsible in large part for the impact of the motion picture industry. And in the Hollywood gallery of great stars must be included such names as Theda Bara, Paul Muni, John Garfield, Edward G. Robinson, Eddie Cantor, Al Jolson, the Marx Brothers, and Lauren Bacall, to list only a few. Among the newer group of Jewish Hollywood personalities are Paul Newman, Barbra Streisand, Dustin Hoffman, Kirk Douglas, Walter Matthau, George Segal, and Woody Allen. The number of Jews who were directors and screen writers is also sizable. But despite these numbers and the importance of Jews both in front of the camera and behind the scenes, the American motion picture industry has done little in probing the Jewish experience up until the postwar era. The television industry is also staffed by a large number of Jews. David Sarnoff of the Radio Corporation of America made the radio and transistor possible, and William S. Paley of the Columbia Broadcasting System, Leonard Goldenson of the American Broadcasting Company, and Robert Sarnoff of the National Broadcasting Company are or were the chief administrators of the three major television networks.

Sports and athletics are also a major part of America's popular culture, and Jews have distinguished themselves on court, diamond, and field. Beginning with such early boxing greats as Abe Attell, the world featherweight champion from 1908 to 1912, Maxie Rosenbloom, who also enjoyed that honor in the early 1930s, Benny Leonard, the world lightweight champion from 1917 to 1924, and Barney Ross, already mentioned, many other Jews helped bring athletic glory to this country. In baseball, there was "Hank" Greenberg, a home-run slugger who threatened Babe Ruth's record, Al Rosen, and Sandy Koufax, pitching ace of the Brooklyn (now Los Angeles) Dodgers, who was inducted into the Baseball Hall of Fame in 1972. Koufax's four no-hitters were momentous feats, but as important to many was his famous decision not to pitch in the World Series on Yom Kippur. Among the leading Jewish football players were Benny Friedman of the University of Michigan, Marshall Goldberg of the University of Pittsburgh, and Sid Luckman of Columbia University and the Chicago Bears. Contemporary Jewish professional football figures include Lyle Alzado, Randy Grossman, Mike Hartenstein of the Cleveland Browns, Pittsburgh Steelers, and Chicago Bears, respectively. Marv Levy is the coach of the Kansas City Chiefs. In tennis, Dick Savitt was outstanding, and his Jewish identification was strong. He captured the Wimbledon Cup and won the national indoor singles title three times.

There were probably more Jews in basketball than in other sports. Among the greats associated with this game were Nat Holman, named in a poll as one of the three greatest players of the half-century, Arnold "Red" Auerbach, the winningest coach in National Basketball Association history, and Red Holtzman of the New York Knicks. Holman, who coached City College of New York for thirty-seven years (1919–1956), is president of the United States Committee for Sports for Israel. Dolph Schayes was once the highest scorer in NBA history. Larry Brown is the coach of the famed UCLA team and Abe Lemons coaches at the University of Texas. Mark Spitz, who won seven gold medals at the same Berlin Olympics where Israeli athletes were murdered, was the outstanding Jewish swimmer.

Thus it is clear that Jews have penetrated effectively all areas of culture. Only selected examples can be included, but the list is representative enough to demonstrate that in America Jews have reached eminence and have contributed to the unique reputation of this country. The story of the Jewish people in the United States and of those who could be listed in its "Hall of Fame" has been, despite some Gentile hostility, one of how a people has become interwoven into the national fabric.

Jewish cultural pursuits also embrace non-elite, popular practices, and indeed, these have often become the stereotype of things Jewish in the minds of non-Jews, and for many Jews themselves, they are the major link to their religious observance. Jewish cuisine is perhaps the most obvious example. Jewish-style foods—hallahs, bagels, knishes, gefilte fish, lox, kishkes, to mention only a few—are enjoyed by Jews and Gentiles alike, so much so that many non-Jews and religiously alienated Jews count themselves as "gastronomic" Jews. As a matter of fact, Jewish cuisine may well be the only bond between some Jews and their heritage, a sort of nostalgic family feeling about Jewishness, even if other identifications have disappeared. This food is often so rich, heavy, and caloric that Jews were reported as being more overweight than non-Jews. Jewish cookbooks, the spread of mass-produced kosher meals, and the nonkosher "kosher-style" delicatessen-restaurant are visible evidences of what some consider to be Jewish life.

The intimate tie between Hollywood and Jews has also been discussed. The list of Jewish-related movies is formidable, certainly compared to the apathy of filmmakers prior to the 1950s. "The Ten Commandments" and "Fiddler on the Roof" were in the top fifteen box office hits as of 1973. ("Fiddler" has had the distinction of being the longest-running musical show on Broadway for many years). Other such films include "Exodus," "Judgment at Nuremberg," "The Diary of Anne Frank," "The Pawnbroker," "Goodbye Columbus," "Jesus Christ Superstar," "The Way We Were," "The Heartbreak Kid," and "Hester Street," to list only a few. The impact of films in creating or reinforcing attitudes about Jews—either negative or positive—is a subject deserving of study. Such movies as "Portnoy's Complaint" and "The Apprenticeship of Duddy Kravitz," depicting Jews unflatteringly, are among those that have aroused angry reactions.

Television also contributes to Jewish popular culture. Some popular programs of the 1970s, including "All in the Family" and the "Mary Tyler Moore Show," had Jewish characters or themes. The 1972-1973 television program, "Bridget Loves Bernie," afforded an insight into intermarriage. But for many Jews, all the unfortunate stereotypes were perpetuated, as they were in a stage play, "Abie's Irish Rose," produced half a century before. Most American Jewish religious leaders voiced strenuous disapproval over the fact that the television adventures of Bridget and Bernie ridiculed religious teachings and condoned intermarriage. At any rate, the show was cancelled. "Rhoda" (1974) was another less offensive TV show that had Jewish characters.

The number of Jewish comedians on television is large. Fortunately or unfortunately, the "Jewish material" or reminiscences of such comics as Lenny Bruce, Alan King, Buddy Hackett, Mort Sahl, David Steinberg, Shelley Berman, Jack Carter, Myron Cohen, Shecky Greene, and Joan Rivers affords at least one view of Jewish life, often the stereotype of the "comic image" of the Jew.

A last example of Jewish popular culture is the preponderance of Yiddish words and expressions in everyday usage. The *Los Angeles Times* even featured an article, "A Nice Guide for the Goyim [non-Jews] to L. A.'s Jewish Community." Words such as *noshes* (snacks), the host of negative descriptions of people (i.e. *nudnik, klutz, shmegegge, meshugge, shlimael*—all basically "fools," "pests," etc.), *kibbitz* ("to talk intimately"), and *ganef* ("thief"), to list only a few, have become part of the American lexicon, often staples of borscht circuit comedians. This cozy good-humored Yiddish has been popularized by Leo Rosten's *The Joys of Yiddish* (1968), a jokebook of Yiddishisms combined with an encyclopedia of Yiddish words and customs.

The teaching of the Yiddish language is another example of how Yiddish has entered the popular realm. Yiddish language teaching was a rarity in colleges in the 1970s but, as of 1980, it is taught in nearly forty, and Queens College even offers a Yiddish major. UCLA has appointed the first tenured professor of Yiddish in the country. Yiddish, of course, has long been a staple in Jewish institutes of education, Jewish centers, and adult education programs in synagogues. Yiddish film festivals and the revival and rediscovery of such movies are quite common and popular. Then, too, there are the Yiddishists, the real scholars of the language and literature and many of whom belong to the Workmen's Circle, a fraternal organization that has furthered the cause through afternoon and Sunday schools, sponsoring Yiddish theater and concert tours. Socialist and worker-oriented in the beginning, the Circle has mellowed and its efforts are largely the propagating of the Yiddish language. Lastly, much of the Polish Yiddish material was rescued during World War II and brought to the United States where it is deposited with the YIVO Institute for Jewish Research in New York City. Max Weinreich (died 1969) authored a four-volume *History of the Yiddish Language*, and his son, Uriel, chairman of Columbia University's Linguistics Department, wrote a modern college Yiddish text and compiled an English-Yiddish and Yiddish-English dictionary. While Yiddish is still a language of older people and a remembrance of the warmth of ghetto and family life, a great deal of it is also in the realm of the literati and academicians. According to sociologist Norman L. Friedman, these examples of contemporary American Jewish popular culture are associated with a mass society; an urbanized Jewish population depends to some extent for its unity and identity upon them. Jewish entertainment, Jewish food, and Yiddish usages are for some a supplement to Jewish elite culture and a link with tradition. They arouse nostalgic recollections of home and the sociability of family. Of course, Jewish religious elitists frequently derogate those of their co-religionists for whom Judaism is gastronomic or who laugh at a comedian's Yiddish remembrances.

The problems of Jewish identification and affluence and the numbers who have become cultural arbiters is intimately related to the importance of higher education for Jews. Unlike Gentiles, whose widespread emphasis on college education dates principally from the end of the Second World War, the Jews became aware of the value of a college degree earlier in the century. In the present day, the Jewish young person who is not a recent college graduate, student, or a prospective collegian is the exception rather than the rule. It is estimated that as many as 85 to 91 percent of Jewish college-age youth are attending institutions of higher education, twice the national average for the rest of American youth. Or put another way, although the Jewish college student makes up only 5 percent of the total college population, he usually accounts for 15 percent of the undergraduate enrollment at prestigious schools. A 1971 study of the American Association of Jewish Education found that 54 percent of Jews twenty-five years or older had attended college or graduate or professional school, and among those Jewish males twenty-five to twenty-nine, the figure is almost 78 percent.

Not only do young Jewish students seek prestigious schools, they often search for prestigious fields as well. While tradition enhances the appeal of medicine and law for Jewish students, other areas like the social sciences continue to attract them because Jews often favor fields with a tradition of social interest through which moral and ethical concern can be expressed. Within the university atmosphere, much is heard of alienation and disenchantment with religion, at least with formal practice and ritual. And it is true that many young people do reject the materialistic ostentation and class consciousness of their parents and, with this repudiation, the religious affiliation as well. However, despite all this, there is evidence of a growing commitment to Jewish matters, if not to religious ritual. This is nowhere more visible than in the number of Jewish studies programs founded in the wake of the black studies movement. Since "black" became "beautiful," as one slogan put it, college campuses have increased ethnic studies offerings, often at the request of the students themselves. About forty universities give a major in Jewish Studies, and there are as many as a hundred full-time Jewish studies professors. In addition to such formal programs, other examples of heightened religious identification include Jewish rediscovery projects dealing with items relevant to contemporary youth concerns, free Jewish universities offering specific subjects initiated by students, and close to forty Jewish student radical presses with a circulation of 300,000. These papers generally reject the anti-Zionism of more extreme campus activists, evince concern for Soviet Jewry and the disadvantaged Jew at home, and editorialize bitterly against the "chopped liver and Mah Jongg" Judaism of establishment elders. The Jewish student newspaper at the State University of New York at Buffalo speaks out for Israel, against Soviet treatment of Jews, in favor of aid for the Jewish poor, and for more religious commitment by Jews. Early in the school year, it also provides a Jewish guide to the city of Buffalo—the location of Jewish agencies, kosher butchers, synagogues, etc. Campus leaders are cooperating more and more with community federations and other agencies on various social welfare projects and Israeli appeals. In fact, the reaction of American-Jewish college students during the latest Mideast war was so activist that many establishment leaders were surprised.

Another popular manifestation of Jewish youth identification is the phenomenon of Chabad, sponsored by the Lubavitcher movement, the group of activists headed by Rabbi Menachem Mendel Schneerson who expound the orthodox Hasidic mystical philosophy, and whose aim is to reclaim wayward Jews. The term Chabad is an acrostic for the Hebrew words for wisdom, knowledge, and understanding. Chabad does not proselytize but, rather, affords students with a traditional setting for study and prayer. And the B'nai B'rith Hillel Foundation, a mainstay of campus Jewry since the 1920s, maintains eighty seven directors on nearly 250 campuses and nearly $4 million a year, almost all raised by welfare funds. All these activities are not only examples of positive concern but also help immeasurably in reducing identity crises so common among youth. The stereotype of a generation lost to Judaism is indeed an exaggeration.

Despite this increased Jewish identification of many college students, there is another assessment, a feeling that many Jewish young people want their lives to be based on a secular foundation rather than on the sacred one of their grandfathers. With the dominance of middle-class secular values and the demise of the specifically Jewish but nonreligious Yiddishist culture, the young Jew is likely to approach his Jewishness through schools. He has to learn how to be a Jew. Many Jewish educational agencies are excellent; yet, many Jewish youth have only a fragmentary Jewish education. Furthermore, the surrounding culture does not necessarily reinforce their Jewish identity. The identity issue of most concern to Jews is that of intermarriage and assimilation. When sociologist Marshall Sklare looked at the intermarriage trends in the United States at the end of the 1960s, he was melancholy about the Jewish future in America if present trends continued.

The growing number of intermarriages is chiefly due to the

increased mobility of the nation whereby Jews are scattered more and more. There is much disagreement not only over the impact of intermarriage, but also over the reliability of national statistics that conclusions must be based on educated guesswork. A study conducted by the American Jewish Committee revealed that 31.7 percent of American Jews who married between 1966–1972 intermarried, while from 1941–1961, the rate was 6 percent. A 1978 report said that at least one third of Jewish marriages were with non-Jews. A report in 1972 stated that as many as 48.1 percent of American Jews marrying in that year were involved in intermarriages, though a positive balance existed in favor of conversion to Judaism. The intermarriage average for 1900–1972 for American Jews still alive was 16.8 percent, and the sober fact of concern to identified Jews was that the rate was increasing, though where the wife was originally Jewish, nearly all the children had been or were being raised as Jews, and in families where the husband was a Jew, the figure was 63.3 percent. But a two-year study released in 1979 was more pessimistic. It found that most non-Jewish spouses do not convert to Judaism, that the Jewish content in mixed marriages is low, that about one third of the Jews in such marriages regard their children as Jewish, and that most offspring receive little training in Jewish culture or religion. Most intermarriages link Jewish men and Gentile women, and, of course, as a result their children are not accepted as Jews within the Orthodox or Conservative branches unless the children or their mothers convert.

In a large population, intermarriage poses no threat, but with American Jewry, with no cushion of extra population, it is the greatest threat to continued Jewish existence. And even with conversion, often the marriage does not last beyond a generation. Related to the question of Jewish survival is the fact that their deathrate is almost as high as the birthrate, an alarming warning about the health of any community and, of all the ethnics, Jews have the lowest birthrate. Thus, intermarriage, together with this declining birthrate, makes the question of survival a very real one.

Another challenge to Jewish survival that has surfaced recently has been the number of so-called Hebrew-Christian groups. One such organization, called Jews for Jesus, is especially threatening to traditional religion because its members are Jews themselves. These groups are essentially missionary in their appeal, attempting to proselytize especially on city streets. College campuses are also attractive centers for their work. Their view is that the two religions are not mutually exclusive, for when a Jew accepts Jesus, he asserts rather than abandons his Jewishness. The American Jewish Committee, however, calls this notion a "theological impossibility" and the Committee and other Jewish groups emphasize combating such missionary efforts.

Secularism and assimilation always negatively influence the Jewish self-image. Many Jews of the prewar period had few qualms about leaving the Jewish community and others took little pride in either Judaism or Jewishness, even to the point of disdaining synagogue affiliation. Their lack of interest often stemmed from a rejection of, or at least an indifference to, the religious element in Jewishness. Instead, they expressed their Jewishness through such secular movements as Zionism or socialism. However, the events before, during, and immediately after World War II changed the religious and secular complexion of the Jewish community.

Nothing better illustrates what has happened since the war than the statistics of congregational affiliation. One may deny that there has been a religious revival, but one cannot negate the fact that there has been a reversal of earlier trends in synagogue membership. According to 1975 figures, a total of 82 percent of Jewish household heads identify with Orthodox, Conservative, or Reform ideologies, though those who are actually congregational members is only 46.3 percent. However, as low as this figure is, between the end of World War II and the 1960s, the Union of American-Hebrew Congregations (Reform) and the United Synagogue (Conservative) more than doubled the number of affiliated congregations and trebled individual memberships (600 and 800 congregations respectively). According to 1978–1979 figures in the *American Jewish Yearbook*, the number of synagogue affiliations is as follows: Orthodox, 83,142; Conservative, 101,449; Reform, 122,447; and others, 37,213. Reform Jews in contemporary America ascribed their increased synagogue membership to a greater religious identity induced by economic depression and disappointing foreign crises. The Orthodox also showed gains. The latter revival in large cities stemmed in part from Hungarian Jews who were saved from Hitler and who came here after 1945. Also, Orthodoxy's vitality is due in part to the growth of the Hassidim, who form a separatist group much like the Pennsylvania Dutch or the Chabad on the campuses. Sociologists and students of religion have noted signs of a new vitality in all American Judaism, but most notably in Orthodoxy. They claim that many young Jews, often children of nonobservant or Reform parents, are gravitating toward the traditional synagogue as an answer to potential assimilation, to offset discontent with modernity, and to seek ways of combatting isolationism.

The reasons for this increase in affiliation did not lie in increased spiritual awareness or more than several days a year synagogue attendance for most, but in a new social awareness developed in the 1950s that Jewishness was bound up with the meaning of Judaism. Attendance at religious services on a daily or weekly basis is quite small and much synagogue attendance revolves around weddings, bar-mitzvahs, and sisterhood meetings, but nevertheless the status of the synagogue as an institution rose in Jewish consciousness and, for one reason or another, it appears as if the centrality of the synagogue will remain.

When many people speak of a return to the synagogue or to its centrality in Jewish life, it is common to equate the return to the synagogue with the move to the suburbs. From a physical and logistical point of view, the dispersion of Jews in suburban settings required new congregations, buildings, and communal organizations. Jews also needed some kind of religious identity. Suburban Christians often thought of themselves and of others in religious terms. To Jews affiliation with a synagogue was a way to conform to the suburban pattern.

The principal reason, cited by almost all observers of postwar Judaism, for the return to the synagogue was an interest in group and family survival. The postwar Jews, the third generation who moved to the suburbs, had no religious quarrel with their parents, felt no restriction in being Jewish, and therefore desired to perpetuate a Jewish identity. That the synagogue is an agency for survival is graphically illustrated in communities where Jews encountered sharp prejudice and discrimination. At such times, increased numbers of Jews seek the protection and security of the synagogue. The synagogue, too, has helped in preventing the erosion of many Jewish families by providing religious consciousness programs, retreats, study groups, and even courses in Jewish cuisine. A specific synagogue service which illustrates a broader orientation to its congregation is provided by one in Minneapolis, Minnesota. This service or "mitzvah" is funerals performed by congregation members. The synagogue membership—a Conservative one—consoles the family, recites prayers, prepares the body, sits with it until burial, and organizes the seven-day mourning period. While caring for the bodies is an ancient tradition, no other synagogue is known to provide such service.

A relatively recent development within Judaism is seen in the *Havurah* "fellowship" movement. Essentially, it consists of small, independent groups combining religious ritual with secularism, away from temples and rabbis and often without reference to Reform, Conservative, or Orthodox practices, or at times, as parts of synagogues. This alternative to establishment religion dates from the 1960s. Often, the *Havurah* meets in a home where there are no pews, altars, etc. Everyone prays together, there is full equality for women and, according to its adherents, spirituality is enhanced by the free-floating nature of this quest for cultural and religious renewal. As of the 1980s, there are as many as several hundred such groups, and one Los Angeles synagogue has sixty of them. Some congregants find the *Havurah* concept more meaningful because they are a part of a small, independently run group as opposed to a large, impersonal synagogue. Important changes mark the internal life of Judaism during the postwar era. Although organizationally the three main groups are separate, there are some evidences of a convergence of practices and beliefs. Reform, for example, which represents approximately one-third of American Jewry, is actually becoming more traditional: there is more Hebrew in the service, Sunday services are virtually abandoned, skull caps are worn, and only a few diehard Reform synagogues preach anti-Zionism. There is also a growing feeling against performing marriages with nonconverted Christians. In Conservative temples, there is more English in services. But, in addition to the subject of women (see below), they are still widely divided about the interpretation of the Jewish law *(Halaka)*.

While there are those who see Reform and Conservative branches coming closer, Orthodoxy seems to be drawing further away from both. Reasons for this include a rising self-confidence among Orthodox Jews and their domination of Israel's religious affairs. And within Orthodoxy, there is a small but discernible liberal ideology. "Modern Orthodoxy" is that movement holding that one can be a practicing Jew and still participate in the general culture. It opposes the older pattern of isolation from secularism and the mainstream of everyday life. A specific branch of this type of Orthodoxy, led by Rabbi Joseph D. Soloveitchik of Boston, holds that Orthodoxy and modern life must proceed hand-in-hand.

An issue of growing interest is the status of women in Judaism. The first woman was ordained into the Reform rabbinate in 1972, and as of 1980, Hebrew Union College (HUC) had graduated twenty three. About 33 percent of the current student body are women. There are also a number of women studying to become cantors at HUC. The Conservative movement's view is unclear. When one Conservative temple agreed to call women to read from the *Torah*, the *New York Times* took note. The Conservative decision to count women for a *minyan* (quorum for religious services) in 1973 attracted attention, the *New York Times* declaring humorously that "the tenth man can be a she." The head of the Conservative rabbinical movement predicted at its 1975 convention that women would serve as rabbis in the foreseeable future. In 1979, the Conservative rabbis decreed that the decision to admit women to the rabbinate would be taken by the Jewish Theological Seminary, but as of 1981, no women had been ordained into the Conservative rabbinate.

Women rabbis serve as educational directors or assistant rabbis of synagogues, or as Hillel rabbis, and there is one woman who serves as a co-rabbi with her husband in a Conservative congregation. In 1979, Linda Joy Holtzman, a graduate of the Reconstructionist Rabbinical College in Philadelphia, was chosen as the sole spiritual leader of a Conservative Synagogue in Coatesville, Pennsylvania. The executive vice president of the Conservative Rabbinical Assembly called her appointment "an historical breakthrough." The Orthodox view is that a Jewish woman's place is in the home, and, in Orthodox congregations, they are segregated from men and take no part in the service. But, inspired by women's liberation, Jewish women are resisting the old stereotypes. Groups have been founded, including the Jewish Feminist Organization in 1974. Feminist *Haggadahs* (Passover ritual books) have increased women's role in the ceremonies. That women are performing a more vital role is seen also in the work of Esther Jungreis. An Orthodox revivalist, this rabbi's wife has attracted large crowds to hear her appeals for increased Jewish identification and for a more fundamentalist practice of the faith. Essentially, her view is that a woman's task is to raise her children as observant Jews. Obviously, whatever the outcome of all these currents, change is in the wind.

As in all religions in contemporary American life, there are conflicting forces of tradition and modernism. Many regard the changes and secularism as a danger, while the dead hand of the past is equally feared by others. The effects of change have long been debated and will remain a perennial issue. The role of the American rabbinate is a case in point. The rabbi bears the imprint of Americanization and suburbanization. He is no longer simply a teacher of *Torah*. He is likely to be a fund-raiser, guidance counselor, educational leader, participant in civic affairs, and interpreter of Judaism for the Christian community. Previously occupied only with pastoral activities such as preaching and teaching, the rabbi is becoming increasingly important as a political activist and community organizer, quite interested, for example, in the outcome of elections. He fulfills the roles that his congregants expect of him as a modern representative of Judaism.

Like other areas of Jewish life, ritual practice has also changed under the impact of America and the suburb. Judaism has become more internalized, with an emphasis upon moral and ethical behavior. And as a result, the sacramental character of the religion has diminished. Secularization has undercut the means by which Judaism sanctified the routine of everyday life. One significant indication of this fact is that over 70 percent of American Jews do not observe *Kashruth* (special preparation of food).

As we have seen, while it is true that there has been a return to the synagogue, for many this return plays a distinctly peripheral role in their lives. As one survey concluded, the synagogue failed to provide a sense of real Jewish community, but rather was more organization and edifice. Larger numbers of Jews affiliated, but except for the High Holidays, fewer worshipped at the regular services. This study noted that the transcendent faith, so prevalent in the past, was being replaced by a type of cultural religion. In the synagogue and religious life as in other phases of Jewish practice, the Jews, like their Christian brethren, have come to reflect more and more stereotyped middle-class values.

One antidote to intermarriage, cultural assimilation, and

religious apathy that some rabbis are now proposing is a Christian-style evangelization program to restore Jewish faith and maybe even to convert Gentiles. The Union of American Hebrew Congregations maintains Judaism has always been a missionary religion, and the primary targeted group for this new thrust are Jews themselves. The Central Conference of American Rabbis has even published a guidebook on Jewish observances for Jews. This missionary drive also aims to convert Gentiles who marry Jews. And some Reform and Conservative rabbis are urging a program among the 61 million Americans who have no religious ties at all. The American Jewish Committee's director of interreligious affairs feels that Jews have a moral obligation to publicize the values and life-styles unique to Judaism. Despite the appeal of missionary activity to many, there is fear among some Jews that evangelical efforts will intensify Christian efforts to convert Jews. Hence, such efforts are at best controversial and afford a very questionable technique to strengthen Jewish life in America.

Whatever the state of the religious life of adults and its meaning for the future, there is no doubt that when it comes to the training of the young, Judaism of every variety is active in teaching the fundamentals of the faith. As stated previously, the main reason for the emphasis on religious education is to assure group survival. Deficiencies, of course, do exist here. As always, one of the great weaknesses is the limitation of most class activity to after the regular secular school routine. Then, too, there are those who feel that the curriculum is impractical and unrelated to everyday life, the caliber of teaching frequently is low, and ambivalent parents often regard Jewish schooling as a peripheral function, not to interfere with their children's music lessons or athletic performance.

But, on the other hand, when compared with the prewar experience, contemporary Jewish education exhibits improvement. Studies both national and local indicate that there is a tendency for increased education of young Jews. In

Rhode Island in 1934, for instance, only 50 percent of the children aged five to fifteen years were in Jewish educational programs, and of that number 60 percent attended only Sunday schools. By the 1960s, however, 75 percent of the children aged five to fourteen were in Jewish schools, and only 40 percent of them were in Sunday classes. On a national level, Jewish educators estimated 53 percent of Jewish children between five and seventeen were receiving Jewish education, and other guesses placed the figure as high as 80 percent. But, more pessimistically, according to 1972 figures, the number of Jewish children in after-school and Sunday school classes dropped from 554,468 in 1966–1967 to 457,196 in 1970–1971. The *American Jewish Yearbook* (1980) estimates that there are 360,000 children in Jewish schools of all kinds, a decline of over 30 percent since 1960. Of the 360,000, about 26 percent are in day schools, 48 percent in afternoon schools two days or more, and 26 percent in a one day a week school. Jewish leaders constantly charge communal organizations with failing to provide a high quality, meaningful educational experience. Ignorance of tradition, indifference among many youth, and a crisis of faith are cited as by-products.

Strongly identified Jews take special pride in the Jewish day school. The growth of such schools has been noteworthy. Growing from 39 schools with a combined enrollment in 1944 of 10,000 to 252 schools with an enrollment of over 60,000 in 1962, to 545 schools with about 92,000 students in 1980, the day schools are now able to provide an intensive Jewish education that is impossible in the limited time available in the afternoon programs. Most day schools are run under Orthodox auspices (86 percent). The very best of these schools are modeled after the most prestigious public and private ones, and they are increasingly becoming more popular as answers to the vexing problem of survival and as substitutes for deteriorating public schools. It has been reported that every city with a Jewish population of seventy-five hundred or more has a day school.

Jewish education on the postsecondary school and adult levels has also been outstanding. For example, Brandeis University in Waltham, Massachusetts, was founded in 1948, the first Jewish-sponsored secular, nonsectarian university. And the Albert Einstein School of Medicine of Yeshiva University is one of the nation's pre-eminent medical centers. The contributions of the Conservative, Orthodox, and Reform seminaries, together with such institutions as Dropsie College, continued into the present era. In 1947, the Jewish Theological Seminary established a West Coast branch in Los Angeles, and the rabbinical college of the Reconstructionist movement (founded in 1967 in Philadelphia), the youngest of these preparatory schools, graduated its first student in 1973.

The widespread Jewish Community Center (or Young Men's and Young Women's Hebrew Association) movement, with its offerings in both general and Jewish subjects, has touched the lives of large numbers of adults and children across the nation. The center, as it is most often called, is an American product whose original purpose was to help Americanize the Jewish immigrant. Unlike other religious and social organizations of the Jews, the community center is intended to appeal to all members of the Jewish community, including the so-called religiously unaffiliated Jews. Centers serve, thus, as a cohesive force within the community and afford a means whereby all Jews can participate in various areas of Jewish interest. Though the centers have offered some typically American adult education fare, such as physical education and arts and crafts, their limited contribution to adult Jewish education has been in those courses dealing with Jewish religion and culture and in the opportunities they have given Jews to express themselves creatively in a Jewish milieu. In the 1970s there were about three hundred centers with almost 900,000 members.

Jewish cultural societies and the Jewish press also attest to the vibrancy of communal life. There is a National Foundation for Jewish Culture, and the work of the American Jewish Historical Society, The Jewish Publication Society, and The YIVO Institute for Jewish Research, to mention only a few agencies, is supported in part by communal funds. The Jewish press is a venerable institution and it is still influential in molding thought and opinion. There are two Yiddish dailies: *The Jewish Daily Forward* (60,000 circulation), and the Communist *Morning Freiheit* (7,000 circulation). Also, more than fifty English-Jewish weeklies in such centers as New York *(Jewish Week)*, Boston *(Jewish Advocate)*, Los Angeles *(B'rith Messenger)*, Miami *(Jewish Floridian)*, Buffalo *(Jewish Review)*, and Philadelphia *(Jewish Exponent)* wield tremendous influence. These papers subscribe to a Jewish version of the Associated Press (Jewish Telegraphic Agency), which brings a kind of unity to American Jewry by providing standardized news. Newspapers, scholarly journals, and periodicals such as *Commentary*, *Midstream*, *Judaism*, *Jewish Social Studies*, *American Jewish Historical Quarterly*, and *American Jewish Archives* serve a community need and reflect the continuous intellectual awareness of the Jewish community.

Another issue that concerned the postwar American Jewish community was that of Zionism and the special relationship between American Jews and the State of Israel. Zionism had come to influence the organizational structure of Jewish life on both the national and local levels. Most synagogues, Jewish community centers, religious schools, and virtually all the organizational societies that composed the American Jewish community espoused the Zionist cause.

With statehood for Israel, the Zionist movement entered a new era marked by confusion about its purpose. During a speech in New York in 1951, Prime Minister David Ben Gurion asserted that a Zionist is one who settles in Israel. His statement initiated an argument which is still not completely resolved. Most American Jews, while eager to assist financially, and while certainly not indifferent to the existence of Israel, rejected the idea of resettlement. From 1948 to 1968, only 8,800 emigrated to Israel and a majority of those returned to America. Even among ardent Zionists there was confusion over the meaning of Zionism. Some held that in theory a Zionist should settle in Israel and that a meaningful life for a Jew is possible only in Israel. Such people often caution that the experience of European Jewry can be repeated in America. American Jews for their part point out that if America is not safe for Jews, then it is doubtful that Jews are safe even in Israel. Despite the arguments of Zionists, American Jews express their brand of Zionism more in giving than in going.

Interestingly, the area in which American Jewry made its greatest contribution to Israel also affected dramatically the quality of American-Jewish life. In their efforts to support the Israeli cause, the Americans marshalled their financial forces and in doing so they had their communal life shaped by this call for assistance. In contrast to the $35 million subscribed in 1945, the United Jewish Appeal raised $101 million the very next year. In 1948, the year the State of Israel was created, donations reached a height of $150 million. In addition to this money, the Israel Bond Drives yielded approximately $365 million in sales during the fifties. Similar large amounts went to Israel during the 1967 crisis, when between May 23 and June 10 American Jews gave $100 million to the Israel Emergency Fund of the United Jewish Appeal (UJA). In 1973 it was estimated that $260 million was raised for UJA; in 1978, Jewish Federation allocations to UJA was 64 per cent and the sale of Israel Bonds amounted to $296 million. Certainly this generosity is a very concrete indication of the closeness which a large portion of American Jewry has felt for Israel.

Besides the weakened American Council For Judaism, the only noticeable Jews who were decidedly antagonistic toward Israel were a number of youth, radical activists, and most often campus-based "New Leftists." These groups surfaced after the Six-Day War and angered establishment sensibilities by likening Israeli action to Nazi slaughter, by describing an imperialistic Israel as a lackey of an aggressor America, and by glorifying the Arab cause. But such sentiments were the voices of a tiny minority. For the great majority of American Jews, there is a commitment to Israel that is as positive as it is powerful, and in the wake of the October, 1973 Yom Kippur war, it became clear that there were few American Jews who would admit to anti-Zionism. Arab intransigence and Soviet hostility pointed up dramatically the need for American-Jewish support of Zionism.

But in contemporary American-Israeli relations there remain philosophical differences of opinion. The fact that being Jewish in America is to be in the minority, while to be a Jew in Israel is to be part of the majority, causes conflicting interpretations of Jewish society. It has been said that because of this minority status American Jews are beset by alienation and marginality and, as we have seen, American Jewish writers often treat this fact as the norm. In Israel, misunderstanding of such alienation contributes to criticism of the American Jews.

The continuing Arab-Israeli crisis, exacerbated by the oil embargoes of the 1970s and '80s and by what some American diplomats have described as Israel's unwillingness to compromise, has created an entirely new dimension in American-Israeli relationships. There are those who feel that because of dependence on Arab oil, the United States is capable of forsaking Israel. But, the independence of Israel remains a priority of American foreign policy, although there is pressure on Israel for some sort of settlement of the festering Arab-Israeli problems, such as yielding land taken in earlier wars. The powerful Israeli lobby in America along with Senator Henry Jackson, ex-Senator Jacob Javits, and others mentioned previously, regarded any possible abandonment of Israel or a diminishing of aid as intolerable. Some Jews even felt that the possible erosion of Jewish influence in America, the decline of sympathy for Israel, and the growth of Arab power all might trigger another wave of anti-Semitism. Thus far, all these tensions and the others detailed in the previous chapter are more possibilities than realities, for American policy is still supportive of Israel. One positive result of the lessened euphoria among American Jews and the increased vulnerability of Israel is the realization that Israel is vital to their sense of identity. In fact, the novelist Elie Wiesel, himself a survivor of the Holocaust, has written in the *New York Times* that he fears the Israelis might become victims of another conflagration. It is no surprise, then, that given this concern for Israel, American Jews raised well over $600 million in the 1974 United Jewish Appeal campaign. And this feeling for Israel's security also explains in part the outcry against General Brown's remarks, the Hassidic activism on campuses, the new ethnic pride that prompted a resurgence of Judaic Studies programs, Jewish Defense League activities, and a more visible concern and lack of inhibition among American Jews.

From time to time, there has been pessimism voiced over the future of the American-Jewish community. Certainly there are challenges to Jewish identity, and widespread alienation is not an optimistic sign. But, on the other hand, the economic comfort of most American Jews, the many evidences of religious affirmation, the more positive feelings about Israel, the number of institutions dedicated to strengthening Jewish identity and to relating it to increased secularization, and the clear record of significant contributions to the cultural health of the nation all mandate optimism. It may well be that the most glorious chapters of American-Jewish history are yet to be written.

Epilogue _____

THE THREE MOST SIGNIFICANT events in modern Jewish history have been the disappearance of the European center as the matrix of Jewish activity, the rebirth of the State of Israel, and the rise of the American-Jewish community to a pre-eminent position.

The United States spawned the development of the largest, most powerful and affluent settlement in all the history of the Jewish people. Almost 6 million Jews (5,920,900 in 1981) out of a world population of over 14 million Jews (14,396,000) reside in the United States, constituting 2.7 percent of the American population. Close to 2 million (1,998,000) live in Greater New York alone, and the next four largest centers of Jewish residence are Los Angeles (503,000), Philadelphia (295,000), Chicago (253,000), and Miami (225,000). Most Jews are metropolitan dwellers, but within these areas, they are concentrating more and more in the suburbs. The South and the West contain 30.2 percent of the total American Jewish population compared to 69.8 percent in the Northeast and North Central United States. The figure for the Sunbelt has been steadily increasing.

The American Jewish community is also an aging one, for one out of nine is sixty-five years or more (compared to one out of ten for non-Jews). The average size of the American-Jewish family is 3.1 persons and the birthrate is quite low—a source of concern.

The noteworthy economic fact of Jewish life in America has been their phenomenal rise in social-economic status. Firmly ensconced in the upper regions of middle-class life, securely buffered from economic reverses by concentration in high-status occupations (almost 8 percent are in white-collar jobs), and armed with more college degrees than the non-Jewish population, the American Jews have become among the most successful and comfortable of all ethnic and religious groups. In the United States the Jews belong not to the "have nots" but to the "haves."

Though education has traditionally been a basic part of the Jewish value structure, Jewish religious instruction has long been and is still rather weak. This deficiency stems largely from inadequate teacher preparation, the lure of secularism, the need for a relevant curriculum, and the part-time nature of most Jewish schooling. On the other hand, many young people attend day schools, and almost 70 percent in the eight to twelve age group are enrolled in some form of Jewish education. These figures confirm the feeling that Jewish education is considered vital for survival.

For Jews, secular education has been the path to upward mobility, professional advancement, and occupational status. In 1960, over 60 percent of the Jews graduated from secondary schools and 22 percent from college. And for the 1970s, the proportion of Jews in universities was twice that of the general population and, for graduate and professional schools, the figure was triple that for other students. Not surprisingly, therefore, the number of Jews in the professions is much higher than that of non-Jews.

The issue of Jewish identification in the secular university environment has been persistent. The Hillel Foundation, founded in 1923 and which still thrives, and the Chabad movement are two attempts to deal with this situation. While there are still problems of identification, there are also positive forces at work among Jewish students—the greater acceptance of their Jewishness, the study of Jewish life and history as part of the curriculum, and the establishment of courses, majors, and chairs of Judaica, relatively recent phenomena. Jewish Studies programs are common in nondenominational and public universities, but courses in this area are also available in sectarian schools. Of interest is the announcement in 1981 that Judaic Studies will be available at the University of Notre Dame.

This driving emphasis on education—both religious and secular—in part accounts for the stellar Jewish role in the cultural and intellectual life of the nation. Those achievements, as we have seen, are apparent in every period of American history, but since the end of the Second World War, there has been a new flowering, particularly in the work of Jewish novelists. Their portrayal of the alienated and complex individual has meaning not only for Jews, but also for the non-Jewish intelligentsia as well.

A positive aspect of Jewish life in America is the bond that has grown with Israel. The United States government and American Jewry have furnished the financial and diplomatic underpinnings of that nation, and Israel for its part has enhanced the self-image and positive identification of American Jewry. We have already seen that the American Jewish financial support of Israel has been enormous. The total U.S. government economic, military, and other aid has also been noteworthy: $15,193 million from 1976 to 1981. A less encouraging aspect of the Israeli-American relationship has been the identification of Israel by New Left radicals with what they refer to as American imperialism. However, with enhanced Jewish consciousness, this feeling has diminished, and for committed Jews, Israel is in large part responsible for this new sense of pride.

The saddest part of the American Jewish experience has been recurrent anti-Semitism. While the blatant forms associated with the years of adjustment early in the century, the conservative twenties, and the Depression tensions of the thirties such as the Ku Klux Klan and the American Nazi movement have been reduced, there are still manifestations. No longer is anti-Semitism, or anti-Zionism, limited to the far right, but it is also to be found in admirers of the Third World and even by other minority groups, especially by some black extremists. Much contemporary anti-Semitic propaganda equates Israel and Zionism and anti-Jewish feeling. Increasing Jewish student disenchantment with the Third World has played a part in the waning of the New Left.

Certain to fill lecture halls and provide heated discourse is the subject of Jewish identification and survival. It has been estimated that 20 percent of contemporary Jewry are committed to the faith, 40 percent admit to nominal synagogue affiliation (meaning attendance on the High Holy Days), 30 percent are unconcerned, and 10 percent deny any loyalty to Judaism. Those who are most concerned over survival cite the tendency toward intermarriage and conversion. While trends are hard to isolate and statistical evidence can be mustered to prove many things, reports indicate a growing number of intermarriages even though most rabbis, especially the Conservative and Orthodox ones, are opposed to marrying such couples unless there is conversion of the non-Jewish partner.

Another problem vexing Jewish thought is the future of the family. Intermarriage, together with declining birth rates, the relaxation of sexual codes, and youthful infatuation with other faiths, has caused Jewish thinkers to seriously reevaluate the future of the Jewish family. A population of only 6 million, increasing intermarriage, and the rise in divorce among Jewish couples are cited as factors causing concern. Even some of the women's liberationist feelings have cut into the traditional cohesive role of the Jewish mother and her insistence on the observation of rituals.

There are other concerns about Jewish security. Black-Jewish relations are more strained in the 1980s than a decade before. The black affinity for the Third World is not always distinguishable from anti-Semitism. And also, the growth of fundamental Christianity, evangelical fundamentalists seeking to elect "born-again" and God-fearing Christians to public office, seems exclusionary to the American Jewish community.

Since the late 1960s, there has occurred a new challenge to the Jewish community—the more than half a million Jews chiefly from Israel and the Soviet Union. Seeking greater freedom as well as improved economic opportunities, these Jews are a problem for the contemporary Jewish community as the East European Jews earlier aroused concern for the established German group. A *New York Times* article (December 7, 1980) estimated that one out of every ten to twelve Jews in America have been here less than a decade. These figures include about 350,000 Israelis, 75,000 Soviet Jews since 1972 alone, and other smaller groups such as 20,000 Iranians, Canadians, Latin Americans, and South Africans. These people have placed an obvious strain on Jewish agencies and their programs of support, but, on the other hand, with a declining birthrate and increased intermarriage, American Jewry needs these newer immigrants as reinforcements.

While predictions for the future of Jews in the United States are often dire and dark, there are also definite areas of hope. As we have seen, all ethnic and religious groups are enjoying a new importance, and increase in pride among Jews is most salutary. A recent survey of eighty major colleges disrupted fears of mass conversions and revealed that only a negligible percentage of Jewish youth were responding to such Christian fundamentalist movements as the Campus Crusade for Christ. Also, there are reports which indicate that where there is intermarriage, the number of conversions to Judaism is increasing, as is the number of children of intermarried couples who are or who will be raised as Jews.

Despite some indications to the contrary, there are also strengths in the traditionally important institutions of family, community, and synagogue. The generation gap, the embracing by youth of radical causes, intermarriage, and divisiveness in the family have not destroyed these areas of Jewish life. The religious press, welfare agencies, Jewish centers, and many other institutions continue to play prominent roles in maintaining the faith. And while secularization has been a long-standing challenge to the synagogue, the temples are not languishing, but remain the most cohesive bond in the entire Jewish complex. Perhaps part of the reason is that the synagogue has responded to American culture in the numerous secular functions that it now performs. English is the language of part of Reform and Conservative services, and in most Orthodox synagogues the sermon is delivered in English. The rabbi has also taken on many functions that are peculiarly American. For many Jews, then, the synagogue performs a greater social and educational than religious function.

Although one can identify a Jewish community, there is no question that its members are part of the larger American culture, and that there has been a great and successful degree of integration within American society. Native-born Jews at various class levels are similar to native-born non-Jews of the same social classes. In matters of dress, speech pattern, and manner there is little difference between most Jews and those of other religious beliefs. But, of course, the Jews are a minority with a heritage, values, and way of life different from those of the majority of Americans. There are certain intrinsic values, such as a liberal political philosophy, a stress on education, and a strong family life, which could be called peculiarly Jewish, but these traits have been woven into the American cultural context. The Jewish community still plays an important part in the lives of most American Jews. There are many reasons each individual chooses to identify with the Jewish community—tradition, common attitudes and interests, a need to belong to some group, a sense of shared destiny, worries about anti-Semitism, and the fact that others who are close to you belong. An American-Jewish community will continue for some to be based primarily on religious beliefs, but for others, a sense of common identity is more important. Whatever the conclusions, one fact is certain. The American-Jewish story has been replete with unprecedented challenges and even traumas, but out of a unique accommodation has come one of the most positive and creative aspects of the entire saga of the Jewish people.

Annotated
Bibliography _____

A BIBLIOGRAPHY COVERING even so relatively short a timespan as the period since 1900 must be highly selective. Only those volumes I consider major or most provocative in theme are listed. I have arbitrarily omitted specific articles in periodicals, biographies, reminiscences, the many fictional accounts of American-Jewish life and those works that cover aspects of American-Jewish history before approximately 1870.

Among the many periodicals and reports that contain valuable information are: *The American Jewish Yearbook* (1899 to date), *Publications of the American Jewish Historical Society* (1893 to date; called *American Jewish History* since 1961), *American Jewish Archives* (1948 to date), *Contemporary Jewish Record* (1938 to date), *Jewish Social Studies* (1939 to date), *Judaism* (1952 to date), *Midstream* (1955 to date), *Commentary* (1945 to date), *Davka* (1970 to date), *American Jewish Committee Annual Report* (1911 to date), *YIVO Annual of Jewish Social Science* (1946 to date), and the Yearbooks and Annual Reports of the United Synagogue of America, the Central Conference of American Rabbis, the Union of American Hebrew Congregations, and the Union of Orthodox Jewish Congregations of America.

The number of adequate histories of the Jews in America is limited. Several are of the elementary-religious school variety, such as Ruth Gay, *Jews in America, A Short History* (New York: Basic Books, 1965); Lee J. Levinger, *A History of the Jews in the United States* (Cincinnati: Union of American Hebrew Congregations, 1935, etc.); Deborah Pessin, *History of the Jews in America* (New York: The United Synagogue of America, 1957); and Jerome Ruderman, *Jews in American History, A Leader's Guide* (New York: Ktav, 1974). Morris U. Schappes *The Jews in the United States* (New York: Citadel Press, 1958) is an interesting pictorial history. Among the more substantial volumes are Nathan Glazer, *American Judaism* (Chicago: University of Chicago Press, 1957, 1972); Oscar Handlin, *Adventure in Freedom* (New York: McGraw Hill, 1954); Judd L. Teller, *Strangers and Natives: The Evolution of the American Jew from 1921 to the Present* (New York: Delacorte Press, 1968); Marshall Sklare, *America's Jews* (New York: Random House, 1971); Rufus Learsi, *The Jews in America: A History* (Cleveland: World Publishing Co., 1954, 1972). In the 1972 edition, there is an Epilogue, "American Jewry, 1954–1971," by Abraham J. Karp. Max I. Dimont, *The Jews in America* (New York: Simon and Schuster, 1978) is a short but provocative text account. The best survey is Henry L. Feingold, *Zion in America* (New York: Hippocrone Books, 1974).

Background historical information on twentieth-century American Jewry is well detailed in Louis Wirth's classic of the ghetto as an institution of social significance, *The Ghetto* (Chicago: University of Chicago Press, 1928); Hutchin Hapgood, *The Spirit of the Ghetto* (New York: Allograph Press, 1965); Charles S. Bernheimer, *The Russian Jew in the United States* (New York and Chicago: A. H. Kelley, 1971; originally published in Philadelphia by John C. Winston Co., 1905); Allon Schoener, ed., *Portal to America: The Lower East Side, 1870–1925* (New York: Holt, Rinehart and Winston,

1967), a handsomely produced collection of readings recreating the cultural climate of the ghetto; Ande Manners, *Poor Cousins* (New York: Coward, McCann and Geohegan, 1972), an appealing, nostalgic, treatment of the East European immigrants; Harry Roskolenko, *The Time That Was Then, The Lower East Side, 1900–1914* (New York: Dial Press, 1971); Ronald Sanders, *The Downtown Jews* (New York: Harper & Row, 1969), a serious study of the immigrant generation (1880–1914); Elkanah Schwartz, *American Life: Shtetl Style* (New York: J. David, 1967). See also Samuel Joseph, *Jewish Immigration to the United States from 1881 to 1910* (New York: Arno Press, 1969). Isaac Metzker has edited *A Bintel Brief* (Garden City, N.J.: Doubleday, 1971), a collection of those famous "Bundles of Letters" that appeared in the *Jewish Daily Forward.* Irving Howe has written an outstanding and lengthy work on the whole question of East European Jewish assimilation: *World of our Fathers* (New York: Simon and Schuster, 1975).

The contribution of American Jews is the subject of Sydney G. Gumpertz, *The Jewish Legion of Valor; The Story of Americans of Jewish Faith Who Distinguished Themselves in the Armed Forces in All the Wars of the Republic and a General History of the Military Exploits of the Jews Through the Ages* (New York, no publisher listed, 1946); J. George Fredman and Louis A. Falk, *Jews in American Wars* (New York: Jewish War Veterans of the U.S., 1942, 1943, 1954), the story of American Jewish war heroes; Rachel DuBois and Emma Schweppe eds., *The Jews in American Life* (New York: T. Nelson and Sons, 1935); and Robert St. John, *Jews, Justice, and Judaism: A Narrative of the Role Played by the Bible People in Shaping American History* (Garden City, N.J.: Doubleday, 1969). On an elementary school level, but still helpful, are Deborah Karp, *Heroes of American Jewish History* (New York: Ktav, 1972); Tina N. Levitan, *The Firsts of American Jewish History* (Brooklyn: Charoth Press, 1952, 1957), and *Jews in American Life* (New York: Hebrew Pub., 1969).

There are many volumes that afford interesting insights into the mind of the American Jew. Elliott E. Cohen has edited a collection of articles from *Commentary* on such subjects as, for example, Jewish college students and the Jewish community: *Commentary on the American Scene: Portraits of Jewish Life in America* (New York: Knopf, 1953). Theodore Friedman and Robert Gordis's edited collection, *Jewish Life in America* (New York: Horizon Press, 1955), contains essays on religion, labor, education, Yiddish literature, etc. A classic is Oscar Janowsky, ed., *The American Jew—A Composite Portrait* (New York: Harper, 1942), also a collection of essays on Jewish life (i.e., synagogue, literature, Zionism, community, anti-Semitism, education, etc.). An interesting anthology containing articles from the *Publications of the American Jewish Historical Society* is Abraham Karp, ed., *The Jewish Experience in America* (Waltham, Mass.: American Jewish Historical Society, 1969). Another collection is from the American Jewish Archives, Jacob R. Marcus, *Critical Studies in American Jewish History* (Cincinnati: American Jewish Archives 1971; New York: Ktav, 1971). Daniel P. Moynihan and Nathan Glazer, *Beyond the Melting Pot* (Cambridge, Mass.: M.I.T. Press, 1962) is an analytical comparative study of several New York City minority groups, including Jews. Ernest Van den Haag, *The Jewish Mystique* (New York: Stein and Day, 1969) combines insights of psychology and sociology to produce interesting and entertaining essays about the significance of being an American Jew. A popular and graphic work that shows much research is James Yaffe, *The American Jews* (New York: Random House, 1968). See also the insightful Sig Altman, *The Comic Image of the Jew: Explorations of a Pop Culture Phenomenon* (Rutherford, N.J.: Fairleigh Dickenson University Press, 1971) and Marshall Sklare, ed., *The Jews: Social Patterns of an American Group* (New York: Free Press, 1958). Sklare's more recent compilations, *The Jew in American Society* (New York: Behrman House, 1974) and *The Jewish Community in America* (New York: Behrman House, 1974), treat such issues as immigration, the "East Side," the Jewish mother, Jewish academics, intermarriage, suburbia, the branches of Judaism, the New Left, Jewish education, and Jewish-Gentile relations. Rudolf Glanz's *Studies in Judaica Americana* (New York: Ktav, 1971), is a collection of essays on such topics as German-Jewish immigration, Jewish peddling, and Jews and Chinese in America. Older, but still important, is *Jews in America* (New York: Random House, 1936), which put to rest a number of myths about American Jews (originally published in *Fortune*, Vol. 13 [February 1936]).

Rabbi Meir Kahane, founder of the Jewish Defense League, has written provocative explanations of his work, presenting himself as a champion of a new, radical Jewish action program, in *Never Again! A Program for Survival* (Los Angeles: Nash Pub., 1971), *The Story of the Jewish Defense League* (Radnor, Penn.: Clifton Book Co., 1975), and *Time to Go Home* (Los Angeles: Nash Pub., 1972). See also Janet L. Dolgin, *Jewish Identity and the JDL* (Princeton, N.J.: Princeton University Press, 1977).

There are a number of works that attempt an evaluation of the quality of American-Jewish life and also in some cases, the American-Jewish future. Only a selected few are listed: David Sidorsky, ed., *The Future of the Jewish Community in America* (New York: Basic Books, 1972); Stuart E. Rosenberg, *America Is Different: The Search for Jewish Identity* (Toronto: Nelson, 1964); C. Bezalel Sherman, *The Jews Within American Society* (Detroit: Wayne State University Press, 1961); Morris N. Kertzer, *Today's American Jew* (New York: McGraw-Hill, 1967); Marshall Sklare and Joseph Greenblum, *Jewish Identity on the Suburban Frontier* (New York: Basic Books, 1967); Charles H. Stember et al., *Jews in the Mind of America* (New York: Basic Books, 1966); Abraham J. Feldman, *The American Jew* (New York: Bloch Publishing Co., 1959); Samuel H. Dresner, *The Jew in American Life* (New York: Crown, 1969); Sanford Goldner, *Perspectives in American Jewish Life* (Los Angeles: Jewish

Information Service, 1959); Benjamin Efron, ed., *Currents and Trends in Contemporary Jewish Thought* (New York: Ktav, 1965); Norman Kiell, comp., *The Psycho-dynamics of American Jewish Life* (New York: Twayne Publishers, 1967); Mordecai M. Kaplan, *The Future of the American Jew* (New York: Macmillan, 1948); John Spargo, *The Jew and American Ideals* (New York: Harper and Bros., 1921); Philip D. Bookstaber, *Judaism and the American Mind in Theory and Practice* (New York: Bloch Publishing Co., 1939); and Albert I. Gordon, *Jews in Transition* (Minneapolis: University of Minnesota Press, 1949).

Gerald S. Strober's *American Jews: Community in Crisis* (Garden City, N.Y.: Doubleday, 1974) deals with such American-Jewish challenges as Israel, Soviet Jewry, Christian and black relations, politics, etc. A classic analysis of the American-Jewish milieu is Mordecai M. Kaplan, *Judaism as a Civilization: Toward a Reconstruction of American-Jewish Life* (New York: Macmillan, 1934). This book is the Bible of the Reconstructionist movement. Joseph L. Blau's *Judaism in America* (Chicago: University of Chicago Press, 1976) contains both a historical sketch of American Jewish history and what he refers to as twentieth century alternatives, i.e., Protestantization, Reform, Zionism, Jews and non-Jews, and an interesting section on the Americanization of American Judaism. Also, Marie Syrkin's *The State of Jews* (Washington, D.C.: New Republic Books, 1980) is what she calls her concerns about "the riddle of Jewish experiences in our times." Milton R. Konvitz's *Judaism and the American Idea* (Ithaca, N.Y.: Cornell University Press, 1978) shows how American and Jewish traditions contribute to human rights and freedom and how they relate to each other. Arthur Hertzberg's *Being Jewish in America: The Modern Experience* (New York: Schocken Books, 1979) is a lucid, provocative examination of Jews and the modern world, the American-Jewish experience, and Zionism and Israel. Specifically, there are essays on anti-Semitism, Negro-Jewish relations, the Holocaust, education, and the rabbinate.

While many of the above works deal with the overall problem of today's Jew in America, the following are more specific in their treatment. For example, there is Roland B. Gittelsohn, *My Beloved Is Mine* (New York: Union of American Hebrew Congregations, 1969), a treatment of marriage, and *Modern Jewish Problems* (Cincinnati: Union of American Hebrew Congregations, 1941), a popular textbook for high school classes and youth groups; Anita L. Lebeson, *Recall to Life—The Jewish Woman in America* (S. Brunswick, N.J.: T. Yoseloff, 1970); Gwen G. Schwartz and Barbara Wyden, *The Jewish Wife* (New York: P. H. Wyden, 1969); Charlotte Baum, Paula Hyman, and Sonya Michel, *The Jewish Woman in America* (New York: Dial Press, 1976), a socio-cultural survey of Jewish women in the United States, especially since 1920, which stresses the forces shaping their activities and their image in American fiction as both domineering mother and "Jewish-American Princess." See also Rudolph Glanz, *The Jewish Woman in America: Two Female Immigrant Generations, 1820-1929:* Vol. I, *East European Jewish Women*; Vol. II, *The German-Jewish Woman* (New York: Ktav and National Council of Jewish Women, 1976). Also quite helpful are David Jay, ed., *Growing Up Jewish* (New York: William Morrow, 1969); Louis A. Berman, *Jews and Intermarriage* (New York: T. Yoseloff, 1968); Robert J. Milch, *How to Be an American Jew* (New York: T. Yoseloff, 1969), a cynical, irreverent, tongue-in-cheek work; and Alan W. Miller, *God of Daniel S: In Search of the American Jew* (New York: Macmillan, 1969).

On the branches of Judaism, see Mordecai Kaplan, *Judaism as a Civilization* (New York: Macmillan, 1934); Moshe Davis, *The Emergence of Conservative Judaism* (Philadelphia: Jewish Publication Society of America, 1963); Marshall Sklare, *Conservative Judaism* (Glencoe, Ill.: Free Press, 1955); Abraham J. Karp, *A History of the United Synagogue of America, 1913-1963* (New York: United Synagogue of America, 1964); David Philipson, *Reform Movement in Judaism* (New York: Macmillan, 1931); and

Julian Morgenstern, *As a Mighty Stream: The Progress of Judaism Through History* (Philadelphia: Jewish Publication Society of America, 1949).

One of the unique, popular, and perceptive commentators on the American-Jewish heritage and contemporary scene is Harry L. Golden, editor of *The Carolina Israelite* from 1944-1968. A few of his books are *Only in America* (Cleveland: World Publishing Co., 1960), a study of the back peddler; *Forgotten Pioneer* (Cleveland: World Publishing Co., 1963); *Your're Entitle'* (Cleveland: World Publishing Co., 1962); and *Long Live Columbus* (New York: G. P. Putnam, 1975).

Unique in its field is Bernard Postal and Lionel Koppman, *A Jewish Tourist's Guide to the U.S.* (Philadelphia: Jewish Publication Society of America, 1954), interesting not only for its handbook aspects, but for its background and history. Postal and Koppman's *American-Jewish Landmarks: A Travel Guide and History*, Vol. I (New York: Fleet Press Corp., 1978) is the first of three volumes to be published and deals with the Northeast; it is a catalogue of hard-to-find information. Also unusual is Richard Siegel, Michael Strassfeld, and Sharon Strassfeld, *The Jewish Catalog: A Do-It-Yourself Kit* (Philadelphia: Jewish Publication Society of America, 1973), a compendium of information about Jewish customs, publications, food, rituals, etc.; and Mae Shafter Rockland, *The Jewish Yellow Pages* (New York: Schocken Books, 1976 and S.B.S. Inc., 1980), a directory of goods and services needed to live a Jewish life. Very useful in understanding some of the ingredients of American-Jewish popular culture is an article by Norman L. Friedman, "Jewish Popular Culture in Contemporary America," *Judaism* (Summer 1975), pp. 263-77. See also Neil Levin, compiler and arranger, *Songs of the American Jewish Experience* (Chicago: Board of Jewish Education, 1971).

General communal issues are the subject of Will Maslow, *The Structure and Functioning of the American Jewish Community* (New York: American Jewish Congress, 1974);

Robert Morris and Michael Freund, eds., *Trends and Issues in Jewish Social Welfare in the United States, 1899–1952* (Philadelphia: Jewish Publication Society of America, 1966); Harry L. Lurie, *The Jewish Federation Movement in America: A Heritage Affirmed* (Philadelphia: Jewish Publication Society of America, 1961); Edward E. Grusd, *B'nai B'rith: The Story of a Covenant* (New York: Appleton-Century, 1966); Maurice J. Karpf, *Jewish Community Organization in the United States* (New York: Bloch Publishing Co., 1938, 1971); Boris D. Bogen, *Jewish Philanthropy: An Exposition of Principles and Methods of Jewish Social Service in the United States* (Montclair, N.J.: Patterson Smith, 1969); Abraham J. Karp, *To Give Life: The UJA in the Shaping of the American Jewish Community* (New York: Schocken Books, 1981); Naomi W. Cohen, *Not Free to Desist: The American Jewish Committee, 1906–1966* (Philadelphia: Jewish Publication Society of America, 1972); Albert I Gordon, *Jews in Suburbia* (Boston: Beacon Press, 1959), a treatment of the suburban scene on a national basis; Peter I Rose, *Strangers in Their Midst* (Ann Arbor: University Microfilms, 1959), on small-town Jews and their neighbors; and Yonathan Shapiro, *The Friendly Society: The History of the Workmen's Circle*, (New York: Media Judaica, 1971). A study of Jewish poverty is *Poor Jews: An American Awakening*, edited by Naomi Levine and Martin Rochbaum (New Brunswick, N.J.: Transaction Books, 1974). Thomas J. Cottle, *Hidden Survivors, Portraits of Poor Jews in America*, (Englewood Cliffs, N.J.: Prentice-Hall, 1980) is another study of economically depressed Jewish Americans. For an examination of a contemporary Jewish communal concern, see William W. Orbach, *The American Movement to Aid Soviet Jews* (Amherst, Mass.: University of Massachusetts Press, 1979).

On Yiddish, see Joshua A. Fishman, *Yiddish in America: Socio-Linguistic Description and Analysis* (Rutherford, N.J.: Research Center for Language and Semiotic Studies, 1965); and Leo Rosten's popular *The Joys of Yiddish* (New York:

McGraw-Hill 1968), which is more than a dictionary. For an interesting study of Yiddish theater see David S. Lifson, *The Yiddish Theater in America* (New York: T. Yoseloff, 1965). For information on immigrants and immigration, see Lyman C. White, *300,000 New Americans: The Epic of a Modern Immigrant-Aid Service* (New York: Harper, 1957); and Sheldon M. Neuringer, *American Jewry and U.S. Immigration Policy, 1881-1953* (Madison: University of Wisconsin Press, 1969, 1971).

On Jewish education, see Alexander M. Dushkin and Uriah Z. Engelman, *Report of the Commission for the Study of Jewish Education in the United States* (New York: American Association for Jewish Education, 1959); Lloyd P. Gartner, *Jewish Education in the United States* (New York: Teachers College Press, 1969); and Jack Cohen, *Jewish Education in a Democratic Society* (New York: Reconstructionist Press, 1964).

Philip R. Goldstein, *Centers in My Life* (New York: Bloch Publishing Co., 1964) traces the development of Jewish Centers from the 1920s to the 1960s. See also Louis Kraft, *A Century of the Jewish Community Center Movement, 1854-1952* (New York: Jewish Community Center Centennial Committee, 1953).

For the Jewish labor movement, consult Melech Epstein, *Jewish Labor in U.S.A.: An Industrial, Political and Cultural History of the Jewish Labor Movement*, 2 vols. (New York: Trade Union Sponsoring Committee, 1950).

There have been a number of helpful histories of American Jewish communities. For example, see Selig Adler and Thomas E. Connolly, *From Ararat to Suburbia: A History of the Jewish Community of Buffalo* (Philadelphia: Jewish Publication Society of America, 1960); Joseph Brandes, *Immigrants to Freedom* (Philadelphia: University of Pennsylvania Press, 1971), on Jewish communities in rural New Jersey since 1882; Sidney Goldstein and Calvin Goldscheider, *Jewish Americans: Three Generations in a Jewish Community (Providence, R.I.)* (Englewood Cliffs, N.J.: Prentice-

Hall, 1968); Arthur A. Goren, *New York Jews and the Quest for Community: The Kehillah Experiment, 1908-1922* (New York: Columbia University Press, 1970); Solomon Poll, *The Hasidic Community of Williamsburg* (New York: Free Press of Glencoe, 1962); S. Joshua Kohn, *The Jewish Community in Utica, New York, 1847-1948* (New York: American Jewish Historical Society, 1959); W. Gunther Plaut, *The Jews in Minnesota* (New York: American Jewish Historical Society, 1959); Moses Rischin, *The Promised City: New York's Jews, 1870-1914* (Cambridge: Harvard University Press, 1962); A. F. Landesman, *Brownsville: The Birth, Development and Passing of a Jewish Community in New York* (New York: Bloch Publishing Company, 1971); Stuart E. Rosenberg, *The Jewish Community in Rochester, 1843-1925* (New York: Columbia University Press, 1954); B. G. Rudolph, *From a Minyan to a Community (Syracuse, N.Y.)* (Syracuse: Syracuse University Press, 1970); and Max Vorspan and Lloyd P. Gartner, *History of the Jews of Los Angeles* (Philadelphia: Jewish Publication Society of America, 1970). See also Leonard Dinnerstein and Mary Dale Palsson, eds., *Jews in the South* (Baton Rouge: Louisiana State University Press, 1973).

Jewish-Gentile problems and anti-Semitism are explored in Benjamin B. Ringer, *The Edge of Friendliness: A Study of Jewish-Gentile Relations* (New York: Basic Books, 1967); Gertrude J. Selznick and Stephen Steinberg, *The Tenacity of Prejudice: Anti-Semitism in Contemporary America* (New York: Harper & Row, 1969); Carey McWilliams, *A Mask for Privilege: Anti-Semitism in American* (Boston: Little, Brown, 1948); Arthur Gilbert, *A Jew in Christian America* (New York: Sheed and Ward, 1966); and Marshall Sklare, Joseph Greenblum, and Benjamin B. Ringer, *Not Quite at Home: How an American Jewish Community Lives with Itself and Its Neighbors* (New York: Institute of Human Relations Press, American Jewish Committee, 1969). Also of interest is Nathan C. Belth, *A Promise to Keep: A Narrative of the American Encounter with Anti-Semitism* (New York:

Quadrangle/New York Times Book Co., Inc., 1979). Two works by Leonard Dinnerstein are helpful in explaining generalizations about anti-Semitism and also in providing specific instances: *Anti-Semitism in the United States* (New York: Holt, Rinehart and Winston, 1971), a collection of essays, and *The Leo Frank Case* (New York: Columbia University Press, 1968), a full treatment of the famous Southern anti-Semitic incident, 1913–1915. Arnold Forster's and Benjamin R. Epstein's *The New Anti-Semitism* (New York: McGraw-Hill, 1974) describes the prejudice that emanates from the so-called "respectable" elements—government, the arts, the clergy—and also discusses the anti-Semitism of the black extremists and the radical right and left. Michael N. Dobkowski's *The Tarnished Dream: The Basis of American Anti-Semitism* (Westport, Conn.: Greenwood Press, 1979) is a convenient summation of anti-Semitism, emphasizing religious factors, the "criminal Jew," the Shylock image, patrician anti-Semitism, radical Jews, and unassimilable Jews. This work, a major re-evaluation of Judeophobia, argues that the link between anti-Semitism and American idology is strong, and much of Dobkowski's conclusion is based on popular literature. *The Dearborn Independent, The International Jew, The World's Foremost Problem* (Dearborn, Mich.: Dearborn Publishing Company, 1920) is a collection of that newspaper's historic articles on anti-Semitism. Will Herberg's famous *Protestant, Catholic, Jew* (Garden City: Anchor Books, 1955) is a classic comparative treatment.

The Nazi influence in America is the theme of Sander A. Diamond, *The Nazi Movement in the United States 1924–1941* (Ithaca, N.Y.: Cornell University Press, 1974); and Leland V. Bell, *In Hitler's Shadow: The Anatomy of American Nazism* (Port Washington: Kennikat Press, 1973). See also Shlomo Shafir, *The Impact of the Jewish Crisis on American-German Relations, 1933–1939* (Washington, D.C.: n.p., 1971).

For the special relationships of blacks and Jews, see

Shlomo Katz, ed., *Negro and Jew: An Encounter in America* (New York: Macmillan, 1967); Nat Hentoff, ed., *Black Anti-Semitism and Jewish Racism* (New York: Schocken Books, 1969); Ben Halpern, *Jews and Blacks* (New York: Herder and Herder, 1971); and Robert G. Weisbord and Arthur Stein, *Bittersweet Encounter, The Afro-American and the American Jew* (Westport, Conn.: Negro University Press, 1970). The strained relation between blacks and Jews during the New York school strikes of 1968 is treated in Maurice R. Berube and Marilyn Gittell, et al., *Confrontation at Ocean Hill-Brownsville* (New York: Praeger, 1969).

Jewish relationships with other white minorities are examined in Rudolf Glanz, *Jew and Italian: Historic Group Relations and the New Immigration (1881–1924)* (New York: Ktav, 1971); and *Jew and Irish: Historic Group Relations and Immigration* (New York: Ktav, 1966).

For American-Jewish political issues, see Lawrence H. Fuchs, *The Political Behavior of American Jews* (Glencoe, Ill.: Free Press, 1956); Nathaniel Weyl, *The Jew in American Politics* (New Rochelle, N.Y.: Arlington House, 1968); Stephen D. Isaacs, *Jews and American Politics* (Garden City, N.Y.: Doubleday, 1974); William R. Heitzmann, *American-Jewish Voting Behavior* (Palo Alto, Calif., Rand Research Associates, 1975); and William S. Berlin, *On the Edge of Politics: The Roots of Jewish Political Thought in America* (Westport, Conn.: Greenwood Press, 1978).

Jewish radical politics are treated in Mordechai Chertoff, ed., *The New Left and the Jews* (New York: G. P. Putnam, 1971); Melech Epstein, *The Jew and Communism: The Story of Early Communist Victories and Ultimate Defeats in the Jewish Community, U.S.A., 1919–1941* (New York: Trade Union Sponsoring Committee, 1959); and Arthur Liebman's *Jews and the Left* (New York: John Wiley & Sons, 1979), which examines Jewish radical concerns from its beginnings in Czarist Russia to the New Left of the 1960s and 1970s.

Of the many works on Jewish-American literature, see Leslie Fiedler, *The Jews in the American Novel* (New York:

Herzl Press, 1966); Sanford Pinsker, *The Schlemiel as Metaphor: Studies in the Yiddish and American Jewish Novel* (Carbondale, Ill.: Southern Illinois University Press, 1971); and Sol Liptzin, *The Jew in American Literature* (New York: Bloch Publishing Co., 1966). Irving Malin, in *Jews and Americans* (Carbondale, Ill.: Southern Illinois University Press, 1965) examines the work of such Jewish-American authors as Leslie Fiedler, Saul Bellow, and Philip Roth and finds that despite a rebellion against traditional Judaism, the authors do express Jewishness. See also his *Contemporary American-Jewish Literature* (Bloomington, Ind.: Indiana University Press, 1973). Another treatment of American-Jewish literati is Max F. Schulz, *Radical Sophistication: Studies in Contemporary Jewish American Novelists* (Athens, Ohio: Ohio University Press, 1969). Allen Guttmann's study, *The Jewish Writer in America: Assimilation and the Crisis of Identity* (New York, Oxford University Press, 1971), treats American Jewish literature in terms of a conflict between the *shtetl* heritage and the emancipated life in the United States and of the resultant fears of assimilation. See also Bernard Cohen, *Sociocultural Changes in American Jewish Life as Reflected in Selected Jewish Literature* (Rutherford, N.J.: Fairleigh Dickinson University Press, 1972).

Yonathan Shapiro has described the history of American Zionism from Herzl to 1930 in *Leadership of the American Zionist Organization, 1897-1930* (Urbana: University of Illinois Press, 1971). See also Samuel Halperin, *The Poltical World of American Zionism* (Detroit: Wayne State University Press, 1961); Melvin I. Urofsky, *American Zionism from Herzl to the Holocaust* (Garden City, N.Y.: Doubleday, 1975); and Urofsky, *We Are One!* (Garden City, N.Y.: Doubleday, 1978), a continuation of the first volume, covering the years 1942 to 1978; Naomi W. Cohen, *American Jews and the Zionist Idea* (New York: Ktav, 1975).

The story of American apathy at the time of the Holocaust is examined in detail by Arthur D. Morse, *While Six Million Died* (New York: Random House, 1968); Henry L.

Feingold, *The Politics of Rescue* (New Brunswick, N.J.: Rutgers University Press, 1970); Saul S. Friedman, *No Haven for the Oppressed: United States Policy Toward Jewish Refugees, 1938-1945* (Detroit: Wayne State University Press, 1973); and Walter Laqueur, *The Terrible Secret, Suppression of the Truth About Hitler's "Final Solution"* (Boston: Little, Brown, and Co., 1981).

On the American role in the establishment of Israel, see Nadav Safran, *The United States and Israel* (Cambridge: Harvard University Press, 1963); Robert Silverberg, *If I Forget Thee O' Jerusalem: American Jews and the State of Israel* (New York: William Morrow, 1970); Jacob A. Rubin, *Partners in State-Building; American Jewry and Israel* (New York: Diplomatic Press, Inc., 1969); Joseph B. Schectman, *The United States and the Jewish State Movement, 1939-1949* (New York: Herzl Press, 1966); and Frank E. Manuel, *The Realities of American-Palestine Relations* (Washington, D.C.: Public Affairs Press, 1949). The exciting story of the American-Jewish underground and its role in the arming of Israel is contained in Leonard Slater, *The Pledge* (New York: Simon & Schuster, 1970). For a revisionist view of the role of Truman in the creation of Israel see John Snetsinger, *Truman, the Jewish Vote, and the Creation of Israel* (Stanford, Calif.: Hoover Institution Press, 1974). Snetsinger contends that the president was ambivalent, deferring to State and Defense Department advice when his policies were pro-Arab and to Democratic party politicians when they were pro-Zionist. See also Zvi Ganin, *Truman, American Jewry, and Israel, 1945-1948* (New York: Holmes and Meier, 1979), Kenneth Ray Bain, *The March to Zion: United States Policy and the Founding of Israel* (College Station: Texas A & M University Press, 1979), and A. Joseph Heckelman, *American Volunteers and Israel's War of Independence* (New York: Ktav, 1974).

Name Index

Subject Index

904328 CENTRAL LIBRARY

973.04924

Plesur, Milton.
   Jewish life in twentieth-century
America : challenge and accommodation /
Milton Plesur. -- Chicago : Nelson-
Hall, c1982.
   xii, 235 p., [8] leaves of plates :
ill. ; 22 cm.
   Bibliography: p. 207-221.
   Includes indexes.

   1. Jews--United States--Social
conditions.   2. United States--Social
conditions--20th century.   I. Title